Political Change in Southea

Southeast Asia is a vast and complex region, comprised of countries with remarkably diverse histories and cultures. Jacques Bertrand provides a fresh and highly original survey of politics and political change in this area of the world. Against the backdrop of rapid economic development and social transformation in several Southeast Asian countries, he explores why some of these countries have adopted democratic institutions, while others have maintained stable authoritarian systems or accepted communist regimes. Bertrand presents a historically grounded account of capitalist countries and state-socialist countries, delving into the historical experience of individual countries, while simultaneously providing a comparative framework with which to draw parallels and foster a better understanding of the political and economic dynamics both within and between the countries. With powerful yet accessible analysis and detailed coverage, this book offers students and scholars a thorough and thought-provoking introduction to the political landscape of Southeast Asia.

JACQUES BERTRAND is Associate Professor of Political Science and a member of the Centre for Southeast Asian Studies at the University of Toronto. For the last few years, his research has focused on the effects of democratization on sub-state nationalist mobilization in Indonesia, the Philippines and Thailand. He is the author of *Nationalism and Ethnic Conflict in Indonesia* (Cambridge University Press, 2004) and co-editor of *Multination States in Asia: Accommodation or Resistance* (Cambridge University Press, 2010).

Political Change in Southeast Asia

JACQUES BERTRAND
University of Toronto

CAMBRIDGE
UNIVERSITY PRESS

CAMBRIDGE UNIVERSITY PRESS
Cambridge, New York, Melbourne, Madrid, Cape Town,
Singapore, São Paulo, Delhi, Mexico City

Cambridge University Press
The Edinburgh Building, Cambridge CB2 8RU, UK

Published in the United States of America by Cambridge University Press, New York

www.cambridge.org
Information on this title: www.cambridge.org/9780521710060

© Cambridge University Press 2013

First published 2013

Printed and bound in the United Kingdom by Bell and Bain Ltd

A catalogue record for this publication is available from the British Library

Library of Congress Cataloguing in Publication data
Bertrand, Jacques, 1965– author.
Political change in South East Asia / Jacques Bertrand, University of Toronto.
   pages   cm
Includes bibliographical references and index.
ISBN 978-0-521-88377-1 (hardback) – ISBN 978-0-521-71006-0 (paperback)
1. Southeast Asia – Politics and government – 20th century.
2. Southeast Asia – Politics and government – 21st century.   I. Title.
JQ750.A58B47   2013
320.959 – dc23   2013011405

ISBN 978-0-521-88377-1 Hardback
ISBN 978-0-521-71006-0 Paperback

Contents

Figures and tables

Figures

Tables

Preface

This book provides a survey of political change in Southeast Asian countries, from independence to the twenty-first century. Any such book makes choices regarding the approach, historical material and nature of the analysis. I present an analytical framework that invites the reader to think about the role of several factors that can be compared across cases, and that frequently have been raised as broad explanations for political change. I also emphasize some of the concepts that specialists of Southeast Asia have introduced to explain more unique aspects of political change, its absence, or the character and quality of the region's political regimes. At the same time, the book remains sensitive to history. The chapters present narratives of political change in each country, in order to both assess the explanatory value of comparative factors, as well as specific historical circumstances that have influenced political trajectories in significant ways. The book's challenge is to provide a relatively cohesive, yet sufficiently complex, explanation that allows for comparison across different countries, while offering a broad historical survey. Southeast Asia is a vast, diverse and complex region that is composed of eleven countries. The book covers all of these except the small country of Brunei. By covering such a broad range of countries, in the exposition of political change I necessarily stress a more specific set of questions and issues that I carry from one country to the next.

The book is therefore by no means exhaustive. I chose to focus on changes in regime type, basic political institutions, as well as governments where they introduced significantly new directions. The presence or absence of democracy determines a terrain that allows or restricts other groups from advancing their interests or pursuing their goals. I view the right of political association and participation, restrictions on political organizations, the ability to express dissent, types of representation, and other such characteristics as basic parameters that define a space in which citizens and groups can operate. For these reasons, I emphasize change in the country's basic political institutions and types of government, while admittedly neglecting a host of other important forms of political action taken by diverse sets of groups in society. More specialized work is best suited for the analysis of these latter groups. I hope to provide with this book a solid base from which to understand the region's diverse politics.

1 | Understanding political change in Southeast Asia

Southeast Asia is a vast region, comprised of eleven countries and incredible diversity. From one country to the next, dominant languages vary, religious groups are different and histories are all dissimilar from one another. In comparison to Latin America or Africa – other large regions of the world – the study of politics in Southeast Asia can be particularly challenging.

Latin America and Africa are also very diverse regions but their respective countries share some similarities that make comparisons somewhat more common. The Spanish language, for instance, binds countries of Latin America where it is dominant in all countries except Brazil. Countries of the region were all colonized, and Spain was the dominant power for several centuries. Latin American countries inherited societies in which descendants of Spanish colonizers and *mestizo* (mixed) classes are now dominant. These common characteristics often tainted their style of politics, with some very interesting parallels among several countries. To a lesser extent, the African experience also generated similarities that have been compared analytically. In Africa, the division of the continent between mostly French and British colonial rule[1] created some homogenizing experiences as well. French and English became common languages of communication throughout West and East/Southern Africa respectively. Colonization by these powers, which imposed bureaucratic structures over societies mostly organized in small political units, created some similar dysfunctionalities that have persisted in the modern independent states (Mamdani, 1996; Young, 1994). Comparisons have often been made between clusters of African countries, where the continued legacies of colonial rule have been blamed for the inability of states to overcome poverty and other major challenges in the continent.

---

[1] While most of the continent was divided up between Britain and France, a few other European countries gained some colonial presence, such as Portugal, Belgium and Germany.

By contrast, Southeast Asia's diversity makes comparison and large generalizations about the region less frequent. Although interactions among peoples stretch back hundreds of years, and cross-cultural influences have left their trace in every country, the region never developed a common language or a common cultural heritage (Lieberman, 2003; Reid, 1988). Several major religions took root. Hindu beliefs spread from India to the archipelagic Southeast Asia, and became widespread among the Javanese and other peoples. Hinduism left its trace in such temples as Prambanan in Java. Theravada Buddhism became a dominant religion in vast areas of continental Southeast Asia, comprising today's Thailand, Cambodia and Laos in particular. Islam, which again came from South Asia, spread through merchants and scholars who travelled to coastal areas. Conversions and the establishment of sultanates displaced Hinduism and Buddhism across the Southeast Asian archipelago, leaving only traces of believers in such places as Bali and the Tengger highlands of Java. Today's Indonesia and Malaysia are predominantly Muslim.

The region was also divided up between several colonial powers, with consequently different effects on the subregions under their respective control. The extent of penetration of colonial rule varied considerably, thereby affecting local political structures in varying ways. Local languages remained dominant, while colonial languages only briefly became the lingua franca. Although some languages eventually superseded others to bind several peoples together and be later elevated as "national" languages, no one language established itself as a regional medium of communication. This prevented the kind of similarity of experience and common trajectories found in some parts of Latin America and Africa.

European colonialism and its influence

When Europeans first reached the archipelago in the sixteenth century, they found well-established societies, solid trading networks and strong kingdoms. For the most part, Europeans came to the region in search of commodities. Markets for exotic spices were rapidly expanding in Europe and entrepreneurial merchants sought new means of profiting from the spice trade. Portuguese merchants created a first trading post at Malacca, which was strategically positioned on the coast that overlooked one of the busiest sea trading routes. They competed with local merchants to seize control over trade in some of the more profitable spices. They set up more trading posts along coastal areas but often clashed with local traders.

Asia was a very dynamic place with advanced civilizations, complex cultures and societies, as well as sophisticated bureaucratic systems, that had been established well before there was much contact with Europe. Yet, it was not isolated. Traders, adventurers and conquerors criss-crossed Asia from the Indian subcontinent to the eastern tip of today's China. With human flows also came the transmission of ideas, such as new religious beliefs. Links also stretched to the Roman Empire and different parts of today's Europe.

Political organization was vastly different from one location to the next. Most prominently, successive Han and Mongul dynasties controlled vast areas of Eastern Asia, spreading their political and cultural influences over neighbouring areas of today's Southeast Asia. After Qin Shi Huangdi created the Chinese empire in 221–210 BC, the Chinese state became highly centralized and bureaucratized, as its influence expanded over the following centuries. Smaller surrounding kingdoms, such as the Viet or Korean kingdoms absorbed some of the Chinese cultural influences, while struggling to maintain their independence. In much of Southeast Asia, polities were a great deal smaller, and tended to change regularly. According to Lieberman, from the fourteenth century onwards, mainland Southeast Asia did see a greater consolidation over time, but archipelagic Southeast Asia remained more fluid. Some kingdoms were formed in parts of today's Java, Bali, Maluku, and Cambodia, for instance, but they were held together often by kinship and religious ties rather than bureaucratic structure or territorial control (Lieberman, 2003). The bases, scale and types of political organization were therefore different across the region, and so were the modalities of legitimacy.

Colonialism set a new course and began to transform this diverse landscape, through integrative and administrative changes that would eventually give way to the emergence of modern states. European influences deeply affected many societies, including their culture and modes of social organization. Politically, colonialism introduced modern forms of warfare, fostered a rapid and deeper integration to world markets, set new and more fixed boundaries and imposed new forms of administrative and political organization. As the historian Anthony Reid has noted, this "imperial alchemy" mixed with a varied landscape of diverse societies and cultures to produce new political forms (Reid, 2010).

Resistance to colonial rule eventually latched onto global political trends as well. The flipside of colonialism's transformative power is the history of popular discontent, resistance and rebellion against European intrusion. Where European powers encountered well-established kingdoms, sometimes military force was the only means by which to subjugate local populations. Muslims in Mindanao and the Sulu Archipelago (in today's Southern Philippines), for instance, militarily resisted Spanish conquest. So did the Acehnese against the Dutch colonial army's attempts to gain full control over the territory representing today's Indonesia. Once consolidated, colonial regimes encountered this type of large and small-scale resistance. Millenarian movements were large-scale peasant rebellions that were mobilized by leaders who were seen almost as prophets or messiahs offering more prosperous and better futures. The Java War of 1825–30, led by Prince Diponegoro in the Dutch East Indies, as well as the Saya San Rebellion of 1930–2 in British Burma both had this character (Adas, 1979). At other times, peasants rebelled in smaller, less visible groups, in villages or more contained locations. James C. Scott wrote about peasant rebellion under colonial rule. He explains how the colonial economy threatened the norms and moral codes of conduct in peasant societies. Peasants rebelled when redistributive norms and survival strategies came under intense pressure from colonial transformation, thereby violating the "moral economy" of the peasants (Scott, 1976). While they might join larger-scale rebellious movements, they could also adopt "everyday forms of resistance", which are individual acts of resistance, often hidden, targeted at local landowners or authority figures (Scott, 1985). By the beginning of the twentieth century, new ideologies and models of political organization emerged globally. They inspired and channeled rebellions into more organized, more modern forms of resistance, such as nationalist and communist movements.

European encounters

Southeast Asian countries were colonized by several different European powers: Portuguese, Dutch, British, French and Spanish conquered different parts of the region, more or less intensively, and with a varied set of goals. Not only did their approach to colonialism vary but, given the wide variety of political, social and cultural contexts, the outcomes of colonialism remained quite diverse as well.

At the outset, Europeans came mainly to establish trading posts, and only much later intensified their involvement. The Portuguese first established a trading post at Malacca in 1511. As with their successors, the Portuguese were lured by spices. While they displaced Arab and Indian Muslim merchants in the Strait of Malacca, they vied mainly for the spice rich Moluccan Islands (present day Maluku). They established forts and trading posts in several locations across the Moluccas, while largely ignoring mainland Southeast Asia. Several local populations and traders later came to resent the Portuguese as they imposed high tariffs and port fees on non-Portuguese merchants who used the Strait of Malacca. Furthermore, Portuguese missionization and attacks against Muslim merchants further irritated mainly Muslim local populations.

Local populations therefore welcomed the advent of the Dutch who easily replaced the Portuguese's waning influence. When the Spanish and Portuguese crowns were combined between 1580 and 1640, the Portuguese section of the empire was largely neglected, thereby allowing the Dutch to establish their supremacy. They also came for the rising profit in the spice trade; the Dutch established a strong footing in the Moluccas, where spice production had continued to rise. Initially, the Dutch were uninterested in either proselytizing or gaining territorial control. As trade was their main interest, they preferred to work with local rulers who maintained their administrative power. The Dutch East India Company, which was the principal Dutch presence in the archipelago, therefore expanded its reach over the densely populated island of Java, as well as the Moluccas and a few other areas, primarily through mutually beneficial agreements to preserve local rulers' power as long as they protected and promoted Dutch trading interests.

In the nineteenth century, Dutch control intensified as new commodities became profitable. In addition to spices, coffee, sugar and indigo also became important. In some areas, the Dutch imposed more direct political control as they established plantations. In others, such as Java, under a system known as the Cultivation System, they forced smallholders to use a portion of their land for export crops. When the Dutch East India Company faltered, the Dutch government became more heavily involved, and some areas of the archipelago were placed under direct rule or more intense Dutch political interference.

The British entered the Malay Archipelago and challenged Dutch control of the Strait of Malacca. In 1819, they gained control of the tiny island of Singapore and proceeded in the following decades to transform it into an important trading post for the region. They also occupied Malacca and Penang, which together became known as the Straits Settlements in 1826. As with the Dutch, the British were interested in trade, so they only reluctantly became more involved in the surrounding Malay states. Nevertheless, as their interest in producing oil palm, tin and rubber expanded, they also established more formal control over Malay sultanates to protect their trading interests and maintain political stability.

Meanwhile, the British transformed Malay society by encouraging large numbers of Chinese and Indians to migrate to their colony. In the 1870s, they expanded their colonial venture into tin-mining areas where Chinese migrants constituted the largest pool of mining workers. Two decades later, they began to establish large rubber plantations, which also attracted Chinese labour as well as Indians. The scale of migration radically altered the demographic landscape of what became British Malaya, as the Chinese represented almost 40 per cent and Indians almost 10 per cent of the population by the middle of the twentieth century. This population change constituted one of the most significant effects of colonialism in the region.

Mainland Southeast Asia became the locus of increasing expansion of British and French colonial powers. For the British, who had occupied India in the eighteenth century, the expansion into Burma initially served primarily as a buffer to protect its crown jewel. Viewing the Burmese kingdom in the same way as they did the princely kingdoms of India, the British sought to impose their dominance. Several treaties failed to give the British the security they needed for their interests in India, as the French expanded their control and Burmese kings refused to recognize British power. It took three Anglo-Burmese wars before the British finally seized control over Burma in 1886.

The French had come late to the region. In the seventeenth century, some missionaries proselytized in Vietnam and, when they were persecuted, sought refuge and established relationships with the Thai kingdom of Ayutthaya. Trade, however, remained minimal as the Dutch successfully contained French attempts to make inroads on the mainland and French kings were not all equally interested in colonial expansion in the region. Nevertheless, by the mid nineteenth century French imperialism intensified. Under Napoleon III, imperial conquest was sought as a source of power and prestige. Vietnam became particularly attractive with increasing opportunities to trade with the south of China. By establishing a base in Saigon, the French intended to compete in this respect with Hong Kong and Singapore. At the same time, despite massive conversions to Catholicism from the last two hundred years of French missionization, threats against missionaries were frequently made. Although reports of persecution were exaggerated, the French state nevertheless used this reason to launch its conquest of Cochinchina in the south of Vietnam and, from there, the entire Mekong Delta.

After their success in 1862, the French continued to expand. For two centuries, Khmer monarchs had been weak. Their more powerful Thai and Vietnamese neighbours repeatedly threatened them. They fell at times under the influence of one or the other, and very briefly protected some of their autonomy by paying tribute to both. By the mid nineteenth century, the Vietnamese and Thai states had been strongly consolidated. Armed clashes occurred on Cambodian territory, leading to much suffering of the Khmer people as well as the seizure of significant portions of the previous Khmer territories. When King Ang Duong sought assistance from Napoleon III in 1853, he could not envision that the French already planned to conquer significant portions of Vietnam. After the French victory in 1862, King Norodom – Ang Duong's successor – accepted Cambodia being turned into a French protectorate. Once Cambodia was secured, the French then eventually further expanded into the Vietnamese provinces of Annam and Tonkin, thereby gaining full control by 1885.

The Spanish came to the region as early as the sixteenth century. In contrast to other European powers, the Spanish crown strongly supported missionization. In the central and northern parts of the Philippines, local inhabitants followed a variety of animist beliefs. With less hierarchical and organized religion, missionaries converted them to Christianity more successfully than elsewhere in the region. Yet, in the south, the spread of Islam across the Malay world had reached the island of Mindanao and the Sulu Archipelago. Moros (Muslims of the southern Philippines) strongly resisted missionization efforts as well as the Spanish conquest. As a result, even though the Spanish had already established a foothold in Manila by 1571, they were only able to defeat the Moros in 1830.

There were few economic incentives for colonizing the Philippines. Having learned from their mistakes in Latin America, where vast numbers of the population died from disease and mistreatment, Spanish colonial rulers prevented Spaniards from living outside the city, and prohibited intensive exploitation of labour in mines or plantations, which had led to huge population losses in Latin America. In the first few years, they conceded a few royal grants to Spaniards, thereby allotting them administrative control over groups of villages in return for Christianizing them and providing employment for the local population. Otherwise, many others worked on friar estates that were mostly granted to Filipino *mestizos* (mixed local and Spanish). Overall, Spanish colonial rule did not significantly transform the local economy until well into the nineteenth century.

Therefore the effect of colonialism in Southeast Asia was profound but very uneven. While some regions were highly influenced by intensive colonial presence, others were barely touched. Economic, political and social transformation left the region with a strong European imprint and laid the basis for the current configuration and character of modern states.

Colonial ventures displaced and transformed local economic networks that already had a global reach. Strong trade networks existed well before colonial times. They connected India to China, and overland routes reached Europe; the appeal of spices from Asia was introduced through these networks. The Portuguese, British and Dutch essentially created competing maritime routes. Over time, their superior maritime power ensured dominance over trade routes. Some land areas, where production of coffee, sugar, rubber, tin, oil palm and other commodities became highly profitable, were transformed systematically to use local agricultural labour and integrate it into colonial priorities. In Java, landholdings remained relatively intact but productivity remained highly contained under the Cultivation System that imposed strict production quotas to the benefit of the Dutch. In British Malaya and parts of Sumatra, however, some areas were converted to plantations, which hired agricultural workers. In the Philippines, perhaps more than elsewhere, large-scale plantation agriculture emerged, later to be seized by a growing Filipino mestizo elite. These transformations created some dependency on external markets for cash crops, and determined to a large extent where small-scale, subsistence

farming remained and where agricultural labour depended more extensively on large-scale plantation farming linked to global markets.

Economic transformation under colonial rule accelerated migration
that was already driven by a number of push factors in the countries
of origin. Most notably, deteriorating economic and social conditions
in China motivated many poor Chinese to seek better livelihoods in
Southeast Asia. Migration to Siam, the Philippines, British Malaya,
Singapore and the Dutch East Indies was already significant in the
eighteenth and early nineteenth centuries. Most migrants tended to
marry locally and mix. In the Philippines, the Chinese population rose
from 6,000 in 1840 to 100,000 by 1890 but many would become *mestizos* and eventually be simply considered Filipinos (Tarling, 1992).
Migration to Siam was similarly strong, and migrants tended to integrate relatively well into the local population. This was also the case
for initial waves of migrants integrating into the Dutch East Indies
and Malaya. By the middle of the nineteenth century, however, and
partly as a result of the scale of migration and colonial policies and
practices, migrants tended to form their own, separate communities.
By the early 1820s, the Chinese population in West Borneo already
reached around 50,000. As mentioned earlier, Chinese migrants came
in much larger numbers to Malaya and Singapore after the 1870s
as labourers in rapidly expanding commercial ventures. Indians also
came in large numbers so that their respective proportion of the population of both colonies was very high. In Singapore, Chinese settlers
became the vast majority. While in colonies such as Burma or the
Dutch East Indies, where the proportion of Indians or Chinese migrants
remained relatively low, they nevertheless came to occupy significant
niches in the colonial economy, as laborers, moneylenders and traders.
These changes prompted the scholar and colonial administrator J. S.
Furnivall to observe the formation of "plural societies", by which
Europeans, Chinese, Indians and "natives" lived in separate commu-
nities, with their distinct religions, languages, and even occupations.
This separation, which was a marked departure from earlier mixing
between migrants and local populations, had lasting effects in modern
Indonesia, Malaysia and Burma/Myanmar,[2] where Chinese and Indian

---

[2] The SLORC regime in 1989 changed the English reference to the country from
Burma to Myanmar, as the latter was closer to its form in the Burmese
language. Several sources continued to use "Burma" after 1989 as the SLORC
regime was highly contested and criticized as illegitimate, particularly after its

communities were subjected to discriminatory policies and largely failed, or were prevented, from integrating even after independence (Furnivall, 1948).

Politically, European colonialism created new states, new identities, and transformed existing political structures. Most dramatically, Dutch and Spanish colonial administration over the Malay and Philippine archipelagos created administrative boundaries, centralized state control where only loose and mainly local political structures prevailed, and laid the basis for new identities to emerge. Modern states of Indonesia and the Philippines were created out of the Dutch and Spanish colonies respectively. Malaysia became its own state, again from loosely related sultanates that had fallen under British colonial control. British rule also left an important demographic transformation, as independent Malaysia inherited a large Chinese population (almost 40 per cent of the population). Ethnic politics have since dominated Malaysian politics, and certainly the strong Malay Muslim identity has grown and been nurtured in juxtaposition with the large Chinese and smaller Indian populations. Singapore was a tiny island with a very small population that only grew in importance as the British transformed it into an important regional hub. Catholic identity, which became so important in the Philippines, was a direct consequence of intense missionization under Spanish rule.

Southeast Asian countries therefore entered the twentieth century with important influences from European colonialism. Some areas remained only subtly touched by European influence, but others were clearly marked, transformed, or even created out of this experience.

Nationalism, communism and the modern state

The first half of the twentieth century radically transformed the region as modern states were crafted. Accompanying the decline of European empires, new ideologies of political organization emerged. Nationalism inspired groups to organize against colonial occupation and to claim their own states as new, modern nations. Communism was also spreading as a radically new form of political organization based on

rejection of election results in 1990. After the return to civilian rule in 2011, the latter issue has become less relevant and the use of "Myanmar" is more broadly accepted in the English-speaking world. Because of the widespread use of Burma up until recent years, I use "Myanmar" to refer to the country after 1989 but "Burma" otherwise.

the empowerment of the working classes, the elimination of wealth inequalities, and the collective ownership of property. Its revolutionary creed appealed to many groups seeking to overthrow colonial powers, displace elites who monopolized local power, and gain access to land and better living standards. Together, these two ideological forces shaped the imaginary thrust of anti-colonial movements. Their success was conditioned in part by global power shifts, including the erosion of imperial power and the Cold War (1945–89) that divided the world into communist and non-communist camps.

Nationalism is a modern ideological form. Its roots lie in the Americas and Europe when groups began to reject imperial and dynastic rulers. Instead, it claimed legitimacy of rule for populations with shared experience and common identity, based on principles of equal membership and participation in new political groupings that we call "nations". As Benedict Anderson has argued, they are "imagined communities" whereby certain populations with a common language and shared experiences on a given territory aspire to rule themselves (Anderson, 1983). It was a powerful idea that inspired populations not only to rid themselves of colonial subjugation but also of forms of rule that reinforced inequality and legitimacy based on dynastic rule.

Nationalism fed some of the early movements against dynastic and imperial rule in Asia. By 1911, nationalists guided by Sun Yat-sen's ideas challenged the long-time dominance of the Qing dynasty and rejected its legitimacy of rule. In Southeast Asia, José Rizal in the late nineteenth century advocated for self-rule by Filipinos. His ideas drove the formation of a nationalist Filipino movement that launched a revolutionary struggle against the Spanish. In Indonesia, Muslim merchants and intellectuals had begun to articulate nationalist ideas in the first decade of the twentieth century but the nationalist movement formally crystallized around the Youth Pledge and the formation of the Nationalist Party of Indonesia in 1928. Young nationalists had by then defined a new Indonesian nation built around a common language, Bahasa Indonesia (a dialect of Malay that had been used as a lingua franca). Their movement led a revolution against the Dutch. Other nationalist organizations similarly arose in other countries of the region but not necessarily with the same revolutionary fervour or outcomes. Aung San, a nationalist leader, intellectual and later general, formed a number of nationalist organizations in Burma, starting in the late 1930s. They culminated in the creation in 1944 of the Anti-Fascist People's

Freedom League, which constituted a broad alliance of nationalists, communists and socialists. While initially these groups supported the Japanese as liberators from British colonial rule, after it became clear that the Japanese intended to maintain control and imposed harsh conditions, they opposed the Japanese occupation and later the return of the British, while demanding that the Burmese control their own land. The formation of the United Malays National Organization (UMNO) in 1946 constituted the clearest expression of Malay nationalism. No strong movement had emerged nor had there been a revolutionary program. Although redefining Malays as a nation, UMNO for some time did not challenge British rule. This form of nationalism also differed from others in the region by claiming Malays as the nation, and reclaiming their legitimacy of rule as "sons-of-the-soil", the original inhabitants of Malaya. Formed around a Malay, Muslim identity, it adopted a much clearer ethnic form that excluded Chinese and Indians from this newly imagined nation. Such exclusion would later limit the ability of Malaysia's leaders to create a common, overarching bond.

Nationalism mixed with other ideological influences to produce various political forms. Liberalism, for instance, propagated ideas of individual freedom and equality. On the economic side, it had led to the enshrinement of property rights, as well as capitalist economies based on notions of free markets and the pursuit of individual wealth. The flourishing of liberal ideas in Europe and the pursuit of personal wealth had fuelled colonial ventures in some respect. The expansion of markets and capitalism in the region presupposed individual liberties and property rights, which among other changes would displace local forms of collective land ownership. On the political side, liberalism shared close affinities with nationalism, in the idea of equality between individuals. But a notion of individual rights, freedom and choice inspired specific forms of democratic politics. Certainly the spread of modern elections based on "one person, one vote" found its roots in liberal ideas.

Communism proposed an alternative societal project, although it could also mix with ideas of "nation" and equality based on different foundations. Rooted in the mid-nineteenth-century writings of Karl Marx, a German intellectual, communist ideas evolved through various practical experiments at societal transformation. Marx had essentially written a critique of capitalism and a theory of the evolution of world history based on an analysis of modes of production and the development of social classes. He argued that capitalism chronologically replaced a feudal mode of production that tied labour to land, restricted the movement of peasants, gave land-owners broad rights over them but also obligations to provide for their subsistence. Capitalism had the unique characteristic of developing a social class, the bourgeoisie, which became the owners of the means of production and whose principal drive was the search for profit. Workers provided labour in exchange for remuneration, in a market transaction that departed from feudal ties, rights and obligations. Over time, Marx contended, capitalist production would maintain the working class mostly close to its costs of subsistence in order to gain maximum labour at the lowest possible cost. Such tendencies would create increasing resentment among the working class, which would rise up against the bourgeoisie and overthrow capitalism by revolution. Workers would then collectively own the means of production and secure a more equitable distribution of the fruits of production in a system that has come to be called "communism".

Revolution in theory became the vehicle for the spread of communism. The first one occurred in Russia, far from the German industrial hinterland that Marx imagined would be the locus of revolutionary potential. Marx had argued that workers in dire factory conditions and impoverished by industrialization would be the primary agents of revolution, not peasants. Yet, Russia, still largely an agriculturally based society with only a tiny industrial sector became the site of communist revolution and the first example of a communist system. Lenin, the leader of Russia's revolution, added pragmatic considerations to Marx's revolutionary theory. He defined a key role for the Communist Party, as he argued the need for leadership, education and awareness for the working class to realize its revolutionary potential. The party therefore became not only the instrument of mobilization and revolution, but also the key political structure around which communist systems were built. In theory, the party played a transitional role until communism could be fully realized. In reality, not a single communist system ever surpassed the stage at which the party occupied a dominant position. A new elite developed around party leaderships, with access to economic opportunities and state resources depending on one's position and relationship to the party.

Following the Russian revolution in 1917, communist parties were formed in several countries of the world. In Southeast Asia, they sprung up in the French colony of Indochina (today's Vietnam, Cambodia and Laos), in the Dutch East Indies (today's Indonesia), in British Malaya (part of today's Malaysia) and in Burma. In their early stage, they promoted the communist alternative, created linkages to Moscow and to the broader communist movement, organized trade unions and fomented occasional revolts. In the Dutch East Indies, a communist revolt in 1926 was quickly repressed. Most other communist parties were formed in the 1930s: the Indochinese Communist Party (1930), the Communist Party of Malaya (1930) and the Communist Party of Burma (1939). Parties focused on organizing labour (factory workers) yet most of these countries remained primarily agrarian. Few tapped initially into their large peasantries to direct their attacks against colonial rulers.

Organized resistance increased during the 1940s. Linkages across Asia were key to developing mobilization strategies. Communists in China were gaining momentum in the late 1940s with Mao Tse-tung's emphasis on organizing peasants, creating an army and using party cadres to recruit, train and mobilize. Largely influenced by the Communist Party of China, the Communist Party of Malaya (CPM) organized along such tactics. In 1948, it launched a guerrilla war against British colonial rulers, primarily by targeting rubber plantations and infrastructure. In 1941, the Indochinese Communist Party also organized a military wing, the Viet Minh, under Ho Chi Minh's leadership. It was able to mount a very strong resistance to the French during the First Indochina War (1946–54). In fact, Ho Chi Minh and the newly formed Vietnamese Communist Party (VCP) were able to occupy and govern a large portion of northern Vietnam during this period. The Communist Party of Burma (CPB) and Indonesian Communist Party, conversely, followed a political route. The CPB joined the Anti-Fascist People's Freedom League (AFPFL) as a united front against Japanese occupation in Burma, but the AFPFL became the dominant organization after the Second World War. Indonesian communists organized a rebellion in 1948 but, again, were swiftly crushed. Communist parties that most relied on peasant mobilization and armed resistance, along the lines of the Chinese Communist Party, gained strongest ascendency.

While communists and nationalists appeared to offer alternative societal projects, they were sometimes conflated. Where parties were organized along each ideological strand, competition arose. The Indonesian Nationalist Party won the upper hand over the

Indonesian Communist Party in the 1940s and 1950s. The United Malays National Organization (UMNO) became the Malays' most important political vehicle, and the dominant party, while the CPM gained support mainly among Chinese. After a decade of guerrilla warfare, the CPM had failed to gain the upper hand and basically dissolved at independence in 1957. At the same time, many communist parties were also nationalist as they organized primarily to resist colonial rule and aimed at obtaining an independent state for Indonesians, Vietnamese, Burmese respectively, in other words for their respective nations. The Vietnamese communist movement was perhaps most clearly conflated with a nationalist project, as communists first led the war against French colonial rule, and then fought in the Vietnam War against American occupation. Their struggle was just as much a war of liberation against foreign occupiers as it was a revolutionary movement aimed at establishing a communist regime.

The Second World War broke the dominance of European power and allowed nationalist and communist forces to establish independent states. The Japanese joined the Axis forces of Germany and Italy. Militarism had risen in Japan, which was then governed by an expansionist military regime. Its goal was to seize control of Asia and establish a "Greater East Asia Co-Prosperity Sphere". In fact, Japan sought to compete with the Europeans and establish its own empire. It had already seized control over Korea and parts of China when the Second World War gave it the opportunity to rapidly expand throughout Southeast Asia as European powers were occupied with the war in Europe. In 1940, Japan signed a cooperation agreement with Phibun Songkhram's government in Siam while the Vichy regime in France, created after Germany's successful invasion, allowed Japan to use ports in Indochina. From this base, Japanese forces first seized full control over Indochina in 1941. After an attack against Pearl Harbor in December 1941, which saw the United States enter the war, Japanese troops rapidly occupied the Philippines, British Malaya, the Dutch East Indies, Burma and Singapore. Although very short, the period of Japanese occupation was brutal and transformative. The Japanese sought to extract as many resources and as much labour as possible for their war effort in the "Co-Prosperity Sphere". Violent methods led to large numbers of deaths, displacement, famine and widespread disease. The economies of Southeast Asia were severely disrupted and many regions rapidly declined. On the political front, however, Japanese occupiers allowed nationalist and some religious groups to expand their influence and hoped to create some loyalty to the Japanese order, by allowing some relief from the otherwise strong imposition of Japanese culture. Nationalist leaders in Burma and the Dutch East Indies were allowed to mobilize masses with the intent of gaining support for the Japanese. In the Philippines and Indochina former colonial administrators were provided with opportunities to fill positions at higher levels of the bureaucracy. Islamic groups were supported in the Dutch East Indies and Malaya. The rise of these administrators and nationalists, combined with the misery the Japanese left behind, provided a strong block against the reimposition of European colonial power when Japan was defeated in 1945.

The Cold War, which began as the Second World War ended, created a new set of international constraints and opportunities that shaped the region. After 1949, the Cold War was in full swing, which added very significant layers of external influence. The Soviet Union and the United States divided the world into East and West spheres of influence. In several regions, they competed for power and even fought proxy wars. Southeast Asia became one of the Cold War's key terrains. The Vietnam War (1955–75) represented the most important application of the United States' containment policy, by which the US sought to prevent the spread of communism. American governments were motivated by the belief that losing in Vietnam might lead to a "domino effect" across Southeast Asia. In this respect, they were somewhat vindicated as the loss of the war in 1975 triggered not only a communist victory in Vietnam but also the downfall of authoritarian rule and replacement by communist regimes in neighbouring Cambodia and Laos. The US government was determined to prevent other communist movements from gaining power. It played a role in supporting the Indonesian military's suppression of communists in Indonesia in 1965, after a failed coup attempt allegedly launched by the Communist Party. It provided further military aid and political support to Suharto's anti-communist, authoritarian regime that began in 1965. In the Philippines, the United States provided military aid, training and strong political support to contain the influence of the New People's Army, the armed wing of the Philippine Communist Party. It gave its unwavering support for the Marcos dictatorship (1972–86), which was strongly anti-communist. It would not be an exaggeration to argue that the fate of many emerging independent states was closely tied to the competition of the United

States and the Soviet Union as well as China in the battle between communist and non-communist states.

Countries in the region therefore gained independence inspired by a variety of ideological projects and under different strategic conditions. Vietnam was perhaps the most complex as the north initially fought and gained its measure of independence from the French. While the south remained under US influence, by the end of the Vietnam War in 1975 the whole country was reunified under the communist regime. Cambodia and Laos initially sustained non-communist regimes after the French departure in 1954 but were overtaken by communist movements in the wake of the victory in Vietnam. The Philippines and Malaya (renamed Malaysia a few years later) gained gradual independence respectively in 1946 from the Americans and in 1957 from the British. In both cases new political institutions resembled the political systems of their former colonial masters. The British subsequently gave independence to Singapore in 1959. Singapore soon chose integration with Malaya and former British territories to form the Federation of Malaysia. Singapore seceded and became fully independent only two years later. In Indonesia, nationalists led a revolutionary movement after the Second World War ended in 1945 and the Dutch attempted to regain control of the archipelago as the Japanese occupying forces retreated. Although Indonesian leaders officially declared independence in 1945, they only succeeded in practice in 1949, when the Dutch finally departed.

Political change: alternative explanations

During the second half of the twentieth century and into the twenty-first, many Southeast Asian countries experienced profound and frequent political change while others remained very stable. Why is it so, and why is it important? There are many explanations that range from unique historical events to broad patterns that we can observe in clusters of countries. History matters and unique events often shape the political landscape. Most countries in the region were set on relatively different paths given varied colonial histories. Large-scale killings often left permanent scars. The Khmer Rouge massacres of the 1970s in Cambodia still have an impact today, including a traumatic relationship to the past and Hun Sen's dominance of the political regime. The 1965 massacre of 500,000 people in Indonesia provided the instability that partially explains the ability of the military-dominated Suharto regime to sustain itself for three decades. The absence of colonial rule in Thailand allowed for the preservation of the monarchy. It has been impossible to understand Thailand's politics without referring to the role that the king has played. Unique events and circumstances therefore provide key aspects to explain political change in each Southeast Asian country.

Yet, broader patterns can be observed. As explained above, ideologies can inspire change, as nationalism and communism did in the formation of independence movements and the resistance to colonial rule. International factors offer opportunities and constraints for political players. Pressures from abroad can allow groups to oppose a repressive regime and participate in its demise. Growth, for example, can be fostered by a change of fortune by which a country might take advantage of its inexpensive labour to boost exports of manufactured goods. Such factors drove the economic boom in Thailand, Malaysia and Indonesia during the 1970s and 1980s. Other times, states can be vulnerable to changes in the international system. Long-term changes in economic development, for instance, provide the basis for democratization, but world economic events such as financial crises and recessions can dampen opportunities for growth and have strong impacts on political change.

International factors in two realms create constraints and opportunities: security and the global economy. Security refers primarily, but not exclusively, to states' military power in the international system. Power is conditioned by a number of sources, including military strength, country size, population, strength of the economy, and other dimensions. Yet, the ability to project military power has historically determined a country's position in the international system. Great powers have been those with strong and effective armed forces. The concentration or diffusion of military power provides a structure from which we can understand how other states position themselves in relation to the strongest ones. From 1945 to 1989, the system was bipolar, featuring two large superpowers: the United States and the Soviet Union. As rival competitive powers, backed by radically different ideologies and regime types, they divided up the world into spheres of influence. Not only did the United States and the Soviet Union project power towards each other, in the form of nuclear deterrence, they competed for the spread of their respective ideologies and preferred regime types, fought proxy wars in various parts of the world, as they funded, armed, or even directly participated in violent confrontations between states and rebel movements.

The United States and the Soviet Union, joined by China in 1949, had considerable influence on the politics of Southeast Asia after the Second World War. The United States' policy of containment, as its active promotion of anti-communist regimes, played a crucial role not only in the Vietnam War but in the support for the Marcos regime in the Philippines or military aid to the Suharto regime, therefore contributing to the longevity of these authoritarian regimes. Soviet and Chinese support for communist movements helped groups, such as the Vietnamese Communist Party, to gain power. In turn, Vietnamese intervention helped to remove the Khmer Rouge from Cambodia but replaced the regime with one initially under Vietnamese control. The leader of this regime, Hun Sen, managed to create a sufficiently strong power base that he remained dominant well after the Vietnamese no longer provided support.

On the economic side, regimes have been strengthened or weakened by world economic trends. Several countries in the region grew very rapidly from the 1960s onwards: Singapore, Malaysia, Thailand and Indonesia. Government policies and private sector strategies – such as the reform of the financial sector or the emphasis on low-cost labour sectors – were crucial but all benefited from large amounts of foreign investment in sectors that were then becoming less competitive in Japan, Taiwan and South Korea but were finding new profit opportunities in countries of Southeast Asia with lower labour costs. Lee Kuan Yew built a highly stable political system in Singapore that fed on the ability to deliver strong economic performance for decades. Suharto's Indonesia profited from this shift as economic growth explained some aspects of its 30-year stability. Conversely, by the end of the twentieth century the same countries faced new challenges. In 1997, Asia was hit with a financial crisis that began in Thailand but rapidly spread to the whole region. Several countries had deregulated their economies and allowed large companies to benefit from bank loans that were risky, in that the loans were not well secured against solid assets. Furthermore, they unintentionally created "speculative bubbles" in real estate and other sectors; the value of real estate artificially rose as a result of speculators obtaining easy loans to buy and sell property for quick profit. Large amounts of foreign investment were pulled out of countries of the region when many of these unhealthy economic practices were exposed. As a result, they were faced with, among other consequences, banking failures and sudden withdrawal of financial capital. Economic growth rates declined as a result. The economic instability partly explained the fall in November 1997 of the Chavalit government in Thailand, the fall of the Suharto regime in Indonesia in May 1998, and the erosion of the stability and confidence of dominant party regimes in Malaysia and Singapore. We can therefore recognize some broad patterns that affect countries in the region and their politics.

Political change, however, is more often than not conditioned by domestic factors. In this book, these factors are emphasized. Countries in the region were highly influenced by the presence or absence of economic growth. How elites responded to crises also could explain moments that allowed for political change to occur. At times, societal movements have also contributed to the erosion of authoritarian rule, or the emergence of democracy. These factors can be compared to assess their degree of explanatory reach in these cases. Yet, we also need to recognize some factors that are more specific to the region or to one or two countries. The following sections present some explanatory propositions for understanding some of the broad strokes of political change in Southeast Asia.

Growth, development and political change

Economic development has long been associated with democratic politics. Seymour Martin Lipset in 1959 established a correlation between high levels of economic development and democracy (Lipset, 1959). He found that the more advanced economies, measured as Gross Domestic Product (GDP) per capita, were all stable, advanced democracies. Lipset postulated that such an association arose out of the greater wealth, education and urbanization of developed economies. Those circumstances created greater demand for openness and competition.

An offshoot of this argument emphasizes the role of the middle class. The argument is a narrower one that emphasizes how the middle class typically prefers more active participation in politics and representation of their interests. Its members tend to be educated, work as professionals or office workers, can be civil servants or teachers and students as well. They are likely to live in urban areas, create associations and organizations to advance their interests and have more time than their poorer co-citizens to be involved in politics.

Why are advanced classes not associated with more democratic politics as well? The argument is not that they shun open and competitive politics. However, they tend to be the dominant groups that control the polity or that are the wealthiest in society. Classic literature in the social sciences postulated that the business classes were in fact the drivers of change historically and that they laid the foundations of emerging European democracies (Moore, 1966). Yet, in Latin America, Asia and Africa the business classes were quite different. The key factor is the relationship between the business classes and the state. If business groups thrived because of their links to the state, they tended to be conservative and mainly interested in preserving the status quo. Scholars such as Peter Evans and Guillermo O'Donnell also saw close cooperation between business and the state as serving the interests of the ruling class (Evans, 1979; O'Donnell, 1973). In the Southeast Asian context, scholars such as Richard Robison, Vedi Hadiz, John Sidel and Paul Hutchcroft, using different analytical frameworks, have all concluded that business groups in the region have been more inclined to be predatory and supportive of authoritarian regimes, often times because their wealth was intrinsically tied to the political regime (Hadiz, 2010; Hutchcroft, 1998; Robison, 1986; Sidel, 1999). In rare cases, such as among some business groups in Thailand or Indonesia, authoritarian controls became impediments to their interests and they therefore more strongly supported political openness, even by entering politics and seeking change from within. Business classes, per se, are therefore likely to support regimes that best serve their interests, whether democratic or authoritarian, but are unlikely to be the drivers of change. On the other hand, to the extent that a large number of small entrepreneurs are less linked to the state, and form part of the middle class, their interests might lie closer to the professionals, students, intellectuals who tend to demand more open and representative politics.

Poverty generally prevents political mobilization. Many poor live in rural areas, where they live on subsistence farming. Because they live in small villages or small towns, they are unlikely to be able to mobilize politically on a large scale. Occasional rioting might occur when they face starvation or rapid decline in their living standards. More often than not, these acts of protest remain localized. Peasants might also engage in "everyday forms of resistance" that nibble at established patterns of local political or economic domination (Scott, 1985). On rare occasions the cumulative effect of such individualized forms of resistance has sufficiently undermined patterns of political and economic control to produce change. Benedict Kerkvliet, for example, has convincingly shown that such individualized resistance sufficiently undermined the communist system of collective farms (collectivization) that it contributed to its demise and abandonment in Vietnam (Kerkvliet, 2005).

In urban areas, the poor also rarely mobilize. They are often migrants from rural areas, work in the underground economy, sometimes in factories, or in small peddler trade. Their preoccupations with survival strategies also make them unlikely to engage in protest or large-scale political movements. Workers in factories or in large-scale industrial sites, however, are likely to be more politicized. Following workers in other parts of the world, they often seek better pay and better working conditions. The labour movement has long focused on unionization and collective bargaining to achieve these goals. Even under authoritarian conditions, union leaders often mobilize workers in strike actions or other forms of protest to voice their demands. Ever since unions appeared on a large scale in Europe and North America in the early twentieth century, labour organizations have been prevalent. Over time, certain forms of collective organizing, various tactics and strategies have been passed on to labour movements around the world. Workers, therefore, sometimes demonstrate, protest or strike at the factory or local level. Other times, as Rueschemeyer, Stephens and Stephens have shown, they have joined the middle class in broader movements demanding democracy (Rueschemeyer, Stephens & Stephens, 1992).

Marxists offer a caveat to the role of social classes in political change. Instead of agents of democratization, Marxists consider the labour movement to be the agent of social revolution. They postulate that workers will create networks and unite for revolutionary change. Lenin in Russia, Mao Tse-tung in China and Ho Chi Minh in Vietnam, led social revolutions based on the mobilization of peasants. By doing so, they showed that peasants, while often powerless and unable to organize, occasionally have engaged in large-scale political action. But revolutions are rare, and we should certainly be cautious of generalizing about the ability of either workers or peasants to generate and produce such profound change.

How do these propositions from political science theory help understand political change in Southeast Asia? We should examine the role of the middle class, the business elites, as well as the working class at moments of political change. A quick survey of the region, however, yields poor predictive value to the role of social classes. Some of the richer, more developed countries with a strong middle class (Singapore and Malaysia) remain stable soft authoritarian regimes. The argument works better in poor countries, with arguably less developed middle-classes such as Burma, Cambodia, Laos and Vietnam that have shown few signs of democratization. It does not mean that pressures for change do not emanate from these classes but that other important factors might delay, outweigh, or even thwart their effects on political change. The following chapters on individual countries examine the role of these classes to better understand the extent to which they have been significant.

Scholars of Southeast Asian politics have emphasized contingent factors. The effect that the social classes might have on political change depends on the institutional starting point. Authoritarian regimes vary enormously in terms of their strength and their style of management. They can be based primarily on personal rule – by which a single leader rules arbitrarily according to his or her will – or they can be highly institutionalized, in which case the leader, or ruling group, abides by a set of formal or informal rules, including at times some form of elections, adoption of laws and decrees and parliamentary roles. Rules of conduct dictate the exercise of power of different elements within the state and guide relations with societal groups. In Indonesia, for instance, the type of authoritarian regime led to a highly institutionalized role of the military, elements of the bureaucracy and connections between the state and the business sector that proved quite resilient to pressures for change. Opposition groups, whether workers, students or other middle class groups, could not necessarily muster sufficient strength to mobilize effectively against the regime (Slater, 2008).

So, while analyzing the role of social classes in political change, we also need to be aware how their ability to mobilize is constrained by the repressive apparatus, incentives to cooperate with the regime, or other ways in which authoritarian rulers might prevent them from being politically effective.

Elites and democratization

Decision-makers and those who hold the strings of power often determine the political rules of the game. Political scientists have grappled with the role of dominant groups, and the extent to which they can control a polity and freely pursue their interests. Critics argue that analyses focusing on these groups sometimes overplay their role. Instead, they point to constraints that prevent individuals or groups from establishing rules or serving personal interests when they do so at the expense of the broader majority. In democracies, legal systems and institutions regulate power and interests in order to limit the power of the few and potential abuses of power in favour of personal enrichment or other forms of personal interest. In authoritarian systems, the small group that controls the regime often appears to create institutions, set rules and accumulate personal wealth with little restraint. Yet, even in those systems, power is not absolute: it is constrained by the leadership's need to obtain sufficient support to maintain stability and control. This fact often means that even authoritarian leaders are constrained by other groups in society. In each regime, there is a balance between the power of the few and the extent to which they are constrained by the majority or groups that are not directly linked to the centres of power.

Analyses focusing on "elites" are primarily concerned with the group or groups that dominate a polity. They typically seek to understand the extent of their power, their motivations, as well as the constraints that they face in the exercise of that power. C. Wright Mills provided an early definition of "elite": the "few who are in command of the major hierarchies and organizations of modern society... They occupy the strategic command posts of the social structure" (Mills, 1956).

Who belongs in the elite? Major hierarchies or organizations, as Mills argues, can vary considerably from one society to another. For sure, the state's major leaders and public policy makers constitute a centre of power. Business leaders and entrepreneurs whose interests are closely tied to the government are also part of the elite, particularly where there are clear networks of interaction and influence between those business interests and the state. The top leadership and executive of political parties are ambiguously linked to the state. Obviously where they directly participate in government or play key roles in legislatures, they are part of this elite. Yet, some parties might be marginal and represent groups that are neither well represented nor powerful. In some societies, other key organizations have lots of influence and their leadership maintains close contacts with the government. These can include religious, ethnic or professional organizations, depending on the society.

The study of political change requires that we pay attention to elites. In stable regimes power and wealth usually keep elites quiescent and sufficiently satisfied to accept the prevailing rules of the game. In their classic study, Guillermo O'Donnell and Philippe Schmitter argue however that elite splits always precede the collapse of authoritarian regimes and transitions to democracy. Splits are not just disagreements about usual policy areas but are fundamental differences in the way a political regime is managed or within the regime itself. O'Donnell and Schmitter emphasized such important moments when these splits occur. They can be combined with factional alliances with groups that have been excluded from the ruling circle. When democratization does occur, it often involves a group of reformists in the ruling elite who then negotiate a path with the regime's opponents to hold elections and craft a more democratic regime (O'Donnell & Schmitter, 1986). In the Southeast Asian context, William Case has extended the argument and argued that elite cohesion or disunity often explain regime sustainability or its instability (Case, 2002).

Elite unity tends to remain stronger in regimes where a single party rather than the military dominates. Within single-party systems, cadres and officials might divide into factions around policy issues but remain committed to keeping the regime intact. Military-dominated regimes tend to be less stable as there are often important divisions over the initiation of a coup and the timeline of remaining in power. Most officers tend to prioritize the survival and efficacy of the military itself. When pressures arise against military regimes, some factions usually prefer to return to the barracks (Geddes, 1999).

When we juxtapose these insights with the role of social classes, an alternative explanation emerges. Democratization or other forms of regime change are predicated less on certain observable levels of development, size of middle class, or type of business class but instead are much more products of choices made by authoritarian leaders at critical moments. Certainly timing of change often requires that we analyze more closely what motivates elites to trigger a process of democratization. For instance, in Burma/Myanmar, after decades of military dominance, the junta introduced in 2008 a new constitution, allowed controlled elections in 2012 and accepted that the popular opposition figure Aung San Suu Kyi could become a member of the new parliament. A focus strictly on development or the growth of Burma's middle class could not explain why the junta moved so decisively towards some measure of political liberalization.

Elite behaviour in itself is not always a good predictor of political change. It rarely indicates long-term processes that might undermine authoritarian rule or sustain democratic politics. New divisions, however, require analysis as they might be precursors to regime collapse. Conversely, when elites seem to be united and profit from the regime, it is difficult to envision cracks that can lead to its demise. In those circumstances, only external factors are likely to bring about political change.

Civil society, oppositional politics and change

Societal groups and organizations make claims on the state and seek to maximize their political space to advance their interests. We refer to civil society as a public space in which organizations and groups can pursue their activities without the state's interference. Civil society is constituted of a large number of groups and organizations with various objectives and goals. These can range from non-governmental organizations operating in a number of areas to religious organizations or even business associations. To think in terms of civil society allows us to grasp the role of seemingly disparate groups that sometimes act concurrently to attain certain political objectives.

As discussed above, there are other ways of conceptualizing politics outside of the state. Sometimes individuals come together and form class identities that become politically significant. We offered a number of propositions relating class to political change. Class analysis emphasizes the stratification of society, and linkages of some classes (the bourgeoisie, for instance) with the state. Organizations and groups can sometimes represent class interests, and therefore we would tend to emphasize that analytical category. Other times, they do not, and their political mobilization cuts across classes. It is often more useful then to think of them as "civil society".

What impact does civil society have on political change? In political science, we often associate a dynamic and thriving civil society with democracy. Democratic politics provide a set of rules that best protect spaces that are autonomous from the state. Where civil society is strong and vibrant, it stabilizes and expands democratic life. Yet, it is not entirely clear whether it can contribute to the demise of authoritarian rule and the emergence of a new democracy. Authoritarian regimes usually allow very restricted spaces that are autonomous from the state, so it is unlikely that civil society can grow significantly under such constraints. There is however a degree of variance among authoritarian regimes and the degree to which they exert vast control over society. Occasionally, therefore, civil society can organize, and even mobilize to build some opposition to the state.

In Southeast Asia, civil society organization has often been weak since states in the region have been predominantly authoritarian. Yet, as Meredith Weiss argues, civil society has not been absent. States in Southeast Asia have often allowed some autonomous political organization in response to rising social forces and economic development. Civil society organizations might not have triggered democratization but have often pressured states successfully to liberalize, allowing more participation and freedom of political action even under sustained authoritarian or semi-authoritarian settings. Their character as well suggests a broader range than usually associated with civil society, including religious organizations and some organizations that are not likely to favour democratic politics. Broadly speaking, civil society organizations might not have the strength to lead political change but have nudged authoritarian states towards more compromise and openness (Weiss, 2008).

Southeast Asia's uniqueness

Broad explanations for political change are always confronted with the complexity and uniqueness of local conditions. While we can observe and compare patterns across cases, sometimes we can only explain political change by very distinct events or factors that are not reproduced elsewhere. At other times, certain regional patterns tend to emerge. Are there regional characteristics that might explain trends in Southeast Asia?

Some scholars long ago emphasized the strong role of patron-client ties in Southeast Asian politics. We sometimes refer to these ties as "patrimonialism". From his deep empirical analysis of the region, James C. Scott argued that dyadic ties between a patron and several clients was a strong feature of socio-political relations from the village to the national level. Typically, a patron nurtures loyalty and commitment from followers by providing resources, sometimes protection, or a safety-net when they are faced with difficult times. In return, "clients" remain loyal and commit to supporting these "patrons". In villages, for example, a wealthy landowner might help poorer farmers needing additional money to fund a large wedding or a funeral. In exchange, the landowner will later ask them to return the favour. In politics, patron-client relations might mean that, in exchange for resources, clients will support a local patron who requires their vote or the support for a particular political party. Political leaders might nurture loyalty from individuals in the armed forces, a political party, or other influential positions by providing some benefits in exchange for their support. An authoritarian leader might help provide resources to loyal generals, politicians or businesspeople in exchange for their support of the regime (Scott, 1972). While we can observe patron-client ties in a broad number of societies, when they become widespread and almost systemic, they need to be placed much more centrally within our understanding of politics. We refer to this kind of phenomenon as patrimonialism when the web of these kinds of dyadic relationships is sufficiently widespread that it becomes part of the character of a society, a state, economic sectors or certain segments of the polity.

Patrimonialism has been a strong feature of Southeast Asian politics. Paul Hutchcroft describes the Philippines as a "patrimonial state". In Indonesia, "bapakism" (from the Indonesian word "bapak", literally "father"), was once used to describe the dense web of patron-client ties that emanated from the top to the bottom of the authoritarian regime, beginning with President Suharto who developed loyalty among key supports by allowing access to state resources, contracts and other material benefits (Jackson, 1978). Many observers of Malaysia's powerful dominant party, UMNO, have emphasized its use of patron-client ties to maintain and reproduce its political success.

Patron-client ties, or patrimonialism, best explain stability rather than political change. A web of such ties tends to create its own strength, in parallel with formal institutions. Patron-client ties are private and informal; they bypass formal ranks or institutional hierarchies, although they often complement them. Because of their vertical nature, they have often been used to explain why Southeast Asian countries have seen fewer large-scale, class-based, or horizontally organized resistance movements than other regions.

In some cases, patrimonialism might have given way to other forms of "dyadic" ties, with a different character. John Sidel for instance uses the concept of "bossism" to describe the particular feature of regional politics in the Philippines by which local bosses dominate regional politics (Sidel, 1999). While they might use a certain mix of coercion and purchase of loyalty, they develop strong bases to exercise power even nationally.

There are other, more unique features that explain political change (or its absence) in Southeast Asian countries. The monarchy in Thailand is a unique feature; the king has played a crucial role during times of crises. Monarchy in Cambodia has also been an important source of political loyalty and division. Mass killings in Cambodia and Indonesia cast long shadows over the politics of these countries.

Broad patterns could therefore be observed across cases but unique features are also important. In the chapters that follow, we will trace how economic growth and development has transformed some of the cases of the region. We will assess the extent to which the middle class was formed in these contexts, and weigh the extent to which it might be behind some of the political movements that have led to political change, in particular democratization. In cases with poor levels of economic development, we will similarly analyse the role of various social classes in the politics of the country, or explain the absence of significant political mobilization where change is absent. At the same time, when political change does occur, we will assess whether identifiable splits in the elites preceded the change.

These broad patterns are conditioned by the international context as mentioned above. In particular, the emergence and stabilization of communist regimes has shaped the way economic growth and development has occurred, as well as the type of political institutions and incentives that maintain elite unity. In comparing authoritarian regimes and their stability, this distinction is particularly important. Similarly, in some cases, change will be linked to international shocks, particularly regional or global economic crises.

Finally, the chapters are organized as a historical narrative of political continuity and change in order to reflect some of the key, and sometimes unique factors, that have shaped political regimes.

PART I

Capitalism, economic growth and political change

Countries in this part have followed a markedly different path from state-socialist countries, which are analyzed in Part II. Prior to independence, they were partially integrated into world markets through the self-serving networks of the colonial economy. After independence, the new governments attempted to retain the profitable ventures established by their colonial predecessors, mostly based on agricultural exports and exploitation of natural resources. They preserved private property, a commitment to capitalist production and their integration to world markets. Over time, they sought to diversify their economies, increase their industrial base and exploit new economic advantages that could foster growth and profit.

The contrast between capitalist and state-socialist countries provides a useful comparison of the different regimes and paths of political change in the region. Since a strong postulate in the political science literature links levels of economic development with democracy, these two parts provide a first-level comparison of levels of economic growth and economic development, with their expected impact on the region's regimes.

Political change has varied among this group of countries. Malaysia and Singapore have been fairly similar despite Singapore's status as a city-state. Ever since they obtained their independence from the British, stable regimes have governed both countries. The People's Action Party (PAP) has dominated Singapore, with opposition parties remaining weak and only occasionally able to mount very small challenges to the regime. The United Malays National Organisation (UMNO) has similarly dominated Malaysia's politics but has always ruled in coalition with other political parties. Initially under the Alliance and later the National Front (Barisan Nasional, BN), other parties such as the Malaysian Chinese Association (MCA), the Malaysian Indian Congress (MIC), or Gerakan have shouldered UMNO and allowed it to retain more than two-thirds of parliamentary seats for most of the post-independence period. In recent years, emerging opposition parties have threatened this dominance but not sufficiently to trigger political change.

By contrast, Thailand, Indonesia and the Philippines have seen lots of political change, against the backdrop of persistent patrimonial ties that reproduce strong oligarchic centres of power. From 1932–73, coalitions of military, bureaucratic and corporate interests ruled Thailand through successive authoritarian governments. After a brief democratic hiatus from 1973–6 – which marks the first successful attempt by societal groups to dislodge these centres of power – authoritarian rule returned until the early 1990s. It is a bit difficult to mark a specific transition even to a minimal electoral democracy in Thailand. In the 1980s, parliament played a more significant role under a prime minister that the military appointed. From 1988–91, democracy increased slightly as the prime minister was then an elected leader of the political party with the largest number of seats. Interrupted by a coup, electoral democracy resumed in 1992. For the following two decades, regular elections were held, and governments succeeded one another through democratic means. Yet, the military was not far behind and even intervened once again in another coup in 2006. Clusters of business interests allied to generals and politicians continued to wield strong power. Thailand also retained its monarchy. As such its political path is somewhat unique, especially the strong influence King Bhumibol has exercised, particularly during episodic political crises.

Indonesia began as a liberal democracy after its independence, followed by a long and stable authoritarian regime from 1965–98. Since then, the country has returned to democratic politics. Yet, as with Thailand, clusters of oligarchic power retain strong influence in the political system. The authoritarian regime of President Suharto during more than thirty years nurtured a patrimonial system by which business interests close to the regime profited from state allocations, regulation and protection. The regime used oil revenues and income generated through economic growth to buy political support from military officers, high-level bureaucrats, politicians and selected businesses. These clusters of power were still present after the fall of the regime; much of the old elite has remained prominent in politics and business.

In the Philippines, a certain form of electoral democracy has taken root, yet it disguises a weak state that political clans have long captured and exploited to their advantage. With the significant exception of a little more than a decade of authoritarian rule under Ferdinand Marcos from 1972–86, the Philippines retained its low-quality democracy. Patrimonialism is an integral part of the political system, which has prevented social groups from exerting sufficient influence to force reform and a more equitable distribution of wealth and political power.

What explains such paths, and how can we compare these countries? Recalling that economic development often produces democracy over time, it is useful to analyze these countries' economic development trajectories in comparative perspective. In the decades prior to independence, these countries had similar economic bases. As with others in Southeast Asia, they were primarily agrarian economies with rice production as the core of subsistence farming. In addition, farmers were often involved in the production of cash crops, which varied by location and world demand. Some grew spices, such as nutmeg or cinnamon; others grew coffee or coconut, which were then sold to the middlemen traders of the colonial economy. In some places, such as Malaya, Sumatra (Dutch East Indies) or the Philippines, European colonial rulers created large plantations and hired contract labour. They also built roads, bridges and other infrastructural needs that served the colonial economy.

At independence, they all had important economic sectors that had been well integrated into world markets through the colonial economy. Some divergence then occurred. In Indonesia, the 1950s were marked by economic stagnation, as successive governments under democratic rule were too unstable to manage the economy effectively. When President Sukarno seized control of Dutch-owned companies still operating in the country, he further contributed to slowing down growth. He came close to steering the country towards state socialism. During this time, Malaysia and Singapore were still under British colonial control. The Philippines also gained independence but economic activity remained relatively similar to the decades under US colonial rule. Increasingly, large landowners exploited plantation-style agriculture, while Americans owned some large plantations. They ventured into some agro-businesses for foreign markets, with not much of a rise in living standards for the very large majority of Filipinos. Thailand became one of the largest rice exporting countries in the first half of the twentieth century and remained so for several decades. Starting

Table 1 *GDP per capita, 1960–2009 (ten-year averages – US$)*

	1960–9	1970–9	1980–9	1990–9	2000–9
Brunei	1 291[a]	7 484	18 111	14 854	24 240
Cambodia	134	85	114	240	473
Indonesia	66[b]	234	590	918	1 425
Laos	–	63	151	283	514
Malaysia	325	839	2 026	3 711	5 506
Burma/Myanmar	–	124	154	155	256
Philippines	210	346	635	920	1 256
Singapore	543	2 280	6 998	19 883	29 114
Thailand	139	353	864	2 175	2 789
East Timor	–	–	–	303	418
Vietnam	–	90	131	247	654

Source: Data between 1970 and 2009 from United Nations Main Aggregates Database. Data between 1960 and 1969 from World Bank Development Indicators.
[a] 1965–9
[b] 1967–9

in 1873 and throughout the following twenty-five years or so, the Kingdom of Siam under King Chulalongkorn (Rama V) pushed ahead with the modernization of its state and bureaucracy in response to pressures of the surrounding colonial powers. It also created conditions that dramatically increased rice production for export. Individual farmers constituted the core of this production and remained an important component of Thai growth until the 1960s. All these countries remained agrarian but had different levels of success with growth in their agricultural production and exports.

If we look at Gross Domestic Product (GDP) per capita for 1960–9, points of departure were quite far apart (see Table 1). This figure is a good indicator of total wealth of the country, divided by its population. A low GDP per capita generally indicates that there is a large majority of the population with very little wealth. A very large, rural-based population usually typifies this kind of profile in Southeast Asia. Singapore was already ahead at $543 per capita,[1] reflecting Singapore's wealth as a commercial hub for the region. Malaysia and the Philippines, as wealthy plantation-based ventures for the British and

[1] Unless otherwise specified, the use of $ in the text refers to US$.

Americans, respectively enjoyed levels of $325 and $210 per capita, although it did not necessarily reflect the wealth of the population as a whole, since distribution particularly in the Philippines was highly skewed towards wealthy landowners. Thailand and Indonesia, as primarily rice-growing economies, remained behind at $139 and $66 respectively. Indonesia was particularly poor given its very large population and the disastrous economic policies of the 1950s. Many of these countries were already wealthier than Cambodia, Laos or Vietnam (see Part II).

Over the following decades, all these countries surpassed their state-socialist peers and most grew at rates that rapidly transformed their economies. Table 2 shows very high growth rates in Singapore during most of the 1960s and 1970s, as the Lee Kuan Yew government intensified Singapore's role as both a commercial and financial hub. Malaysia and Thailand grew rapidly under government policies that stimulated the development of low-cost manufacturing. Growth was near or above 7 per cent in Thailand for most of the 1960–95 period, whereas Malaysia's was well above 6 per cent. The exceptionally high growth rate in the early 1970s (11.7 per cent) reflects the development of the oil sector at a time when oil prices boomed internationally. After lagging behind, Indonesia followed a similar path with rates mostly at or above 7 per cent from the 1970s to the early 1990s. Oil and gas, as well as the mining sector, represented a good portion of this growth but, from the early 1980s onwards, low-cost manufacturing assumed an increasingly larger share of this growth. The Philippines remained a laggard in this group, with growth rates generally lower than 6 per cent. Figure 1 shows the disparity between the Philippines and others, only reaching similar growth rates in recent years.

Does political change in these countries follow patterns of economic development? Does democracy emerge in countries with high levels of development? The modernization thesis would predict that sustained levels of economic growth would create pressures for democratization as a middle class develops and expands, and as the greater complexity of economic relations produces business groups and professionals whose interests are best served with a more open political environment, such as democracy.

Countries in the region, however, defy to some extent this thesis. The countries with the highest growth and those with highest per capita income – Singapore and Malaysia – remain authoritarian, with

Table 2 *GDP growth (%), 1960–2009 (five-year averages)*

	1961–4	1965–9	1970–4	1975–9	1980–4	1985–9	1990–4	1995–9	2000–4	2005–9
Brunei	–	–	10.3	12.2	–4.4	–2.2	2.5	1.7	2.6	0.5
Cambodia	–	–	–8.7	–5.8	0.9	9.0	5.5	6.6	8.5	7.6
Indonesia	2.3	4.9	8.7	6.9	7.2	5.6	8.0	1.7	4.6	5.6
Laos	–	–	5.2	1.3	7.9	4.9	6.3	6.5	6.0	9.8
Malaysia	6.7	6.4	11.7	7.2	6.9	4.7	9.3	5.2	5.5	4.1
Burma/Myanmar	3.0	3.1	2.7	5.2	5.8	–2.0	5.1	7.2	12.9	10.7
Philippines	5.2	4.9	5.4	6.2	1.3	2.7	1.9	3.7	4.7	4.4
Singapore	5.8	12.8	11.5	7.4	8.5	6.3	9.2	6.1	5.0	4.8
Thailand	6.9	8.5	6.9	8.0	5.5	9.0	9.0	1.5	5.1	3.0
East Timor							10.3	–2.6	3.5	5.9
Vietnam			1.7	7.2	5.2	4.3	7.3	7.5	7.2	7.3

Source: Data between 1970 and 2009 from United Nations Main Aggregates Database. Data between 1960 and 1969 from World Bank Development Indicators.

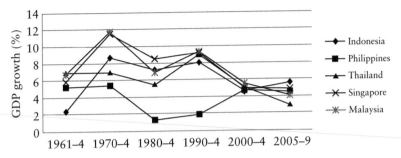

Figure 1 GDP growth in non-socialist Southeast Asia

the PAP and UMNO maintaining political dominance. Only in very recent years have significant pressures appeared in Malaysia, where the Malay middle class has shifted its support towards the opposition. In Singapore, no similar pressures have been sufficiently strong to produce real challenges to the PAP's dominance. Yet, both have a strong middle class. The Philippines, conversely, has enjoyed neither the growth rates of its neighbours nor the development of a large middle class, yet except for the Marcos regime, it has remained an electoral democracy.

Only Thailand and to a lesser extent Indonesia reproduce the expected modernization pattern. After two decades of economic growth, demonstrators brought down Thailand's military regime in 1973. When the military then returned in 1976, it soon realized that it could not maintain tight control as before. Parliament was allowed to function throughout the 1980s, yet still under military control. Since 1988, the country has been mostly democratic, interspersed with coups and brief periods of military rule. By the 1980s, Thailand's middle class had grown considerably. Its business class had also expanded and diversified with some significant portions of it seeking more political clout. Together these factors have helped to create pressures initially for the establishment and later the maintenance of democracy. Indonesia in turn remained authoritarian from the late 1950s until 1998. During these decades, a growing middle class had pressured the regime for reform and demands for more democracy had become widespread. The regime of President Suharto collapsed in 1998 and was quickly replaced with electoral democracy. On the whole, even though economic development has created some pressures for change, the results have not been straightforward. When looking at Malaysia,

Singapore, Thailand, the Philippines and Indonesia, there is enough variance in outcomes to suggest that there is only a weak relationship between economic development and the emergence of democracy in the region.

Factors such as party dominance, military cohesiveness or shared predatory interests leading to elite unity under authoritarian rule can help to explain some of the discrepancies. Singapore has had the most united elite while Thailand's elite has probably been the most divided. The PAP's dominance in Singapore has largely defied modernization expectations, given the leap in Singapore's total wealth as well as its spread to large segments of its population. Decades under Lee Kuan Yew's leadership helped to stabilize a ruling elite very closely tied to the regime. The PAP has been an elitist party that recruits the best and brightest. Its leadership profits from stable and lucrative careers. In the private sector, entrepreneurs also profit from close ties to the PAP, and barriers between the public and private sector elites have often been quite porous. Such party dominance reproduces some of the advantages of communist parties in state-socialist systems. Malaysia's UMNO has been similar in this respect but not quite as dominant. UMNO built a very strong loyal elite as it backed political success with a vast network of patronage. Ethnic divisions created rival groups within the political elite, yet UMNO could create and nurture unity through alliances with non-Malay based parties. Elites in these parties maintained close ties with UMNO, given that Malays were assured control of the political system and links with the Malay political leadership were necessary for their community's protection and interests. Nevertheless, occasionally elite unity has eroded and splits have occurred even among the Malays, yet not sufficiently deep or strong so far to trigger a move away from the status quo.

Indonesia and Thailand's elites have only occasionally been united, and mainly under military dominance. Indonesia's elite remained highly divided throughout its initial period of liberal democracy in the 1950s. After the armed forces became dominant in 1965, however, the authoritarian regime maintained elite unity for more than thirty years under Suharto's rule. When factions emerged within the military or the bureaucracy, Suharto managed to sideline emerging rivals or ensure cooperation through an extensive patronage network. Similarly many political opponents were attracted to support the regime through a mix of patronage, protection of their interests, or fatigue at lack of alternative political options. By the 1990s, however, more serious cracks appeared within the armed forces and within the ruling elite more broadly, including pro-Islamic politicians who had become more assertive within the regime and demanded political reform. Indonesia followed a classic democratization path by which such elite divisions strongly contributed to the regime's fall and the establishment of a democracy. Thailand had a notoriously divided elite that pitted against one another various factions of military officers and bureaucrats. Coup and counter-coups occurred frequently. Rather than democratic breakthroughs, authoritarian leaders replaced previous ones that had fallen in part because of a shared interest in maintaining military and bureaucratic dominance. Military dominance eroded during the 1970s, with the emergence of a brief democratic period (1973–6), a decade of semi-authoritarian rule in the 1980s and finally a return to full civilian rule and electoral politics after 1988. Although coups subsequently occurred in 1991 and 2006, the military maintained direct control only briefly and then returned power to civilians, while maintaining a more indirect influence. It is less obvious to identify clear splits in the elite prior to periods of regime collapse in Thailand. Nevertheless, chronic factionalism in the armed forces certainly prevented it from maintaining strong unity while other factors, such as a rising middle class, created increasing pressures for more open politics.

Finally, the Philippines are a slightly different case. The country's political and economic elite have long shared common interests, as large landholders formed political clans that captured the presidency, parliament and local political positions. These family-based clans continue to dominate the political landscape as well as the country's wealth, as they migrated into different areas of the economy. A large wealth gap separates this elite from the vast majority of the population. While the elite remains united in its broad interests, family-based political clans compete for power. Elections and democratic process have provided the framework for these clans to compete, sometimes violently, to capture the state and its resources. The authoritarian regime, under President Marcos, represented less a new regime than the temporary success of one political clan to impose its dominance over others. Elite division remained and, a little more than a decade later, competing clans found allies in mass rallies to overthrow the Marcos regime and reinstate the competitive framework that had long allowed them to pursue their interests. In this sense, democracy in the Philippines does provide an expected framework for political competition but, ironically, remains of poor quality as it maintains and reproduces elite dominance and stark inequality.

Elite unity and institutions that support it, alongside the effects of economic development, explain a larger part of the maintenance of authoritarian regimes. When elites are divided and economic development has produced a burgeoning middle class, pressures for democratization are very strong. Some unique factors such as the political institutionalization of ethnic divisions in Malaysia or the maintenance of the monarchy in Thailand provide unique factors that are also considered in the following chapters.

2 | *Indonesia and Timor-Leste*

Indonesia

In Indonesia, several regime changes have occurred since independence. From 1950–7, Indonesians were governed under a parliamentary democracy. After several crises in the late 1950s, President Sukarno abandoned this regime and proclaimed "Guided Democracy" instead, which was essentially the beginning of authoritarian rule. This regime lasted from 1957–65, and was then replaced with the New Order government of President Suharto, after a failed coup attempt allowed the military to establish a stronger hold on the country. Finally, after thirty-three years, the New Order regime ended when President Suharto resigned in May 1998. His successor, B. J. Habibie, began a process of democratization. Indonesia now constitutes one of the most vibrant electoral democracies of the region, although it continues to be dogged by many problems.

Much of the scholarship on Indonesian politics has attempted to draw continuities across different time periods and regime types, to identify similarities that apparently created some fundamental characteristics in the Indonesian state or practice of politics more broadly. From this scholarship, two kinds of approaches are worth noting: one using the concept of patrimonialism; the other emphasizing cultural practices that are reproduced from one period to the next. These kinds of approaches both emphasize continuities.

During the long period of authoritarian rule from the late 1950s to the late 1990s, several scholars used patrimonialism or a variant thereof to explain the longevity and resilience of authoritarian rule. For instance, scholars such as Jackson characterized the Indonesian state as a bureaucratic polity but emphasized that its strength lay in the close ties between the ruling group and the bureaucratic elite (Jackson, 1978). Especially under the New Order regime of President Suharto (1965–98), they noted the extensive web of material benefits that flowed to elites in exchange for supporting the regime. Harold Crouch also analyzed the pervasive nature of patrimonial ties and explicitly linked these features of Indonesia's authoritarian period to a much longer tradition of "patrimonial" style of rule among Javanese rulers (Crouch, 1978). In this respect, patrimonialism can be viewed as a variant of a cultural explanation, rooted in a traditional type of rule that has persisted over time.

Cultural explanations also emphasize continuities. Among scholars of Indonesia, Benedict Anderson provided such an explanation to account for some of the features of the authoritarian styles of Presidents Sukarno and Suharto, as well as Indonesia's rejection of parliamentary democracy in the 1950s or the style of political and administrative management that emerged in the 1960s and 1970s. For Anderson, some of these features were steeped in a distinct concept of power in Javanese culture. The Javanese are the largest ethnic group in Indonesia. All Indonesian presidents have been Javanese and a good portion of the ruling class as well. Therefore Anderson saw Javanese culture as having a strong effect on post-independence Indonesian rule. The Javanese see power as concentrated in the hands of an individual or a group. If not concentrated, it would weaken and dissipate. Such views would explain, for instance, why Indonesian rulers have been very anxious about national unity and held strong tendencies to centralize power (Anderson, 1990).

Such notions of culture or patrimonialism have appeared in many analyses of Indonesian politics. While not always prominently featured, they are frequently mentioned as persistent features that defy periods of important political change. For instance, persistently high levels of corruption in today's democracy are often seen as remnants of patrimonial styles of rule.

Nevertheless, these features do not explain change. Given its previous instability and dramatic demise in the 1950s, what explains a return to democratic rule in the 1990s?

First, over the long run, economic development seems to have produced expected results. Under New Order rule between 1965–98, the country's economy grew around 5–6 per cent annually, thereby creating an increasingly large and politicized middle class. At first, most of this middle class was composed of Chinese-Indonesians, an ethnic minority representing around 4 per cent of the population. Chinese-Indonesians fared very well in the business sector, with several large business conglomerates owned by Chinese-Indonesians, some of whom maintained close ties to the New Order regime. These conglomerates employed large number of Chinese-Indonesians, whose standards of living remained steadily above most other Indonesians. Over time, the middle class expanded and diversified as more Indonesians obtained higher education and the business sector continued to grow. This broader middle class, many of whom were mainstream Muslim Indonesians, began to demand political reforms several years before Suharto's resignation. Many of them had entered the dominant political party and were also part of the regime. They worked from within for political reform. As Edward Aspinall has noted, in Indonesia the expected direct and rapid effect of middle class growth on democratic change did not materialize. The growing middle class eventually produced political change but not through strong oppositional resistance and broad pressure for change. Instead, the middle class formed different types of opposition, some outside, some within the state, and brought about political change through more gradual nibbling of the regime's legitimacy (Aspinall, 2005).

Second, economic crisis constituted a catalyst. The Asian financial crisis of 1997 hit Indonesia more than other countries. When the effects of the crisis were felt in urban areas, this led to anger and unrest. Months of riots and demonstrations contributed to convincing a reluctant elite to oust Suharto. The movement spilled beyond the middle class as many working class and poor Indonesians joined street demonstrations. Is this evidence of a civil society movement that successfully pushed for democratic reform? Such an analysis would be an exaggeration. Civil society played a crucial role in the form of mass demonstrations but mainly when in combination with broader factors of change (Aspinall, 2005).

Third, elite disunity played an important role in weakening Suharto's grip on power. As the authoritarian ruler grew older, a succession crisis unfolded. By the mid 1990s, a relatively quiescent political elite that had supported the regime divided into factions, each supporting different scenarios for Suharto's succession.

The stability of Indonesia's democracy, not its quality, is more difficult to explain. For the most part, after the sudden resignation of Suharto, a gradual democratization allowed various political forces to align themselves within the new institutional configuration. The old elite could reinvent itself within the new democracy and, in fact, provided a strong measure of continuity as most prominent political figures remained the same as before. A politically weakened armed forces chose to stay away from a central role in politics, partly in exchange for disregarding past abuses.

Some weaknesses persist, and contribute to undermining the quality of democracy. Corruption is endemic, as well as nepotism. Although some analyses link these practices to long-standing patrimonial practices and a political culture supportive of such informal ties, another perspective sees these practices as remnants of authoritarian rule that encouraged patrimonial ties beginning with Suharto himself. The patterns are much more fleeting and subject to constant changes than sometimes assumed.

As seen below, the emergence of democracy in the 1990s was very different than its conditions in the 1950s. Deep ideological divisions drove politics, which were mainly centered on a small elite, while those divisions were largely resolved by the 1990s. Furthermore, a stronger and more diverse middle class, after decades of authoritarian rule, has sustained a return to democracy.

Liberal democracy and Guided Democracy, 1959–1965: elite divisions and ideology

The "Revolution" was a defining moment of state and nation creation in Indonesia. After the Japanese lost the war in 1945, nationalist leaders proclaimed a new independent Republic of Indonesia. Yet, the Dutch refused to relinquish their colony and instead sought to regain control. Over the next four years, the Republic and the Dutch fought over the future of Indonesia. Under international pressure, the Dutch finally relinquished their claim in 1949. Nationalist leaders, with Sukarno at their helm, proclaimed the victory of their "Revolution", as they called the resistance movement. It formed the basis of rhetorical appeals to the unity of the Indonesian state and nation that would shape the strong centralizing thrust of the government for the following five decades. Furthermore, it provided the armed forces with a rationale to participate in politics, as the state elevated their role to heroes of the Revolution. Although not yielding an immediate impact, this rhetoric was used extensively by the late 1950s to justify the military's increasing role in state governance and its eventual dominance after 1965 under the New Order regime of President Suharto.

After the Dutch left Indonesia in 1949, Indonesia's new leaders established a fragile parliamentary democracy. They adopted a temporary constitution in 1950, with the provisions that elections would be held and a new constitution adopted by referendum within a few years. It took until 1955 before free and fair elections were held, and a Constituent Assembly was created to draft a new constitution. By then, various political factions had split along deep ideological lines. Compounded by regional instability, the crises soon led to the demise of the democratic experiment.

The first decade of democratic rule was very unstable. Formed as a parliamentary system in which coalitions were necessary if parties wanted to rule, few governments were able to maintain themselves in power for more than a year. Among the parties, a few were more powerful than others. The Nationalist Party of Indonesia (Partai Nasional Indonesia, PNI) maintained a strong following as Sukarno's party, the party that had led the Revolution and the party that had given birth to the idea of a unified Indonesian nation. As a country in which a vast majority of people are Muslim, parties based on Islam also gained strong support. Among these, two were most significant: Masjumi, which originally gained a strong following among all major Muslim organizations; and Nahdlatul Ulama, a party whose following was based mainly in the large Islamic organization of the same name, and based in the densely populated island of Java. Nahdlatul Ulama had originally been part of Masjumi but eventually split because of internal disagreements. Masjumi retained a strong following among supporters of Muhammadiyah, the second largest Islamic organization in Indonesia and also the "Outer Islands", which refers to the islands outside of Java (Feith, 1962).

The distinction between traditionalist and modernist Islam is important for understanding politics in Indonesia. Traditionalists, perhaps best exemplified by followers of Nahdlatul Ulama, Indonesia's largest association of religious scholars/leaders based in Java, practice Islam but its rituals and beliefs have been highly influenced by local conditions. In Java, for instance, some Muslim practices and beliefs are reminiscent of the past dominance of Hinduism before most of Java converted to Islam in the sixteenth century. Modernist Muslims emerged from a revivalist movement in the early twentieth century that advocated a more textual practice of Islam, less imbued by local traditions and rituals and reflecting more universal Islamic practices, while acknowledging the need to adapt to the modern world. Modernists were at the forefront, for instance, of creating educational institutions and providing health care, rather than emphasizing tradition and past customs. For the following decades, this division marked some of the political lines between Islamic groups and parties.

Finally the Communist Party, initially less important, represented a third kind of political ideology and program. In spite of their weakness, communists had twice before attempted to foment revolutions but were crushed. Towards the end of Dutch colonial rule, the communist leadership had organized small revolts in 1926 and 1927, but Dutch authorities strongly repressed them, arresting 13,000 people, and sending several hundred into internal exile (McVey, 1965). Again in 1948, in the chaos of the Republican resistance to Dutch attempts to regain control, the communist leadership proclaimed a mass revolt against the Republic, and organized a mass uprising in Madiun. Republican forces swiftly crushed the rebellion. The Communist Party had very few roots across Indonesia and did not organize the kind of armed organization that characterized, for instance, Mao Tse-tung's Red Army in the successful revolution in China in 1949. Instead, after two failed rebellions, Indonesian communists shifted strategies and chose to join established democratic institutions, while gradually expanding their organizational strength at the grass roots.

Leading up to the 1955 election, the three streams became even more entrenched. The electoral results, surprisingly enough, closely reproduced the allocated seats that had been given to various parties when the temporary legislature was set up. The Nationalist Party won the plurality of votes, followed by the two Islamic parties Masjumi and Nahdlatul Ulama. The Communist Party of Indonesia came close behind. Results confirmed the divisions between supporters of nationalist, Islamic and communist visions for the country.

This division was reflected, and intensified, in the Constituent Assembly that was formed to draft a final version of the Indonesian constitution. The Constitution of 1950 had been adopted temporarily with the expectation that a new constitution would be drafted following a democratic process. Voters in 1955 also elected parties to this Constituent Assembly, with results being very similar. From the outset, the Constituent Assembly became deadlocked over the fundamental principle that should underlie the Indonesian state. Nationalists espoused Sukarno's vision of a secular society organized around the five principles outlined in Sukarno's Pancasila ideology, namely: belief in the one and only God; just and civilized humanity;

unity of Indonesia; democracy through deliberation; and social justice. Communists supported the nationalists strategically; they had an alternative vision for Indonesia but temporarily found their interests better served with nationalists rather than Islamists. The main contenders were Islamists, who wanted Islam as a basis for the state. Because neither could muster sufficient support, the Constituent Assembly remained deadlocked (Feith, 1962).

Other challenges contributed to political instability. Many regions began to resent control by the central government, especially the large presence of civil servants from Jakarta and Java. Furthermore, the military had been divided into various factions, some of which were formed around regional commanders who were growing more independent from the central command and who took advantage of their position to engage in profitable business ventures. By the late 1950s, some of these tensions produced regional rebellions as armed forces commander A. H. Nasution re-established firmer control and centralized the army to increase its unity. In 1957, some of these commanders launched regional rebellions, which further destabilized the country. The declaration of an alternative Revolutionary Government of the Republic of Indonesia (Pemerintah Revolusioner Republik Indonesia, PRRI) was the ultimate challenge to Sukarno's increasingly authoritarian approach, sealing a coalition between disgruntled army officers, regionalists and members of the Masjumi party. In response, the armed forces successfully crushed the rebellion, and Masjumi was banned in 1960. From then on, the armed forces became increasingly influential as authoritarian rule deepened.

Liberal democracy formally ended, and was replaced with Guided Democracy, when Sukarno dissolved the Constituent Assembly in 1959 and parliament in 1960. He had begun to develop the concept in earlier years, focusing primarily on denouncing the ills of "Western-style" democracy, and espousing a system that he deemed more appropriate for Indonesia. The central concept entailed representation of all political parties in the Cabinet, including the Communist Party, which had never joined the government; functional groups into a national council; consensus rather than voting as a principle of decision making; yet also a strong central authority. The president's powers had been curtailed under the temporary constitution under which Indonesia had been ruled since 1950. Scholars have contested whether in fact the Assembly had no chance of finding a compromise despite ideological divisions. It is equally plausible that Sukarno was essentially frus-trated with a system that reduced his powers, and prevented him from advancing his agenda. In the end, the decision to dissolve the Assem-bly and move to Guided Democracy left a long-lasting impression that the experiment with liberal democracy had been a failure (Lev, 1966; Nasution, 1992).

There are two main reasons why democracy failed in Indonesia. In addition to the immediate causes relating to the political instability described above, a few broader factors are important. First, the ideo-logical divisions of the 1950s were profound and hit at the heart of the fundamental basis of the state. Democratic institutions often provide a framework to resolve conflicts but, when foundational principles are involved, it can be limited. The deep divisions between nationalists, communists and Islamists could have been resolved but with difficulty in that context. Until Islamists could accept less than an Islamic state, they would clash with nationalists and communists for whom such an option was unacceptable. Similarly, communists could remain loyal to democratic politics, as long as they were willing to compromise and advance their interests within an essentially capitalist market economy. With increasing power in the early 1960s, however, and the growth of communist movements in Asia, communists would become increas-ingly likely to advance revolution rather than compromise, again pit-ting themselves fundamentally against Islamists and nationalists.

Second, there was a very small middle class and no strong economy to support the democratic regime. At the time of independence, only a very small number of Indonesians were educated. The economy was mainly agriculturally based and, aside from some plantations that reverted to the state, self-sufficient agriculture from small landholdings provided Indonesians with their main livelihoods. There was virtually no manufacturing sector and only a very limited agro-industrial sector employing a tiny fraction of Indonesians. As a result, only civil ser-vants constituted a small middle class with livelihoods so closely tied to the state that they would not rebel against attempts to transform the regime. Furthermore, the economy was stagnant throughout the 1950s and 1960s. Political parties disagreed over economic policy. Coalition governments were concerned more about survival than actual policy, as governments changed almost every year during the period of liberal democracy. Regional instability created havoc in the economy. With a stagnating economy and inflation running very high, Indonesians saw few benefits from liberal democracy, but there was very little opposition from the middle class against the rise of authoritarian rule. Instead, impoverished Indonesians were lured by the appeal of land reform and transformation that the communists had promised but had been too weak to deliver during that period.

Guided Democracy marked the beginning of authoritarian rule, as Sukarno relied increasingly on the armed forces. He attempted to reduce ideological divisions and consolidate elite unity under authoritarian rule but had limited success. Guided Democracy remained a transitional regime that saw two major players struggle for supremacy and the support of the charismatic Sukarno: the armed forces and the Communist Party.

The armed forces had become more centralized and consolidated. They played a greater role as political parties were increasingly emasculated. Much stronger presidential leadership, large rallies and mass appeals, characterized the regime. At the same time, as a civilian, Sukarno mistrusted the armed forces and was reluctant to rely extensively on them. He was well known for his skillful ability to balance political forces. By the early 1960s, he saw great political potential in nurturing support from the Communist Party (Partai Komunis Indonesia, PKI) without ever clearly siding with its program or leadership. He played a delicate balancing act between the communists and the army, which had a strong anti-communist core. A third political force, Islamist parties, had been severely weakened and sidelined after the defeat of the PRRI and the banning of Masjumi.

This delicate balancing act proved to be Guided Democracy's death knell. The communists and the armed forces increasingly clashed in the last couple of years of the regime, and it became obvious that one or the other main political force attempting to sideline the other would resolve a severe power struggle. Furthermore, President Sukarno was more concerned with his confrontational foreign policy than keeping his regime stable. He relied on his rhetorical appeals to nationalist claims rather than other means to stabilize the regime. He challenged British plans to create Malaysia, out of their colony of Malaya and adjoining colonial territories, and threatened war to "recover" West New Guinea from the Dutch, as the most eastern part of the former Dutch East Indies had remained in Dutch hands at independence. Sukarno considered the territory to belong rightfully to Indonesia and therefore escalated the confrontational stance against

the former colonial ruler. In addition, his government decided to
seize control of Dutch companies, thereby placing in the state's hands
the management of the only large companies that were operating in
Indonesia. These nationalist policies not only contributed to unstable
political conditions but also economic decline. With splits at the heart
of the regime between the armed forces and the rising Communist
Party, Sukarno failed to manage and contain these opposing forces.

New Order regime, 1965–1998: military rule, elite consolidation and weakened opposition

The New Order regime came to power violently. The crisis that led to
its establishment defined its character and, to some extent, its longevity.
It sealed and institutionalized a much deeper form of authoritarian
rule, based on the strong control of the armed forces. The regime
ended when the legitimacy of the armed forces was undermined, the
president lost his authority and severe economic crises weakened the
regime's extensive patronage.

The regime began with a massacre. The Communist Party had been
on the rise in the early 1960s and, with some support from President Sukarno, began to take increasingly bold actions. It organized
a campaign of land seizures destined to force land redistribution in
areas where large landowners were powerful. It held mass rallies
and excelled at organizing large numbers of people around the country through its various functional organizations. The armed forces
saw a mounting threat as the PKI's confidence grew. At the same
time, the nearby escalation of the Vietnam War fed some sense of
threat, as the United States intensified its involvement in Vietnam and
became concerned at the rising power of communists in Indonesia. On
30 September, 1965, seven of the highest-ranking generals of the
Indonesian armed forces were assassinated, in a coup attempt for
which the Communist Party was accused. One of the few remaining generals, Suharto, who was commander of the Jakarta garrison,
stepped into the leadership vacuum, took charge and secured the capital. The official version blamed the Communist Party for launching
an attempted coup that failed because of the successful intervention of
the armed forces and Suharto's leadership role. Historians still debate
this version of events and question the exact role of the Communist

Party in the generals' assassinations as well as Suharto's role during those crucial days.

Nevertheless, subsequent events were much clearer. The armed forces swiftly purged communist sympathizers from within its ranks. The Communist Party was blamed and banned. During the following months, a climate of fear spread across the archipelago as the armed forces urged citizens to seek out and even kill communist supporters. In the confusion, thousands of people were killed for a variety of reasons, whether they had or not supported the Communist Party. The estimated numbers of victims range from 100,000 to 500,000 people, with the armed forces giving its tacit support as well as having direct involvement in some locations. The shadow of this massacre continued to hang over Indonesians for the subsequent few decades, as the government routinely used accusations of being communist to suppress dissent (Cribb & Coppel, 2009).

The armed forces, and its new leader Suharto, became almost the only significant power in the country. Suharto became president in 1966 after gradually sidelining Sukarno. The Communist Party was crushed. Under Guided Democracy, Sukarno had already weakened other political parties. Islamic organizations, which had represented a third pillar of power in the 1950s, were rapidly sidelined after rising momentarily to the fore. As the new regime had turned against the Communist Party, Islamic organizations and parties had seen an opportunity to regain the upper hand. Most notably, the youth wing of Nahdlatul Ulama, the largest Islamic organization, participated in the regime's anti-communist purge. Its leaders, as well as former members of Masjumi, hoped for a stronger role of Islamic parties and organizations under the New Order but their hopes were dashed. The regime consolidated the power of the armed forces but remained suspicious of political mobilization on the basis of Islam.

Over the course of the following years, the regime's consolidation and stability relied on several sources of power. First, the armed forces were deployed across the archipelago and maintained a presence down to the village level. In order to ensure its loyalty and its unity, Suharto routinely reassigned regional commanders and top generals, particularly when any one seemed to rise above the fray. By doing so, Suharto skilfully prevented the emergence of potential rivals. Second, the regime built a sophisticated corporatist structure that created bureaucratic tentacles linking the state to all levels of society. The state sponsored and organized groups along functional lines: business associations, women's groups, youth groups and even organizations to manage religious groups. These organizations were linked to bureaucratic layers at the provincial, district and village levels. Furthermore, they formed the core, along with civil servants, of *Golkar* (Golongan Karya, literally functional groups) that served as the governmental political party during elections. Third, it placed a high priority on economic development, as a lesson learned from the earlier regime when poor economic performance contributed to the rise in support for the communists. Fourth, the regime used patronage to buy support from the elite. With economic growth, Suharto benefited from an increasing amount of financial resources to buy support from the bureaucratic and military elite. The military became more heavily involved in business ventures, Suharto family charities were used as sources of patronage distribution, and civil servants benefited from lucrative opportunities to siphon off resources. At the apex, Suharto skilfully managed this sophisticated system of authoritarian management (Crouch, 1978; Liddle, 1996).

In the first couple of decades, the New Order regime crafted the institutional and economic structure that ensured its longevity. Although the armed forces were the main power holders, and strongly represented at all levels of government, over time they left an increasing amount of space for civilian allies, particularly from the government party Golkar. Suharto was concerned with increasing the regime's legitimacy by respecting a certain number of institutional rules. First and foremost, he maintained the Constitution of 1945, which had been revived by Sukarno when liberal democracy was suspended. This Constitution gave strong powers to the president but made him accountable to a People's Consultative Assembly (Majelis Permusyawaratan Rakyat, MPR), which was comprised of members of parliament (the People's Representative Assembly, Dewan Perwakilan Rakyat, DPR), as well appointed members including representatives from the armed forces and from the regions. The MPR adopted broad guidelines of state policy for five years, and elected the president and vice-president, as well as accepted the president's accountability report.

The DPR was mostly an elected body, although some seats were reserved for the armed forces. Elections were held in 1971 and then every five years from 1977, although they were far from free and fair. Political parties were initially reduced to ten, and subsequently to three when, in 1973, the government forced the amalgamation of nationalist and Christian parties into the Democratic Party of Indonesia (Partai Demokrasi Indonesia, PDI); Islamic parties were forced into a single Unity Development Party (Partai Persatuan Pembangunan, PPP). Golkar, as the government party, formally an association of functional groups, constituted the third. Suharto remained fully in control of the electoral process, as Golkar was the only party permitted to organize and mobilize at all administrative levels outside of electoral campaigns; civil servants were all required to vote for it; the leadership of the PDI and PPP usually required Suharto's assent; intimidation was frequently used during campaigns; and appointed members of parliament were firmly under Suharto's control. Yet, small marginal changes in electoral results often constituted indicators of regional or broader discontent with the regime. Political campaigns allowed citizens to demonstrate and voice some discontent in what became known as "festivals of democracy", and the mere presence of alternative parties gave Indonesians a sense of choice.

These institutions and rules did not truly provide either legitimacy or representation, but injected some predictability and small sense of participation among the elite. Even though elections and the party system were mostly a masquerade, they nevertheless cushioned the effects of authoritarian rule by providing some regularity, some ability to express discontent, and reduce the arbitrariness often associated with military dominated regimes. In this sense, it contributed to some regime stability and, ironically, later provided the basis for relatively smooth democratic transition.

In the economic realm, the transformation was also significant. Soon after rising to power, Suharto hired professional economists to manage the economy. He entrusted them with the mandate to stabilize inflation and create conditions for rapid growth. Under his predecessor, the economy had plummeted. High inflation and stagnation contributed to rising poverty. Suharto attributed the strong support that communists had received to poor economic conditions. He would continue to rationalize his regime, and explain away other problems, through the belief that economic development would raise support for the regime and prevent rebellion or strong discontent.

Economists successfully created a framework that stabilized the economy and laid foundations for more development. At the same time, the discovery and subsequent exploitation of large oil and gas reserves, starting in the early 1970s, gave a huge boost to the economy.

Furthermore, it provided the regime with a very large, autonomous financing basis, since the oil and gas sector was controlled by state-owned Pertamina, in partnership with foreign companies. Oil and gas revenues provided huge patronage resources, some of which were filtered down the administrative ladder and others provided the foundations to start state-sponsored companies.

In the mid 1980s, the price of oil declined and threatened Indonesia's economic health. Suharto again turned to his team of professional economists. They began to deregulate the economy and created a number of incentives to stimulate investments in the non-petroleum export sectors. In the following two decades, the manufacturing and agro-industrial export-oriented sectors grew rapidly, even overtaking the oil and gas sectors. Indonesia sustained economic growth rates of 5–7 per cent until the late 1990s. Large numbers of Indonesians benefited from the manufacturing boom, which contributed to the creation of an expanding middle class. There is no doubt that many Indonesians found economic opportunities and more stable conditions appealing. While perhaps not actively supporting the regime, they were willing to tolerate it as long as benefits flowed.

The flipside of economic growth was the elaborate structure of patronage that helped to strengthen and sustain the regime. Top military officials linked to wealthy businessmen obtained lucrative state contracts. Large conglomerates owed much of their wealth to their connections to the regime. Private sector enterprises, state companies and large foundations became various outlets by which the New Order fostered loyalty through the provision of economic opportunities and side payments. Civil servants at all levels regularly siphoned away state resources in exchange for supporting the regime. Oil money and eventually other state resources from economic growth fuelled much of this patronage.

Overall, the regime relied on a mix of patronage and development to create support, in addition to repression and coercion as would be expected in a military-dominated authoritarian regime. Patronage helped to buy out an elite that benefited from the system. At the same time, the regime had sufficient resources to direct some state funds to development at various levels of government. Some of these funds actually contributed to providing clean water, and building bridges and roads. Others allowed even low-level civil servants to benefit from the state's patronage. For many Indonesians, more stable food prices, fuel subsidies, agricultural subsidies and a generally well-functioning economy raised living standards and therefore ensured a fair amount of compliance with the regime.

Nevertheless, the New Order regime was not without its challenges. In 1974, riots broke out in Jakarta, when students protested against corruption and economic inequalities. Combined with urban discontent at unstable rice prices, the rioting, looting and burning was widespread, in particular since a few disgruntled generals manipulated the events. Protesters were strongly repressed. At the same time, the regime continued to foster economic growth in the hopes of limiting the rise of such discontent.

Other crises were prompted by the regime's repressive approach to the management of religious and ethnic groups. In 1984, the regime was highly criticized when the armed forces opened fire on Muslim protesters who voiced their discontent at government plans to force all organizations to adopt Pancasila as their basic ideology. From the 1970s to the 1990s, the regime suffered external criticisms and growing domestic unease at its handling of insurgencies in East Timor, Aceh and Irian Jaya. East Timor became a particular sore point when a videotape was broadcast internationally in 1991 showing soldiers opening fire on demonstrators during a funeral procession. In Aceh, when the Free Aceh Movement rose in protest against the government, it was strongly repressed. During the final decade of the regime, the armed forces considered Aceh a "military operations zone", and harshly treated civilians suspected of supporting the movement. In Irian Jaya, the regime also conducted regular military operations to suppress strong secessionist sentiments. Over time, Indonesians became increasingly aware of the abuses of the armed forces in these regions. Criticism arose even among some of the regime's supporters.

Finally, even the regular manipulation of the electoral process caused discontent among supporters of the regime. In 1993, the armed forces for the first time openly rejected Suharto's choice of vice-president and imposed their own. From this point on, factions within the armed forces appeared to be eager to regain some independence from Suharto and remain influential for an eventual succession.

In the face of these crises, the regime was responsive not only through coercive means, but by making adjustments to its institutions, its use of development funds, and its patronage system to incorporate and appease sites of opposition, especially from within the regime.

This very sophisticated, hierarchically organized system began to change in the early 1990s, and came under intense strain by 1997. First, the regime made overtures to Islamic groups, some of which wanted reforms and were willing to push for them from within the system. A sociological transformation had occurred in the previous decade, particularly after the regime had forced Indonesians towards religion, in order to avoid being accused of communist sympathies. Combined with growing religiosity, a greater number of Indonesians had become more devout Muslims. Furthermore, as the regime continued to curtail Islamic organizations and channelled Islamic aspirations into the relatively powerless PPP, educated Muslim intellectuals, administrators and activists chose instead to work from within the regime to transform its political orientation. Eventually, pressures led to the formation of the Indonesian Association of Muslim Intellectuals (Ikatan Cendekiawan Muslim Se-Indonesia, ICMI). Suharto named as its leader his controversial protégé and Cabinet minister, B. J. Habibie, and provided him with an opportunity to build a political constituency. ICMI became a powerful organization in the last years of the regime.

Opposition also grew outside, among secular oriented organizations. Beyond the urban, educated Muslim middle class, many secular-oriented groups also called for democratic reform. Tired of the regime's manipulation, one of the opposition political parties, the PDI, challenged Suharto's preference for its leader in 1996 and selected instead Megawati Sukarnoputri, one of the daughter's of the late President Sukarno. Within a few months, Megawati became a symbol of democratic opposition to the Suharto regime, as she enjoyed the nostalgic aura of her father's past and her willingness to challenge Suharto. In return, Suharto cracked down on the PDI and declared it illegal, thereby forcing Megawati and her supporters to become an unrecognized party, which they named Democratic Party of Indonesia for the Struggle (PDI-P). Instantly, Megawati was transformed into an even stronger representative of democratic opposition.

Second, a succession crisis had been looming for almost ten years when the regime fell. Suharto's success at manipulating the elite and sidelining potential challengers left him alone at the top. As Ed Aspinall has argued, the New Order regime increasingly resembled a personal dictatorship in its last few years, as Suharto placed trust only in family members and cronies (Aspinall, 2005). As he was ageing, members of the armed forces and the political elite manoeuvered to position potential contenders for succession. The space to do so was certainly narrow given the tendency to remove challengers. Succession issues partly lie behind the confrontational refusal of the armed forces to endorse Suharto's vice-presidential candidate in 1993. Vice-presidential nominations in 1993 and 1998 created intense debates about suitable candidates for succession, with various groups attempting to position favoured candidates. B. J. Habibie succeeded in becoming vice-president in 1998 despite past tensions with the armed forces, which had partly imposed their own candidate in 1993 to prevent Habibie from obtaining the position. By 1998, however, Habibie enjoyed strong support from ICMI and managed to yield a sufficiently strong following to withstand opposition. Suharto placed even greater effort to ensure his selection. Yet, at the same time, the regime was on its last legs.

The third, and last straw, that gave the final blow to the regime was the Asian financial crisis of 1997. The crisis first hit Thailand before it spread to Indonesia and other Asian countries. It began as a currency crisis but investors fled as the crisis unveiled the degree and extent of corruption that eroded the economy. Large amounts of short-term debt were held in foreign currency, which put downward pressure on the local one. Banks had overextended, non-economic loans. Combined with increasingly open criticism of the regime's corruption, the economy plummeted. Under intense short-term pressure, and a sudden reliance on the International Monetary Fund for a bailout, the government began to slash subsidies that mattered to the urban poor. The crisis created a sense of heightened panic and anger at its suddenness and depth.

In May 1998, Suharto resigned as the crisis reached its peak. Riots broke out in Jakarta, mainly protesting against the rise in prices, elimination of subsidies, and adjustment policies the government was taking to tackle the country's financial problems. Although he attempted several times to reorganize his government and stay in power, Suharto finally resigned when the armed forces and his closest allies abandoned him. His vice-president, B. J. Habibie, was sworn in and became Indonesia's third president despite being fairly unpopular among several elite circles, especially parts of the armed forces.

The new democratic era: the emergence of the middle class?

Since 1998, Indonesia has enjoyed a relatively stable and promising democracy. In spite of many initial doubts, Indonesia's democracy has proven remarkably resilient. Yet, there have also been some important limitations, including continued secessionist challenges, human rights abuses and especially high levels of corruption.

Habibie was a transitional president who surprised everyone by his bold decision to democratize the political system. Within a few months he relaxed constraints on political parties, announced free and fair elections and allowed the media to report freely. The New Order institutions, including the sitting DPR and MPR members had not changed. Habibie, as Suharto's protégé, was strongly associated with the New Order and was not expected to be a reformer. Yet, the "Reform movement" that ousted President Suharto continued to ask for democracy, many members of the political elite also asked for political change and international donors pressured the government to reform in order to escape the financial crisis and build a sounder economic base. Habibie then moved ahead with reforms and announced elections for June 1999.

Three free and fair elections were held in 1999, 2004 and 2009, thereby setting Indonesia in a stable, democratic path. In 1999, Megawati's PDI-P won the largest numbers of votes and seats, whereas Golkar came in second. PDI-P did not have sufficient votes, however, for Megawati to become president. Instead, Islamic parties that had split the "Islamic" vote managed to garner support from Golkar after Habibie's chances of becoming president were lost because of a banking scandal and because of fury over his decision to allow East Timor to leave Indonesia after referendum results showed strong support for independence. This coalition of parties settled on Abdurrahman Wahid, leader of the largest Islamic organization (Nahdlatul Ulama) and its political party, the National Awakening Party (Partai Kebangkitan Bangsa, PKB), and long-time defender of democratic rights. Following rules established under the previous authoritarian regime, the MPR elected him president and Megawati as vice-president. After two years, however, the MPR overstepped its authority when, disillusioned with Wahid's performance and erratic style, it latched onto a scandal and impeached him. Megawati ascended to the presidency in 2001.

The next two elections were different in one important respect. A constitutional amendment introduced direct presidential elections for 2004. Under the new rules, Indonesians elected Susilo Bambang Yudhoyono (widely known as "SBY" in Indonesia). He was re-elected again in 2009. The legislative elections in 2004 returned a plurality of votes for Golkar and were mainly noticed for a confirmed rise in support for a new Islamic party, the Prosperous Justice Party (Partai Keadilan Sejahtera, PKS), which rode an anti-corruption campaign and won 8 per cent of the votes. It maintained its share of votes in the 2009 elections as well. Another surprise was the strong showing for the newly established Democrat Party (Partai Demokrat, PD), which was essentially SBY's political vehicle. After 2004, SBY relied mainly on Golkar and other parties for political support. By 2009, the Democrat Party became much stronger and won 20 per cent of votes (26 per cent of seats), followed by Golkar and PDI-P. The Democrat Party won largely on the popularity of SBY, who then gained a much stronger and more independent political base.

Overall, Indonesia became a healthy electoral democracy with different parties winning each election, and incumbent presidents being replaced, except in 2009. The array of political parties became much more stable, after some fine-tuning of party laws and regulations and some strengthening of party programmes. After an initial boom in the number of parties leading up to the 1999 elections, parliament adopted some restrictions to stabilize the party system and reduce numbers to more manageable levels. At the same time, these restrictions were not so strong as to prevent the rise of alternative parties. The ability of the Democrat Party to gain a plurality of votes in 2009, as well as the rise of the Prosperous Justice Party, shows evidence of this flexibility.

Other aspects of Indonesia's democracy are noteworthy. The media is now one of the freest in Asia. Parliament is more subjected to scrutiny since the creation of a Constitutional Court, which has ruled several times against legislators. The military no longer holds formal positions in the political system. Initial plans to reduce reserved seats for the military in the parliament and MPR were accelerated, so that the military no longer had representation in these institutions after 2004. It has since remained uninvolved in Indonesia's formal politics. Regions have been given much more representation by the formation of an elected second chamber dedicated to regional representation and sweeping legislation that decentralized administrative and fiscal powers to the benefit of provinces and districts. In some respects, then, Indonesia's democracy has become relatively healthy, with elections at all levels of government, including direct presidential elections. It also resembles federal systems where power is broadly distributed among regions and the central government holds only a few powers.

In spite of these changes, there are still significant limitations to Indonesia's democracy. Certainly in its first five years, from 1999 to 2004, democracy remained fragile. Ethnic and religious violence spread to several regions, including Maluku, Sulawesi, Kalimantan and Aceh. In Maluku and Sulawesi, Muslims and Christians fought each other over land, resources, employment and a certain amount of uncertainty surrounding the country's future for religious minorities. Militant groups such as the Laskar Jihad and Front Pembela Islam fuelled the violence. In Kalimantan, Dayaks and Madurese fought again over local resources. In Aceh, a civilian movement demanded a referendum on independence but was subsequently eclipsed by renewed mobilization of the Free Aceh Movement (Gerakan Aceh Merdeka, GAM). The worst ever violence between GAM and the armed forces occurred in the new democratic era. By 2004, much of the violence had been reduced, as the government was more stable, militias were more contained and the military and police exercised better discipline over their members. Furthermore, many of the opponents to the Indonesian state were lured into the system of patronage and lucrative opportunities that have continued after the transition to democracy (Bertrand, 2004).

The military continued to hold on to some previous authoritarian practices. Although it agreed to relinquish its role in formal political institutions, it was not as readily amenable to civilian control. President Wahid faced many obstacles in his attempt to favour reformist generals and ultimately failed. Furthermore, many retired generals entered politics, thereby maintaining some relatively direct linkages between the political arena and the armed forces. President Susilo Bambang Yudhoyono is the most prominent former general in power. The armed forces were given stronger independence to manage the country's crises under President Megawati at the cost of human rights protection. During significant operations, the armed forces placed Aceh under martial law, with presidential approval, and prevented the media and outsiders from observing their activities. Several human rights abuses were reported. Although on a much smaller scale, in Papua the armed forces also infringed on human rights. The crisis in Aceh was resolved when the Indonesian government and GAM signed a peace agreement that opened a path towards the normalization of politics in the province. But in Papua, problems have persisted. Furthermore, in the rest of Indonesia, the military maintains its territorial command structure that gives it a presence across the archipelago and that can be used for rapid military intervention. Finally, the military has maintained many of its business ventures that were created under the New Order, including hotels, shopping centres, landholdings and a number of other enterprises, even illegal ones. In spite of a 2004 law to curb the military's non-state sources of financing within five years, the military still continues to tap into sources of financing outside of the state.

Decentralization had mixed results. While it did increase regional representation and spread power more evenly across the Indonesian landscape, it also increased opportunities for corruption. Many regional governments used their newly acquired powers mainly for graft rather than sound policy implementation. Hopes of attracting more private investment through infrastructural investment and incentive programmes yielded to more pessimistic assessments of corruption and inefficiency (Aspinall, 2010).

Some institutions have fallen short of being properly reformed. The Supreme Court, for instance, has been notoriously corrupt, open to outside pressure and inefficient. It succeeded in resisting reform and the window of opportunity then waned. The judiciary remains far from being sufficiently competent and independent to provide strong oversight over democratic institutions and practices (Davidson, 2009).

Overall, Indonesia changed quite rapidly from a fairly stable, long-standing authoritarian regime to a fairly healthy democratic one, with free and fair elections, a good amount of civil liberties but with some limitations in terms of deepening the quality of this democracy. How can we explain such a change?

The initial attempts to establish democracy in the 1950s were fraught with weaknesses. In spite of the unifying thrust of the revolution, such common purpose to develop a new Indonesian nation and state was insufficient to deepen and preserve a fragile democracy. Instead, deep ideological divisions soon ripped it apart as Islamists, nationalists and communists presented different visions for Indonesia's future. Furthermore, democracy in the 1950s remained limited to party elites and their debates in Jakarta, with virtually no attempt to extend the reach of political participation. Conversely, Indonesian society emerged from colonial rule still primarily agrarian and poorly educated. With a small middle class and little economic development, the regime collapsed under the weight of ideological division and elite competition.

Authoritarian rule was consolidated and preserved for over three decades. There are four broad sets of factors that explain its longevity. First, the armed forces were able to consolidate their power and displace rivals. Repression was an important instrument of power but not sufficient. Second, the regime built an extensive corporatist structure resembling some of the organizational tentacles of communist regimes. Organized around a hierarchical bureaucracy and functional organizations, the regime included a large number of groups, with a variety of interests, within its institutional structure. Third, a sustained commitment to economic development produced economic growth that strengthened regime support. Fourth, a large number of state funds and revenues were distributed as patronage to supporters of the regime. As a result, repression combined with inclusiveness widened the beneficiaries and supporters of the regime while periodically weakening opposition.

In structural terms, Indonesia was "ripe" for democracy in 1998. Growth rates were high during the three decades of the New Order regime. When oil revenues began to decline, government policies attracted investment in a large number of export-oriented businesses. State resources were poured into raising educational levels, as universities and colleges rapidly expanded. By the 1990s, therefore, the Indonesian middle class was fairly large and well educated.

Yet, we need to be cautious about the role the middle class played in the opposition that brought down the regime. In many respects, it was not the middle class that brought down the regime but a set of alliances between mainly the lower middle class in urban areas, the working class and the rural population. For much of the New Order years, the middle class appeared mainly apolitical and only swung in favour of change when it seemed inevitable. Nevertheless, more segments of the middle class and other opposition groups had become much more vocal in their opposition by the end of the regime, and their mobilization occurred both within the state and in alliances between state reformers and societal groups (Aspinall, 2005).

In addition, as pointed out by O'Donnell and Schmitter, no transition occurs without a split in the ruling elite (O'Donnell & Schmitter,

Table 3 *Indonesia*

Population (rank)	Land area (rank)	Main ethnic groups (%)	Main religions (%)	Regime type (transition)	GDP per capita (rank)	GDP growth rate (%) (rank)
248 216 193 (4th) (2011)	1 811 569 sq km (15th)	Javanese 40.6 Sundanese 15 Madurese 3.3 Minangkabau 2.7 Betawi 2.4 Bugis 2.4 Banten 2 Banjar 1.7 Other/ unspecified 29.9 (2000 census)	Muslim 86.1 Protestant 5.7 Roman Catholic 3 Hindu 1.8 Other/ unspecified 3.4 (2000 census)	Democracy (+1998)[a] Republic	$4 700 (154th) (2011 est.)	6.4 (37th) (2011 est.)

Source: CIA, *The World Factbook*; Polity IV Project, Polity IV Individual Country Regime Trends, 1946–2010.

[a] The year indicates the most recent transition; (+) means a transition towards democracy and (−) denotes a transition towards authoritarianism.

1986). Such a split was apparent already a decade before the transition as various groups within the regime positioned themselves for an inevitable leadership succession. Such elite divisions within the regime occurred earlier as well, certainly in 1974, to some extent in the 1980s, and more frequently in the 1990s. Yet, Suharto skillfully managed to control these potential challenges, by establishing early on a practice of displacing rising rivals, and manipulating the elite to strengthen his grip on power. Ideologically, the regime kept a veil of fear over the elite and the broader population by constantly reminding them of the instability of the 1950s, accusing democracy for such ills and, more importantly, pointing to the rise of the Communist Party and the violence of 1965–6 as possible outcomes of destabilizing the regime. These factors helped to shield Suharto until the succession problems became much stronger, and the financial crisis provided a catalyst that dried up resources to maintain elite loyalty and crushed one of Suharto's main sources of legitimacy: his continued ability to deliver economic growth and rising living standards.

These factors combined with mass mobilization to trigger political change. The mass mobilization in 1998 contributed to the regime's downfall but was mainly a catalyst. It explains the timing of political change rather than its causes. The 1998 movement did not arise out of a well organized and purposeful set of civil society groups seeking reform but grew out of the dislocation and frustration from the Asian financial crisis. Leaders successfully channeled this resentment into sustained demonstrations against the regime. Structural factors and divisions in the elite had made the regime particularly vulnerable to such a challenge.

Timor-Leste

The tiny country of Timor-Leste occupies the eastern half of the island of Timor, along the Indonesian archipelago. After obtaining independence from the Portuguese in 1975, the territory was invaded and then integrated into Indonesia. After the downfall of President Suharto and the demise of the New Order regime in 1998, a referendum held in 1999 strongly supported independence. The Indonesian government gradually transferred power to a UN Transitional Authority, not without a traumatic transition by which the Indonesian armed forces destroyed the capital, Dili, and several other areas, while displacing thousands of Timorese. Timor-Leste became formally independent in May 2002. The newest country in Southeast Asia adopted a democratic regime that remains challenged by some of the traumas of the past as well as the absence of strong roots. As with other externally designed democracies, without a strong internal constituency rooted in the middle class, democracy remains at risk. Nevertheless, Timor-Leste appears to have surmounted some of its most significant challenges in this respect, and democratic politics have become more stable.

In 1974, the fall of the Caetano authoritarian regime spelled the end of Portugal's colonial venture. The Portuguese had held onto the eastern part of the island of Timor when the Dutch had forcibly displaced them from the rest of the East Indies during the seventeenth century. East Timor remained a Portuguese colony until 1974, when the successful revolution against Caetano brought in a democratic government that moved swiftly to grant independence to its colonies.

In preparation for independence, various political parties that had been formed proposed different visions for the future. Fretilin most clearly espoused independence. It offered a revolutionary alternative along the lines of left-wing decolonization movements elsewhere and in particular of the Frelimo movement in Mozambique, another Portuguese colony. Its rival, the Timorese Democratic Union (União Democrática Timorense, UDT), originally worked with Fretilin towards independence in 1975. Concerned about the rather extremist Fretilin members who were more dedicated to a socialist path, and seeing its popularity losing ground, the UDT was swayed by the Indonesian armed forces to integrate to Indonesia. The UDT launched a coup and invited the Indonesian armed forces to enter East Timor. After months of brutal war, the Indonesians established firm control in East Timor, which later became one of its provinces against objections from many foreign countries.

The Indonesian government maintained tight control over the province as it sought to integrate it more fully into Indonesia. For several years, Fretilin and its armed wing Falintil retreated to the mountains and pursued resistance through guerilla warfare. In response, the Indonesian armed forces launched successive operations to weed out the rebels. By doing so, it also displaced thousands of Timorese. Under war conditions, at least a hundred thousand Timorese died from direct or indirect consequences of the war, including disease and malnutrition.

Meanwhile, the government adopted measures to integrate the population to Indonesia. Bahasa Indonesia became the only official language, including for education at all levels. The use of the local lingua franca, Tetum, was discouraged and displays of Timorese culture were restricted. The curriculum emphasized Indonesia's common history and culture, its heroes, symbols and the national ideology Pancasila, while ignoring East Timor's specific circumstances. Migration from other parts of Indonesia was encouraged. In particular, the government regularly appointed civil servants from other parts of Indonesia to serve in East Timor's local administration. The military controlled some key business sectors, such as its monopoly over the coffee industry. A climate of fear hovered over the province, as the military frequently resorted to repression and intimidation.

The military approach combined with strongly centralistic policies seriously undermined any effort to integrate the territory into

Indonesia. Not only were historical trajectories different, as the East Timorese had not been part of the Dutch East Indies, but no effort was made to make integration attractive. Instead, repression was dominant while policies were imposed from the top.

When Suharto resigned and the New Order ended, President Habibie offered East Timor a choice. On 30 August, 1999 the East Timorese voted massively in favour of independence in a referendum that had also offered wide-ranging autonomy within Indonesia. In the weeks following the results, however, pro-Indonesia armed militias supported by factions of the Indonesian armed forces rampaged the capital Dili, and attacked large areas of the countryside. Hundreds of thousands of East Timorese fled the mass destruction, many across the border into West Timor. The United Nations sent troops, which arrived a month later to restore order. For the following three years, the United Nations Transitional Authority administered East Timor, until it finally obtained full independence on 20 May, 2002.

The Indonesian occupation brought in very significant transformations. Education levels rose dramatically. While only 10 per cent of the population was literate and there were only two lower secondary schools in Dili in 1974, this number had risen to 103 by 1994 and literacy levels were much higher. Although most Timorese resented the Indonesian occupation, at the same time they had learned Indonesian and been socialized into many aspects of Indonesian culture via television and other media. At independence, a diverse set of groups competed to shape the future of the new country. Some spoke Indonesian fluently and saw the need for continued close relations with Indonesia. Others had lived in exile during the whole occupation. Resistance fighters, who had hidden from Indonesian authorities for decades, also vied for influence. As a result, although there was new enthusiasm for the new country, divisions surfaced over its shape (Simonsen, 2006).

Few disputed the moral high ground occupied by Fretilin and its former leader Xanana Gusmão. Long imprisoned after Indonesian troops captured him in 1992, Gusmão emerged as the almost undisputed leader. After Fretilin formally adopted Marxism-Leninism in the late 1970s, Gusmão distanced himself from the party and eventually left it all together in 1987. He remained the leader of Falintil, Fretilin's armed wing, and retained the kudos of being the front-line resistance leader against the Indonesian military. He also created in 1986 the National Council of Maubere Resistance (Conselho Nacional da

Resistência Maubere, CNRM). The CNRM used "Maubere", a term to refer to Timor's unique tradition, to build a broader political front and reach out to former rivals, such as the UDT. Falintil at this point claimed to represent all Timorese under the CNRM umbrella and distanced itself from Fretilin. In 1998, the CNRM was renamed CNRT, dropping Maubere for the Timorese to appear even more inclusive. Fretilin, by its long political struggle against Indonesian occupation, still enjoyed strong popularity. Mari Alkatiri led Fretilin from abroad during the years of occupation. In the first elections after independence, Fretilin won by a wide margin in parliamentary elections and its leader, Alkatiri, became prime minister. Gusmão ran as an independent in presidential elections and won with 82 per cent support.

Beneath the surface of national unity, the newly elected government also reflected a divided elite. With a semi-presidential system that forces collaboration between an elected president and the prime minister, a political struggle was embedded into the institutional structure. Gusmão emerged as a strong supporter of multiparty democracy and believed that Fretilin should become a regular party alongside others. Alkatiri accepted multiparty democracy but believed that Fretilin should enjoy a privileged position. Other political leaders from the resistance also occupied significant positions, such as José Ramos-Horta, who for some time had been Fretilin's main spokesperson abroad and who became foreign minister in the new government. Many opposition politicians also hailed from the 1975 period, including the former leader of the rival UDT, Mario Carrascalão who formed the opposition Social Democrat Party (Shoesmith, 2003).

The new government faced enormous challenges. After the destruction of 1999, East Timor was completely dependent on foreign aid. Following UN troops, a large number of foreign aid organizations competed to reconstruct it. Over 75 per cent of the population had been displaced and over 70 per cent of public buildings, homes and utilities had been destroyed. Oil and gas revenues were the only hope, as East Timor began to exploit jointly with Australia vast offshore oil and gas reserves. Nevertheless, unemployment was extremely high, with very few viable business opportunities (Simonsen, 2006).

Division in the security forces was another obstacle to the stabilization of democracy. At the time of Timor-Leste's transition to independence, Falintil was gradually disbanded. Some former rebels were integrated into the newly created armed forces but many others were not. They joined the ranks of large number of unemployed, while resenting that they could not gain "peace dividends", even after their contribution to the resistance. The problem was compounded by a perception that favoritism guided inclusion in the new security forces. In particular, those closer to Gusmão and former members of Falintil were favoured, as were those from the east. Regional divisions therefore developed (Shoesmith, 2003).

The crisis reached a climax in 2006. In March, 600 members were dismissed from the army after they had protested and went on strike over their working conditions. They also accused the government of treating them differently because they were from the western part of the country. By April, violent clashes began to occur. The crisis escalated during the following two months, as mobs burned buildings in Dili, and clashes pitted former soldiers against military and police personnel. Again, thousands of people fled their homes in the fear of a renewal of the 1999 slash and burn violence. Prime Minister Alkatiri resigned after suspicions that he might be connected. President Gusmão replaced him with José Ramos-Horta.

Since then, the country has stabilized and democratic politics have persisted. Although President Gusmão had declared martial law during the crisis, he had swiftly restored democratic government as soon as the violence ebbed and a new prime minister was appointed. In 2007, Gusmão ran under the Alliance for a Parliamentary Majority (Aliança Maioria Parlamentar, AMP). The party won a majority and Gusmão became Prime Minister. Its main opponent, Fretilin, accepted its new status in the opposition in spite of its previous parliamentary dominance and its long-time symbolic status as the party of resistance to Indonesian rule. José Ramos-Horta traded places with Gusmão as he was elected president (Gunn, 2010). In 2012, elections were held once again and returned results that were healthy for democracy. In the April presidential elections, the incumbent, José Ramos-Horta, failed to gain sufficient votes to mount even a serious challenge. Instead, a former commander of Falintil, Taur Matan Ruak, won and became president. In the parliamentary elections in July, the CNRT of Prime Minister Xanana Gusmão won the most amount of votes and formed a coalition government, while Fretilin remained in opposition.

Despite relatively healthy democratic politics, the country remains fragile. Corruption is high, particularly since the economy offers few opportunities. East Timor's main revenue comes from petroleum, from

Table 4 *Timor-Leste*

Population (rank)	Land area (rank)	Main ethnic groups	Main religions (%)	Regime type (transition)	GDP per capita (rank)	GDP growth rate (%) (rank)
1 172 390 (159th)	14 874 sq km (159th)	Austronesian (Malayo-Polynesian) Papuan Small Chinese minority	Roman Catholic 98 Muslim 1 Protestant 1 (2005)	Democracy Republic	$3 100 (171st) (2011 est.)	7.3 (18th) (2011 est.)

Source: CIA, *The World Factbook*; Polity IV Project, Polity IV Individual Country Regime Trends, 1946–2010.

its fairly recent exploitation of offshore reserves. Although growth in the non-oil sector was relatively high after 2007, the country was still ranked one of the poorest in the world. Aside from a little construction in Dili, there were few avenues for employment. The Gusmão government used petroleum revenues to spend on a variety of social programmes, including rice subsidies, pensions for veterans and cash to internally displaced people who had fled the 2006 violence. While these programs helped to maintain some social cohesion, they drew down Timor-Leste's Petroleum Fund without stimulating much new economic activity. Furthermore, the use of these funds were controversial as the Petroleum Fund had been set up with a provision to use only 3 per cent per year, in order to encourage fiscal responsibility. The Gusmão government, however, used emergency provisions to spend beyond that limit, thereby triggering accusations that it was misusing the fund to artificially increase economic growth and buy political support.

Comparisons to other cases are difficult, given Timor-Leste's history. After colonialism, the territory was essentially under a state of occupation, with attempts to fully integrate to Indonesia. Timor Leste's recent independence resembles in some respects the fragile state of new regimes in many Southeast Asian countries when they gained independence mostly in the 1940s and 1950s. With levels of economic development being relatively low and with a relatively small middle class, Timor-Leste lacks the kind of structure that, in many cases, sustains democratic politics. Yet, its unique history of Indonesian occupation, resistance and the broad suffering shared by the Timorese during the occupation and the violent transition to independence remain strong factors uniting much of the elite and the population behind democratic principles.

3 | The Philippines

The Philippines is the longest lasting democracy in Southeast Asia, but its quality has been persistently poor. American colonial officials organized elections under the Commonwealth system in the 1930s, after setting up political institutions on the US model. Post-independent governments continued to hold regular elections after the Philippines gained its independence in 1946. The system proved unstable, however, as it produced tensions that opened the door to authoritarian rule. First elected as president in 1965, Marcos declared martial law in 1972 and officially disbanded the Philippines' long-standing electoral democracy. The authoritarian regime lasted fourteen years before a "People Power" revolution brought it down in 1986. This marked the Philippines' transition to its current democratic regime. Rather than build a new democratic system, however, the crafters of the Philippines' new constitution returned to the previous model of a US-based presidential system. Established elites recaptured it, and recreated many of the problems that marked the pre-Marcos democracy. As a result, the new democracy has held regular elections but its quality remains low.

We can explain this pattern of transformation and continuity by focusing on some comparative similarities with other cases while also recognizing some factors specific to the Philippines. As in the case of Indonesia, some scholars such as Carl Landé have emphasized the continuity of practices across time (Landé, 1965). Patrimonialism, they argue, has been a persistent feature of Filipino politics. Close ties between patrons and their clients allowed wealthy families to strengthen and maintain their political and economic power. From this perspective, there was little difference between democratic regimes before and after Marcos, as well as his authoritarian period, since wealth concentration, and the use of state instruments to enhance private wealth have been persistent features of the system, whether authoritarian or democratic. For Paul Hutchcroft, such as a system has been sufficiently entrenched and pervasive to be called "booty capitalism" (Hutchcroft, 1998).

An alternative perspective casts some doubt about the strength of this characterization of Filipino politics. Benedict Anderson viewed "cacique" – a term for local political bosses in Latin America – as a characteristic feature of Filipino politics, marking continuity between wealthy patrons turned politicians before and after Marcos, which he saw as the ultimate "cacique" (Anderson, 1988). John Sidel emphasized further this practice of "bossism" and argues that it is less a cultural or persistent pattern than a malleable and ultimately persistent practice that is reinforced through constant reconstruction of power bases. Sidel also adds a corrective to the view that the state has been weak and merely plundered by the wealthy elites but, instead, has been itself a strong instrument of resource extraction that has benefited the ruling oligarchy (Sidel, 1999). As such, he emphasizes less the unique features of Filipino democracy and instead draws parallels to the collusion between business interests and the state that also characterizes Indonesia and Thailand.

Distinctions aside, both perspectives share the view that a powerful oligarchy has developed over time. Originally a few families controlled most of the country's economy. While others eventually joined this elite, they were few in numbers and grafted themselves to the existing patterns of economic power rather than becoming sources of change. This business elite has formed political clans that dominate positions at all levels of government.

While such a system might favour authoritarian rule, electoral politics have actually served the existing elite quite well. The political system was used to strengthen and enhance the elite's wealth, while creating an arena to compete and balance personal interests. In the past, competition included not only elections but also the building of private armies to defend one another's turf. This practice has diminished, but nevertheless the elite shares a certain sense of the rules of the competitive game that sustains the Philippines' poor democracy. It would be an exaggeration to speak of an "elite unity", but even though there is a common understanding that elites compete with each other, even violently at times, there is a shared interest in preserving the existing system, with its elite dominance, patronage and weak institutions.

The anomaly in this respect was the Marcos dictatorship. Marcos violated these rules by attempting to eliminate rivals and gain greater control over the state, the economy and opportunities for private gain. In many ways he was an outgrowth of the same oligarchy but tried to transform it to his advantage. His cronies constituted new wealthy patrons with their own political clans loyal to Marcos. In the aftermath of Marcos' downfall, they were less visible for some time but slowly reappeared to rejoin the political game. Meanwhile, the rise of Marcos in the late 1960s could be explained partly by the economic and political decay, which provided a short-lived opportunity for him to dominate.

Yet, the oligarchs proved resilient. The explanation for a return to democracy as much reflects Marcos' inability to fully consolidate his authoritarian regime, the rival elite's determination to return to the former system, as well as alliances with some emerging social forces that became instrumental in Marcos' downfall. Although Marcos built up the armed forces, they became more his expanded personal army rather than a professionalized instrument of authoritarian rule. The regime never became an institutionalized military-dominated system such as Indonesia and remained more vulnerable due to its dependence on Marcos himself. Furthermore, once cracks emerged among the high ranks of the armed forces, and among Marcos' supporters, rival political and economic elites created alliances to further weaken Marcos and push for his removal. Finally, what emerged as the "People Power" revolution in 1986, as Eva-Lotta Hedman argues, resulted from a crafty alliance between the anti-Marcos oligarchs and a number of organizations that shared the common purpose of removing Marcos but differed with respect to the shape of the future democracy. The movement that removed Marcos from power therefore could only superficially be seen as the result of an emergent and strong civil society (Hedman, 2006).

Against this backdrop, what is the political role of the middle class? It has developed much less than in Singapore, Malaysia, Thailand or Indonesia. With growth rates in the Philippines remaining lower than these faster growing countries, the middle class developed at a slower pace. Up until 1986, it is difficult to argue that it played any significant role in sustaining democracy prior to Marcos, or placing much of a block on authoritarian rule. "People Power" in 1986 was a much broader alliance that showed some evidence of an assertive middle class but also of marginalized sectors. Furthermore, it was linked to some of the anti-Marcos elite. Since 1986, the middle class has continued to expand yet there is little evidence of its capacity to transform the political landscape. Nevertheless, Filipinos have a long tradition of democratic politics so that many groups remain highly vocal and easily mobilized to place pressure on the political system. Such a factor should not be exaggerated, as societal sectors have been unable to effectively broaden representation within the political system and the quality of democracy remains quite low.

Long but weak democratic tradition: 1946–1972

The period of democratic politics between 1946 and 1972 focused mainly on elections but produced very ineffective and unresponsive governments. The upper class that dominated the economy also produced the politicians that filled the seats of the upper and lower chambers of parliament. Senators reflected the power of regional clans. Meanwhile, state resources were siphoned off to serve this elite's interests with few benefits filtering down to the population at large.

Local clans were built from families that once held large landholdings. Under Spanish colonial rule, these families had come to own plantations that were modelled on the hacienda of Latin America. Many Filipinos worked on this land as wage-labour, in higher proportions than in other Southeast Asian countries. Others held family-owned, small plots mainly used for a rice cultivation system similar to the rest of the region. Under American colonial rule, the wealthy families were well positioned to take advantage of growing agro-industrial business and resource export opportunities opened up by American investment. While it could be considered an overstatement to say that the Philippines is more similar to Latin American countries than its Southeast Asian neighbours, nevertheless it did develop a pattern of large plantations and concentration of wealth that were comparable to some degree.

Under the Commonwealth system, the American colonial government allowed Filipinos to govern but kept their ultimate control. In previous decades, it had created a quasi-bicameral legislature. In preparation for the Commonwealth government, a constitutional convention adopted a framework that strongly resembled the US constitution while preserving aspects of the previous institutional structure. A

Congress and Senate, as well as a strong elected presidency governed the Commonwealth after its inauguration in 1935. These institutions functioned under American tutelage from 1935–46, and were subsequently preserved after independence in 1946.

Patronage and pork-barrel politics dominated the political system. With few other groups capable of mounting significant competition, wealthy families competed against each other for political office. Two political parties dominated the landscape: the Nacionalista and Liberal parties. While they alternated in power, very little distinguished them. Party switching was very frequent as members pursued personal interests rather than party loyalty. They were party machines that functioned as vehicles to gain office and distribute patronage, rather than espousing any particular ideological or policy direction. Under this system, Congressional members and Senators used state resources to give benefits to their friends and followers. This system of patron-clientelism became firmly institutionalized.

Wealth concentration continued after independence. Sugar, coconut and banana plantations provided the major plantation-based crops. American firms joined this economic elite and expanded the production for export. The same families also owned most of the business corporations that emerged from diversification and industrialization. By the early 1970s, the top 10 per cent of stockholding families controlled 77.6 per cent of the 1,511 corporations with assets over half a million pesos (Wurfel, 1988). Much of the economy depended on US markets and investment. From the 1940s to the 1970s, the US remained the main export market and, in the 1960s, US investment constituted four-fifths of total foreign investment in the Philippines.

Aside from their dominance of the economy, wealthy families also dominated politics. Relatives entered politics and provided services for their families from within the state. The political system became an arena to play out rivalries between wealthy dynastic families. Elections became bloody, violent affairs as family clans built private armies to intimidate or eliminate opponents in their quest for power. Press freedom flourished as various outlets, also owned by the same families, launched attacks on the corruption and abuse of politicians, without ever leading to any prosecution or other judicial measures.

The United States provided some measure of influence over the system. In addition to strong economic ties mentioned above, the US also supported the regime. Under an agreement reached at the time of independence, the Americans maintained a very strong military presence by establishing the Subic Bay and Clarke Air Base on large tracts of land leased to them by the Philippines government for ninety-nine years. This base served at the Americans' launch pad for operations in the region, particularly when it increased its involvement in Vietnam in the 1960s. Even as early at the late 1940s, the US worried that the communist victory in China would spread communist influence across the region. Its policy of "containment", intended to prevent the spread of communist revolutions, dictated US support for regimes that suppressed rebellions and thwarted communist influence. The US therefore gave its support against the Huk rebellion, even though its linkages to communism were very weak. Furthermore, it interfered in elections to support pro-American presidential candidates. Given a significant resistance to its military presence among Filipino nationalists, the Americans were particularly concerned with preventing the election of governments that might question this presence. They intervened behind the scenes in the election of almost every president between 1946–72 (Wurfel, 1988).

While the system worked to preserve the political and economic power of the wealthy families, it also bred decay. Politicians protected family interests by exploiting state resources that included granting monopolies in certain sectors, huge bank loans at cheap rates with no guarantees of repayment and pork barrel disbursements. While the Philippines had been on a relatively high growth trajectory in the early 1950s, it was lagging behind its neighbours by the 1970s. Combined with a high birth rate, the continued plundering of state resources and unproductive economic practices increasingly impoverished the country and its population.

Deprived of political participation, the rural poor gave their support to armed rebellion. During the Second World War, peasants joined guerillas in Hukbalahap (Huk) armies that resisted the Japanese occupation. After independence, they rebelled against the independent state when it became clear that the government had no intention of implementing land reform and addressing the needs of the poor. The Huk rebellion was crushed in 1954 and many peasants were sent to the southern island of Mindanao where they were given tracts of land. Although this outmigration from the densely populated region of Central Luzon removed potential rebels, nevertheless, continued poverty fuelled the emergence of another rebel group, the New People's Army, with links to the Communist Party of the Philippines (CPP). By the 1970s, this group became very significant and proved to be difficult to crush.

As in many other post-colonial countries, at independence the Philippines began with democratic institutions. Surprisingly, they lasted until the 1970s whereas in many other countries, such as in Indonesia and Burma, they collapsed after only a few years. The reasons for their stability were also the reasons for their weakness. First, aspects of these institutions, such as the bicameral legislature, were already in place well before independence. The US colonial government nurtured them and allowed the wealthy families to capture and control them. Second, after independence, the new constitution ensured that the powerful economic elite could expand and preserve its control. Elections, political parties and representation in Congress suited the wealthy families that competed for power and used the political system to siphon off resources. Because it served them well, these families worked to keep it stable. Third, with such an established civilian government, the armed forces developed little independence or involvement in politics, while the wealthy families built private armies. Fourth, poor peasants continued the main opposition to the regime but they had insufficient resources to mount a significant challenge. Fifth, with a sustained military presence, the Americans preserved some influence and continued support against rebels, in their quest to contain the regional spread of communism. US investments and business interests also fuelled the established elite's productive ventures (Putzel, 1999).

The Marcos regime and its downfall

Given its stability and the absence of powerful opposition, it is somewhat surprising that the democratic regime broke down. Nevertheless, when President Marcos declared martial law on 23 September, 1972 he ended several decades of a weak but stable electoral democracy. Its breakdown came not from strong opposition but precisely from internal decay. Beneath a veneer of regularity, the competition between wealthy families invited increased competition and plundering of state resources. Marcos, in some respects, represented the ultimate extension of this competition by which he gained the means of winning over his competitors. At another level, the regime was breeding increasing opposition as the economy faltered. Marcos initially gained popularity for his bold policy to break the power of the economic elite and steer the economy in a more productive direction. But he ended up espousing its ways and became, with his cronies, the ultimate plunderer of state resources. Under his leadership, the economy plummeted, violent mass mobilization rose and corruption reached unprecedented levels (Thompson, 1995).

In his first mandate, Marcos initially seemed to espouse change but ended up consolidating his power and abusing it. He ran in 1965 on a platform to eliminate corruption and reform the ailing economy. Once in power, he used public spending, executive agencies staffed with "technocrats" and the military to bypass Congress and implement development strategies that included vast rural infrastructural programs, road construction and the building of schools. He also borrowed heavily from external sources of credit and implemented incentive schemes to attract foreign investment in export-oriented industries. This developmentalist push was accompanied by widespread corruption no different from past administrations. Yet, the results were disappointing, as large debts to finance development yielded relatively poor economic growth, certainly not sufficient to boost the Philippines' export-based economy and create sufficient revenues to refund this debt. The country began to falter under heavy debt and declining external sources of investment and credit.

Crisis accompanied his re-election in 1969. Marcos was re-elected because of an unprecedented $50 million used to finance his campaign, much of it from public funds. Soon after, opposition began to increase. Leftist opponents reorganized, and the Communist Party re-emerged after a near decade of silence. Jose Maria Sison and his Nationalist Youth organization became most vocal. In association with other, more radical members influenced by the Vietnam War and inspired by Mao's revolution in China soon sidelined their elder communist leaders and officially relaunched the party in 1968 as the Communist Party of the Philippines (CPP). The CPP now attracted mainly urban-based intellectuals and middle class activists, as it had been cut off from its peasant and worker base. They organized demonstrations against the government but greatly benefited from an opportunistic alliance with anti-Marcos members of the landed elite, such as the Laurel and Lopez families, whose interests Marcos had targeted. They provided radicals with access to television and newspaper outlets under their control, and thereby greatly amplified the radicals' power.

Marcos used the crisis to justify his declaration of martial law on 23 September, 1972. Although he was losing support from party members and parts of the civil service, he managed to retain strong control over key players. Most notably, the military stood firmly behind him. He had already promoted to key positions allies from his Ilocano base and had increased the military's budget. Some civil servants continued to believe that he had a strong vision for the country, which included redirecting investments, promoting exports and reducing the power of wealthy families to stimulate new forms of development. American businesses also supported a greater centralization of power if it produced more stability and security for their investments.

Marcos built the regime on three sources of power: the military, external support and economic patronage. He poured unprecedented amounts of money into building a strong and loyal military, as he centralized its leadership and brought under its purview the Philippine Constabulary (the national police) and municipal police forces. The US encouraged the World Bank and other donors to support the regime, which it saw as a key ally in its anti-communist efforts in Southeast Asia. Marcos built support among emerging businessmen whom he favoured and nurtured, while curbing the political and business interests of rival families. For instance, upon declaring martial law, he had dismantled the private army of his greatest rival, Benigno Aquino. He subsequently targeted the Aquino clan's business interests, while promoting new allies to build their own business empires.

Marcos expanded the system of corruption and patronage that had dogged the Philippines under successive democratic governments. He became an ultimate "warlord" as he used the whole apparatus of the state to serve his personal and family interests. Whereas local clans often created personal armies to protect their interests, Marcos used the Philippine Constabulary and the army to serve his. Instead of influencing particular judges, Marcos made the Supreme Court pliable to his wishes (Anderson, 1988; Thompson, 1996). He built his own political party, the New Society Movement (Kilusang Bagong Lipunan, KBL) before the 1978 elections. The KBL became a magnet for patronage resources, and a structure to centralize power and control over local clans. Billions of dollars in foreign aid were diverted to private bank accounts.

The military grew considerably during this time period. In order to sustain its support, Marcos allotted key leadership posts to officers from his region (the Ilocano-speaking northwestern Luzon). For instance, he named Fidel Ramos as Chief of the Philippine Constabulary (the police, but also a branch of the armed forces). Marcos ensured a steady rise in pay and access to opportunities for graft and corruption.

In spite of this consolidation of power, the authoritarian regime remained relatively weak. Compared to other such regimes in Southeast Asia, the fifteen years under Marcos' authoritarian grip was relatively short. In part, its demise came from its inability to deliver on the rationale for its existence. Authoritarian regimes often have legitimation problems that make them difficult to sustain. In many cases, they justify military intervention in politics as a temporary solution to a crisis, with an expectation that democratic politics will return when such a crisis is resolved. Since the Philippines had been a long-standing nominal democracy, authoritarian rule was difficult for Marcos to justify, especially when the economy began to falter. With widespread awareness of Marcos' cronyism and a weak economy, initial promises of reform were largely discredited. Repression and military dominance only added fuel to the fire among Filipinos who had enjoyed a fair amount of freedom up until martial law.

As the opposition to the regime grew, Marcos scrambled to find new ways of enhancing his legitimacy. In the south of the Philippines, educated Muslims formed in 1972 the Moro National Liberation Front (MNLF), which rebelled against decades of Muslim marginalization, displacement and repression that reached a peak under the Marcos regime. The MNLF waged a fierce war of resistance during the 1970s. On another front, the communist New People's Army (NPA) grew considerably under the increasing impoverishment of Filipinos who also resented the regime's arbitrary repression. The NPA expanded from 8,000 in 1980 to 20,000 in 1983 despite the fact that the armed forces grew three times during this period (Thompson, 1996). In addition to repressive responses towards the NPA, the MNLF and other critics of the regime, Marcos attempted to use elections and referenda to attract broader popular support, beyond the circle of cronies and beneficiaries of his patronage.

After 1981, Marcos lifted martial law and attempted to bolster his support through democratic mechanisms. Already, in 1978, he had organized an election for a new assembly, largely in response to international pressure. He had allowed the opposition to run under the umbrella LABAN (Lakas ng Bayan meaning "fight" and also an acronym for People Power), which was led by Benigno Aquino from his prison cell. As the election was rigged, Marcos won the election without a problem but his tactics increased the opposition's strength. Under domestic and international pressure, he sent Aquino into exile. Aquino was allowed to return in 1983 but was assassinated as soon as he arrived in Manila. The event was a catalyst for even greater opposition to the Marcos regime. Marcos sought to appease the growing protest by organizing a snap election in February 1986. Cory Aquino, Benigno's wife, emerged as the new leader capable of uniting the opposition, as she was bolstered by sympathies for her late husband. She drew large support during the election campaign. After delays, the regime announced that Marcos and his KBL had won with 54 per cent of popular support but it was widely obvious that the elections had been rigged. Instead of bolstering the Marcos regime, the election marked its demise.

The People Power revolution was a massive, organized set of demonstrations that contributed to the downfall of the Marcos regime. After the results of the rigged elections were announced in 1986, Filipinos descended in the streets of Manila by the thousands. They occupied the capital city's main roads and demanded Marcos' departure. As such, it would appear that civil society played an important role in triggering regime change.

Demonstrations alone, however, could not have brought down the regime. Civil society was instrumental but not decisive in the regime's demise. Division within the military was an important precondition. During the previous decade, Marcos had consolidated support among military troops by raising salaries and offering more patronage. Yet, the armed forces were not strongly united. When Marcos appointed Fabian Ver as head of the armed forces, he alienated Fidel Ramos, the head of the Philippine Constabulary, who was more professional and less "political". Ver also sidelined Defence Minister Juan Ponce Enrile, who was eventually sacked altogether. Enrile joined a group of junior officers to create the RAM movement (Reform the Armed Forces movement), which began to plan a military coup in the early 1980s. Ramos was aware of this group's activities and supported its efforts to remove Marcos. However, the group never mustered enough power to reach their objective. While Marcos loyalists attempted to suppress them, the People Power movement created a temporary alliance with the RAM group that became instrumental in the removal of Marcos and his supporters. The head of the Catholic Church in the Philippines, Cardinal Sin, also supported the demonstrators, thereby adding support from one of the most respected institutions, as the Philippines had a highly devout majority Catholic population. In the end, Marcos fled the country on a US helicopter and ended his days in a secluded villa in Hawaii.

Perhaps more importantly, the style of authoritarian regime also contributed to its demise. In comparison with the New Order regime in Indonesia, or the years of military dominance in Thailand, the Marcos regime was poorly institutionalized. Marcos changed the constitution, built up the military, or created a political movement to bolster his own position rather than to solidify the regime's foundations. The military became an instrument of his plunder and cronyism rather than a professional army with clear lines of succession. As a result, there were no mechanisms for a transition to a new leader of the regime, and Marcos became isolated and resistant to change (Thompson, 1996).

Economic crisis further eroded the Marcos regime. Elsewhere in the region, "performance legitimacy" had sometimes provided some support to authoritarian regimes. In the case of the Philippines, promises of economic reform and development initially bolstered Marcos' popularity before martial law. After a few years, however, it was evident that such rhetoric was followed by no action and, instead, Marcos and his cronies proceeded to plunder the economy even more than the oligarchy had done in the past. Consequently, the economy faltered, Filipinos became more impoverished and greater numbers either joined the ranks of the communist opposition or waited for a window of opportunity to bring down Marcos.

The return to democracy

The return to democracy also marked the re-establishment of the power of the oligarchs. While civil society organizations celebrated People Power and hoped for a broader participation in the political system, the euphoria was short as it soon became apparent that old political clans had reinstated their basis of political and economic power. The new democracy, as with the old, was recreated as an arena for their struggles and competition, rather than a true representative and accountable political system. The middle class and marginalized groups that had stood behind People Power continued to raise criticism against the system but held little power to transform it.

Cory Aquino was popular but her administration remained fragile. The first couple of years were focused on the new constitution, which included many progressive features to enhance the role of civil society organizations and recognized the need to accommodate Muslims in the south and indigenous peoples. At the same time, it restored the institutions that were in place prior to the Marcos regime: a presidential regime, with a senate and House of Representatives and a single-member district system. The constitution imposed one significant countermeasure against the abuse of power by introducing a one-term only limit on presidents. Nevertheless, by bringing back the same institutions, old networks around family clans could be quickly revived (Abinales, 2001).

Only two years after the People Power revolution, the old oligarchy had been restored. The 1987–8 elections saw a return of the old politicians and political clans of the pre-authoritarian period. They returned to the rent-seeking and political violence by which they maintained their power over state institutions. By creating and maintaining little fiefdoms in their electoral regions, they used their local power and position in the national legislature to siphon away state resources for private advantage. John Sidel has dubbed this phenomenon "bossism", arguing that these local politicians and clans act more as mafia-style bosses than politicians or administrators (Sidel, 1999).

Decentralization increased resources available to these local politicians. The Local Government Code of 1991 greatly increased the powers of local governments and also provided funding that was transferred from the central government. Local "bosses" benefited from using these resources to their advantage.

Finally, Aquino's regime was never really stable. Groups within the military, including the RAM group and some officers closer to Marcos, launched several "coup attempts". Although they were never successful, they showed that important groups from the previous regime continued to operate within the Philippines. The armed forces included many officers with patronage links to wealthy politicians or civilians, some of whom stood to benefit from returning to a Marcos-style regime. In addition, Aquino's government remained too weak to successfully repatriate the large sums that the Marcos family hid abroad. The Marcos family was even able to return and run in elections only a few years after the People Power revolution. The promise of reform and empowerment of the poor and marginalized seemed very remote by the end of Aquino's mandate. The NPA's and MNLF's continued mobilization also contributed to regime instability (Thompson, 1996).

Fidel Ramos' presidency brought in more stability and economic growth to the Philippines. As a former general, Ramos commanded respect from fellow soldiers. Coup attempts ended and the armed forces accepted civilian rule. Ramos had formed an electoral coalition that included the popular sectors and social movements that had led the People Power revolution, but also corporate elites who longed for a more stable environment to pursue their business interests.

Close ties with the business elite and willingness to reform produced economic growth. He deregulated some major industries, such as airlines, banking and telecommunications. He privatized some state enterprises and sponsored congressional bills to reform the health and housing sectors. Under his mandate, economic growth was much higher than it had ever been, reaching the 6–7 per cent rates that were more common in other Southeast Asian economies (Abinales, 2001). The stability and growth of the Ramos years seemed to set the Philippines into a new path. Mark Thompson in 1996 wrote of the Philippines as being "Off the endangered list", arguing that its democracy was becoming more consolidated and its future looked better than ever.

Ramos was also more inclined to pass major reform bills. He had gained support from the non-governmental organization (NGO) sector, whereas the political clans had supported his opponents. He pushed through a long-awaited electoral reform bill that created a party-list system alongside the single-member districts. The reserved seats gave greater opportunities for smaller parties to obtain representation, thereby increasing possibilities for civil society groups to enter the legislature. Yet, the mechanisms were so limited and constrained that it failed to fulfill such promises (Eaton, 2003).

That year however seemed to be a turning point. Ramos' administration became tarnished as rumours spread of President Ramos' support of a constitutional change that would have allowed him to remain in power. Ramos failed to win support for his proposals, as he faced massive opposition from NGOs, and prominent figures such as Cardinal Sin and former President Aquino. His plans were defeated (Eaton, 2003).

The Estrada administration marked a return of the Marcos family and cronies into the political realm. Estrada was elected on a pro-poor platform. He was popular as well because of his previous career as a movie star. He won the election partly because of financial backing from former supporters of the Marcos regime. He had been elected mayor of Manila and was vice-president at the time of the election, but was still considered an outsider given his lack of connections to the traditional political clans. Once in power, it quickly became clear that his populist approach had been rhetorical as he failed to deliver any programs that were favourable to the poor. Instead, he enhanced the position of his friends and former Marcos cronies. Eduardo Cojuangco, a business tycoon who had made a fortune as head of the Marcos-era coconut-marketing monopoly, had also been made chairman of the San Miguel corporation's board and allocated large amounts of shares. He had lost this position under Aquino's presidency but Estrada restored it soon after his election. Similarly, Lucio Tan, owner of Philippine Airlines, had been charged for tax evasion under the Ramos adminis-tration but benefited from a tax amnesty under Estrada (Landé, 2001).

Estrada's style and corruption soon led to his downfall. His late night parties, his "midnight Cabinet" with friends drew harsh criticism as he made official decisions while drinking and gambling with his bud-dies. Economic mismanagement contributed to declining growth rates and the decline in the value of the peso beyond the effects of the 1997 Asian financial crisis. When in 2000 a scandal broke out around allegations that Estrada had received a cut in an illegal gambling scam, Congress began a formal investigation, which led to the initiation of impeachment proceedings. People power was revived as large num-bers of people demonstrated in the streets of Manila. When the senate refused to open bank accounts in January 2001, and therefore failed to seek crucial information in the impeachment trial, mass demon-strations intensified. Under pressure, the armed forces withdrew their support for Estrada, and he was replaced by his vice-president, Gloria Macapagal-Arroyo (Landé, 2001; Eaton, 2003).

Oddly enough, despite a second massive mobilization of Filipinos in the streets of Manila, again little seemed to change. As Eva-Lotta Hedman notes, such mobilization tends to be a recurring phenomenon in Filipino politics. While the 1986 and 2001 uprisings were most notable, other forms of mobilization involving different segments of society preceded them. She cautions that, while demonstrating the vivid willingness of broad sectors of society to protect electoral democracy, these movements were always backed by the dominant business and Congressional elite whose interests were mainly to preserve the minimal democratic procedures serving their interests rather than real political change. It is hardly surprising therefore that mass mobilization has generated little deepening of democracy (Hedman, 2006).

In fact, under the administration of Gloria Macapagal-Arroyo, Philippine democracy steadily eroded. In the words of Nathan Quimpo, it increasingly resembled a "predatory regime". He distinguished it from the clientelism and patrimonial politics that have characterized the country by outlining its "pervasive corruption, systematic plunder of government resources, and rapid corrosion of public institutions" (Quimpo, 2009).

Corruption expanded, while checks on government abuse declined. Her administration was implicated in a number of scandals, some of which included her family members, close associates and herself. Kickbacks were awarded to high-raking officials for lucrative government contracts. In 2005, Arroyo's husband, son and brother-in-law were accused of involvement in the same kind of gambling racket that brought down President Estrada. Patronage and control over appointments ensured, however, a high degree of loyalty to the president. Arroyo maintained a strong pro-administration majority in Congress through her control of the Priority Development Assistance Fund, which is the "pork barrel" funding that is distributed to congressional representatives. By doing so, she was able to fend off several attempts at impeachment. At the same time, investigations into alleged kickbacks and other scandals were most often dropped as the bureaucracy was full of appointees loyal to the president, even disregarding required eligibility criteria for many key positions (Quimpo, 2009).

Authoritarian tendencies could be observed in particular with the rise of violence perpetrated by the armed forces or suspected of being linked to the government. Several journalists who reported on corruption scandals, gambling or other illicit activities were killed. Leftist activities were also targeted. They were subjected to repression, arbitrary detention and extra-judicial killings. After Arroyo declared in 2006 a massive counter-insurgency campaign against the persistent mobilization of the NPA, the United Nations reported a dramatic rise in extra-judicial killings and disappearances of leftist activists. Arroyo then declared a state of emergency after a failed army mutiny in February 2006. Justifying these actions by pointing fingers at the communist movement and a conspiracy to overthrow the government, she lifted it after a week under public protest. She nevertheless soon followed suit with the "Human Security Act" in March 2007, supposedly an anti-terrorist law to give means of crushing the Abu Sayaff terrorist group in the south of the Philippines, but widely seen as providing increased powers to curtail civil liberties and human rights (Quimpo, 2009).

Elections in 2010 appeared to bring a fresh new start. When Benigno "Noynoy" Aquino was elected president, Filipinos hoped for a reinjection of democratic values and principles. Noynoy Aquino gained power from the legacy of his mother's leadership of the People Power movement that ousted Ferdinand Marcos, as well as the continued respect for his popular father, Benigno Aquino. Yet, he faced serious challenges, including the ability to implement promises to reduce corruption and reach peace agreements with the NPA and the MILF. In 2012, he had succeeded at least in reaching a cease-fire agreement and adopting new policies to address the long-standing conflicts with the MILF.

The Philippines is a somewhat unique case. It has been an electoral democracy for several decades but its democracy has been persistently weak. Given its economic base, theoretical propositions on economic development and the role of the middle class would not predict that the Philippines would be the country in the region with the longest history of democracy. It has persistently lagged behind Singapore, Malaysia, Thailand and Indonesia in terms of its levels of economic development and growth rates. Consequently, its middle class has been smaller, even though often vocal and active. To explain democracy in the Philippines, and its type, therefore requires that we go beyond such structural propositions.

The Philippines' colonial history and American inheritance certainly laid the basis for the democratic system in place. Patterns of landownership and economic power allowed this elite to seize control of the political system, tailor it to their interests and agree on its perpetuation as long as they all abode by their established rules of the game, which included electoral competition and a recognition of shared spreading of the benefits of political control. As a result, these families managed to control the economy, and adapt to economic and technological change. They harnessed their wealth from land to control emerging sectors of the economy during the twentieth century. Furthermore, they extended their power into the political realm, where they competed for positions in parliament, the executive and in local provinces. Typically, they dominated politics in their own region, and used that base to gain power in the House of Representatives and Senate. The elite has been perpetually divided and competitive, therefore, but has shared a general understanding that the minimal electoral democracy serves their interests.

Two different interpretations characterize this pattern of political and economic power. One emphasizes the pervasiveness of patron-client links that maintain the ties of political clans and wealthy oligarchs. The other, "bossism", allows for some variation in the reproduction of the pattern by emphasizing the resources and practices necessary not only to build but also to sustain power over regions, economic resources and political positions. These different characterizations of the political system also differ with respect to their views on whether the oligarchy simply plunders state resources or whether the state has been a crucial instrument to extend economic power in many sectors. The net effect remains, however, that the wealthy elite has maintained control over the state and its resources, and has used it to further its interests. Consequently, Philippine democracy has been weak, with limited broadening of participation and very low quality in terms of providing services and benefits to the broader population.

The authoritarian period under Ferdinand Marcos is therefore best understood as an extension of this competition for power. Marcos mainly disregarded the unwritten rules that maintained competition between political clans. He deepened the system by which the state was used for personal profit. He could temporarily reduce the power of his rivals, mainly by using the armed forces as his personal militia. Over time, however, he failed to secure enough power to eliminate opponents. The armed forces never professionalized, nor did they become central to the regime. As a result, Marcos remained at the apex with no ability to introduce reforms or organize a succession when pressure mounted for him to leave.

The return to democracy in 1986 was as much a restoration of past competition between the elite than the establishment of a new regime. The weaknesses of the Marcos regime prevented its resilience in the face of growing elite division and social forces rising against it. Long-standing elite division prevented Marcos from concentrating sufficient power over the longer term, and rivals remained powerful economically. When these were coupled with divisions in the armed forces and among some of Marcos' collaborators in the mid 1980s, the fate of his regime was sealed and its demise was inevitable. Rival elites allied with social forces that were increasingly disgruntled by the regime's deep corruption, human rights abuses and economic misman-agement. In this case, elite division was an important precondition of democratization.

Can "People Power" be taken as evidence of the importance of civil society in democratic transition? It can to the extent that the mobi-lization of social forces was key in pressuring Marcos to leave and in gaining momentum among the elite to push him out. It can therefore explain some of the timing of the regime's downfall. Furthermore, the United States encouraged him to leave in large part because of the scale of anti-Marcos demonstrations. Yet, the movement had not emerged out of a strongly organized civil society. The mobilization was cob-bled together from a large number of loosely organized groups. Anti-Marcos elites were also crucial supporters of the movement (Hedman, 2006). As in the case of other instances of people power, such as the mobilization against President Estrada, these mass movements appear weak after a few months.

As Kent Eaton (2003) has argued, civil society has been repeatedly prevented from playing a strong role. Civil society actors have emerged as a check on abuse of power despite a restoration of the powerful political clans that have dominated the Philippines. The constitution of 1987 provided for much greater involvement of civil society groups. In the Aquino and later Ramos administrations, several prominent civil society leaders gained positions in government. Organizations proliferated, and were vocal critics of government policies. In some cases, civil society actors played important roles in lobbying Congress. They also played a key role in the removal from power of Joseph

Table 5 *Philippines*

Population (rank)	Land area (rank)	Main ethnic groups (%)	Main religions (%)	Regime type (transition)	GDP per capita (rank)	GDP growth rate (%) (rank)
103 775 002 (12th) (2011 est.)	298 170 sq km (72nd)	Tagalog 28.1 Cebuano 13.1 Ilocano 9 Bisaya/Binisaya 7.6 Hiligaynon Ilonggo 7.5 Bikol 6 Waray 3.4 Other 25.3 (2000 census)	Catholic 82.9 – Roman 80.9 – Aglipayan 2 Evangelical 2.8 Iglesia ni Kristo 2.3 Other Christian 4.5 Muslim 5 Other 1.8 Unspecified 0.6 None 0.1 (2000 census)	Democracy (+1986)[a] Republic	$4 100 (159th) (2011 est.)	3.7 (110th) (2011 est.)

Source: CIA, *The World Factbook*; Polity IV Project, Polity IV Individual Country Regime Trends, 1946–2010.

[a] The year indicates the most recent transition; (+) means a transition towards democracy and (–) denotes a transition towards authoritarianism.

Estrada. Nevertheless, politicians have maintained an upper hand and civil society groups' calls for reform have been successfully curtailed. They have had very limited influence on policy and so democratic politics continue as they always have. Democracy has returned to an elite-controlled, low-quality state, despite several instances of people power.

Re-democratization was not an outgrowth of economic development or of the growth of a strong middle class. Instead, it occurred as a result of a combination of the relatively weak institutionalization of the authoritarian regime, unprofessional and eventually divided armed forces, elite division and sustained economic power of rivals, as well as civil society mobilization.

The democratic system that was re-established very much preserves the weaknesses of the past. Political clans continue to exercise oligarchic power over the state and the economy. Although the middle class is critical and vocal, and marginalized sectors have been politicized through repeated mobilization, they have gained little space in the country's representative institutions. The Philippines maintains its low-quality democracy based on electoral competition between elite political clans.

4 | *Malaysia and Singapore*

Malaysia and Singapore have shared relatively similar paths. Both former British colonies, at independence they formed parliamentary systems along the British model. In each case, a dominant political party gained ascendency at independence and managed to reproduce its power base until today. In Malaysia's case, the dominance of the United Malays National Organization (UMNO) was maintained within coalitions, first the Alliance and next the National Front (Barisan Nasional, BN). Singapore's People's Action Party (PAP) has been more strongly dominant as opposition parties have only recently managed to gain a few seats in parliament and remain very weak. At the same time, both states developed strong, professional bureaucracies and the judicial system has exercised some degree of autonomy and authority. Against the backdrop of this political stability, the middle class has grown remarkably since independence, as both countries have developed rapidly and the proceeds of economic growth have been widely shared. Theories of democratic transition would therefore predict that such high levels of economic development and the large middle class should have made both countries prime candidates for democratization, yet they have maintained soft authoritarian systems. How can we explain such persistence?

Malaysia's post-independence politics have been remarkably stable. Except for ethnic riots that shook the country in 1969, political life has been even, regularized and to some extent devoid of open conflict. No significant regime change occurred and the structure of the political system remained the same, with only few occasional reforms. The state has kept control over simmering ethnic tensions, resentment at persistent inequalities and other forms of discontent through a sophisticated institutional structure that has outlived moments of crisis. The United Malays National Organization (UMNO) remains dominant in a coalition that has ruled Malaysia since independence, although the results of the 2008 elections came close to challenging its position.

The regime is not democratic but its brand of authoritarianism is much softer than many other forms in the region. William Case has referred to it as "electoral authoritarianism" (Case, 2009b) or "pseudo-democracy" (Case, 2004). Harold Crouch has dubbed it "neither authoritarian nor democratic" (Crouch, 1996). It cannot be called democratic because no opposition political party has ever come close to winning an election. Except in 1969 and 2008, UMNO and its electoral partners have managed to win more than two-thirds of the parliamentary seats. At the same time, the military has never intervened in political affairs, the government has some respect for the rule of law and there is some serious electoral competition within UMNO. At the state level, such as in Kelantan and Terengganu, opposition parties have won in successive elections. These characteristics render the regime somewhat less authoritarian than others.

Its stability and longevity can be explained by two main factors. First, institutional manipulation and patronage have allowed UMNO to maintain its strength, even beyond any single leader's control over the party. Successive governments have manipulated electoral rules, constitutional provisions and various laws to preserve UMNO's dominant status and elite unity. UMNO's dominance allowed the coalition (initially the Alliance and later the BN) to maintain the two-thirds majority required to modify the constitution. When challenges to UMNO's dominance were raised from within the state, the government modified the constitution. For instance, Prime Minister Mahathir Mohamad introduced constitutional changes in 1993 to remove Malay traditional rulers' immunity from prosecution. Malay rulers – who rotated as heads of state – had often challenged the government and the measure was designed to curb some of their authority. Various laws, such as the Internal Security Act or Sedition Act, gave the government extraordinary powers of arrest while preserving a semblance of respect for the law.

Patronage has produced continued benefits to UMNO's supporters. Gomez and Jomo have argued that links between state and business have provided resources and incentives for select businesses to grow in exchange for continued support of UMNO. A strong economy enabled this relationship to consolidate and ensured a continuous stream of patronage (Gomez & Jomo, 1999), even down to the local level, where the wealthiest farmers have been generally those supporting UMNO and benefiting from state resources (Scott, 1985).

Second, UMNO-led governments turned Malaysia into a rapidly growing economy. Their policies raised living standards of large numbers of Malaysians who gratefully supported the regime during elections. "Performance legitimacy" developed from successful economic development that continuously promised better livelihoods to a broad segment of Malaysians. In return, they would support the regime that continued to deliver such results.

Nevertheless, other factors also set Malaysia apart from other cases in the region. Most notably, UMNO has maintained its dominance in part through its ability to exploit deep ethnic divisions between the Malay and Chinese. Balancing between policies that favoured the Malays while reassuring the Chinese, UMNO skillfully manipulated ethnic tensions to its advantage. Ethnic riots in 1969 have been repeatedly used as a point of reference to reinforce ethnically based policies. While many parties have organized along class or ideological lines, their efforts have been dampened by ethnic divisions and state policies that institutionalized and intensified them.

Singapore shares many features with Malaysia. Its political regime has been remarkably stable since the 1960s. As with its larger neighbour, civilians dominate the regime, which is authoritarian with some soft features. The government has no chance of losing elections. Singaporeans are highly restricted in attempts to organize opposition groups or openly criticize the government. Yet, they can easily travel outside of the country and do not face direct evidence of authoritarian rule, such as the daily presence of soldiers on the streets.

Single-party dominance best characterizes the regime. While in Malaysia, UMNO has required allies among other parties to maintain power, in Singapore the People's Action Party (PAP) rules alone while it faces only a handful of opposition members in parliament. Almost no riots, demonstrations, or public protests ever disrupt this political tranquility.

"Performance" legitimacy, institutional control and some unique features explain this stability. Originally a thriving trading post under British colonial rule, Singapore became a wealthy, modern city-state over the last six decades. Its population remained supportive of a regime that successfully engineered steadily high levels of economic growth with remarkably well-distributed benefits. Rather than enriching itself and concentrating wealth at the top, as has been characteristic of authoritarian regimes elsewhere in Southeast Asia, Singapore's political elite ensured that a fairly broad segment of the population benefited from economic growth. It consequently has enjoyed some degree of legitimacy in spite of its authoritarian tendencies.

Its political institutions and the legal apparatus have also contributed to the regime's longevity. In general, the government has followed well-defined constitutional and legal procedures, including regular elections. It has skillfully manipulated electoral districts and rules to ensure PAP dominance, while allowing opposition parties to run. It has used the law rather than force to repress opposition parties and groups. Legal instruments also allow the government to create incentives for individuals to support it. Most Singaporeans depend on the government for housing, pensions, health and a number of other services. They are reluctant to criticize or oppose the government by fear of losing them. As a result, a whole web of institutions and laws strengthen the PAP's hold on the country.

Political adaptation has been also a hallmark of the PAP's strategy. It has made adjustments to its institutional controls to allow for more consultation, more feedback, or to loosen some of its stricter controls to regain its upper hand over rising opposition.

As in Malaysia, the government has also used ethnic diversity to bolster its rule. Ethnic divisions have been less institutionalized than in Malaysia, where political parties were organized along ethnic lines. Singaporean political parties, from the PAP to major opposition parties, bridge the ethnic divide. Nevertheless, even though Singapore did not have riots on the scale of Malaysia's in 1969, tensions between ethnic groups have occasionally risen. The government has used such tensions to promote government measures and ideology presumably to strengthen national unity but providing it with further instruments to control.

Finally, this tightly knit web of control would not be possible without Singapore's small size. Because it is a city-state, the government can be present everywhere. The population is sufficiently small that the government can reach all citizens through its policies and programmes. Larger countries would never be able to create dependence on a housing scheme. In comparing this case with other authoritarian regimes, therefore, such unique characteristics need to be taken into account.

Malaysia

British colonial rule laid the basis for Malaysia's political system. The multiparty parliamentary system, elections from municipal to national level, an independent judiciary, professionalized military and good bureaucratic capacity were part of its legacy, which gave Malaysia a strong base for democracy. Yet, these were undermined by the structure of economic and social relations that the British also bequeathed. The exploitation of large rubber plantations and mines required labour that Malays were reluctant to provide. The British recruited instead large numbers of migrant Chinese and Indians. They also segregated racial groups through residency restrictions and policies designed to give Malay sultans authority over their subjects, with the objective of preserving their rural-based political control over the Malays. It allowed the British to maintain a separate status for the Chinese and Indians, and therefore better control over them as well (Case, 2009b). Racial segregation had the most long-lasting effect by institutionalizing ethnic differences. Once carried over into independent Malaysia, these divisions remained at the core of political life.

In preparation for independence, the British decision to propose a Malayan Union after 1945 had profound consequences. The proposal gave equal citizenship rights to Chinese migrants and Malays. For Malay aristocrats who had served the British as civil servants, such an option was unacceptable as it reduced their status and that of their Malay followers. UMNO was formed in 1946 out of a protest against equal rights. In the face of such protests, the British withdrew the proposal and, instead, recognized Malay special rights, thereby enshrining a status difference for the Malays. Unsurprisingly, in reaction to UMNO's formation, alternative political parties also organized along ethnic lines. In 1948, the British proclaimed the Federation of Malaya, which placed at its core the enshrinement of Malay "special rights".

Meanwhile, the Cold War left a different mark than elsewhere in the region. The Malayan Communist Party (MCP) declared an armed struggle in 1948. In response, the British passed a number of regulations to contain the armed insurrection. The period that became known as "The Emergency" (1948–60) had significant consequences for the political system. First, it deepened already tense relations between Malays and Chinese. The MCP was almost exclusively Chinese and drew very little support from Malays or Indians. Malays saw the MCP not only as an enemy of the British but as a party that sought to deny them a privileged status. Second, the British Emergency Regulations had a lasting impact. One of these allowed for detention without trial;

the authorities could arrest and imprison people without a trial for up to one year if they were deemed to threaten security. By the end of the "Emergency", the newly independent government passed the Internal Security Act in 1960, which essentially preserved and continued this precedent that the British had established. Originally intended as a tool to arrest communist supporters, the law was later used to intimidate and detain opponents to the government (Bedlington, 1978).

The first elections in 1955 and the subsequent Constitution of 1957 sealed the regime's structure. What was initially an ad hoc arrangement for municipal elections became a winning strategy in the 1955 elections: with the Malayan Chinese Association (MCA) and the Malayan Indian Congress (MIC), UMNO formed an alliance that secured almost all the seats in Parliament. The Alliance was formalized, and remained a winning strategy for subsequent elections until 1969. The 1957 Constitution maintained British parliamentary institutions but institutionalized Malay dominance. It created a Conference of Rulers that included the traditional Malay Rulers and governors of states that did not have Rulers. On a rotational basis, the Conference selected one of the Rulers to act as the largely ceremonial head of state, Yang di-Pertuan Agong. The Constitution also assigned it the role of protector of Malay special rights. These rights included quotas for the civil service, scholarships and training privileges for Malays. With Islam enshrined as the state religion, and the Malay language given preponderance, Malays enjoyed a clearly dominant status. The Chinese reluctantly accepted this political arrangement on the understanding that their community would be free to pursue their business interests and to play a greater role in the economy, as they had done in the past. This quid pro quo created a stable balance that lasted more than a decade.

In the first decade of independence, two issues prevailed. The first involved the creation of an expanded Federation of Malaysia that included Singapore. The second was the question of Malay privileges. The first Prime Minister Tunku Abdul Rahman (the "Tunku"), proposed in 1961 a new Federation of Malaysia that would include the newly independent Federation of Malaya, Singapore, as well as the British territories of Sabah, Sarawak and Brunei. Partly under British pressure, the Federation of Malaysia was proclaimed in 1963. The inclusion of Sabah and Sawarak counterbalanced that of Singapore, with its majority of Chinese, as the "Tunku" and his government deemed it crucial to preserve the existing ethnic balance. Brunei became its own independent country. The creation of the Federation of Malaysia provoked a confrontational policy from Indonesia's leader, Sukarno. Known as the *konfrontasi*, this policy first began as a vocal protest against the Federation, which Sukarno saw as a "puppet state" to perpetuate British colonial control in a different guise. While tensions rose, there was little interest in war, so that the worst of the confrontation essentially consisted of a few Indonesian incursions on Malaysian territory. A more significant challenge happened a little later, when tensions were heightened between Singapore and the Federal government. In 1965, Malaysia decided to expel Singapore after Lee Kuan Yew, the leader of Singapore, repeatedly interfered in the Malaysia-wide elections despite an agreement that Singapore should stay out of national elections.

The question of Malay privileges, particularly the national language, was a second thorny issue. After the adoption of the 1957 Constitution, the government followed preferential treatment policies for Malays. The question of the national language, however, became a high point of contention. The Constitution provided for a ten-year retention of both English and Malay as official languages. While the Singapore controversy was developing, there was strong Malay pressure to adopt Malay only as a national language by 1967. Non-Malays strongly resented this movement. In the end, the Tunku ended the dispute by suggesting that Malay would be the only national language but that English could continue to be used for official purposes where it was appropriate. This vision was enshrined in the National Language Act of 1967. While the Tunku emerged as a figure that could balance Malay and non-Malay interests – and indeed was key for maintaining the fragile understanding holding the Alliance together – he was increasingly resented by a segment of Malays who wanted stronger measures to protect and support the Malays.

1969 riots, the New Economic Policy and the formation of the National Front (Barisan Nasional)

Simmering ethnic tensions broke into open conflict when the results of the 1969 elections triggered riots that disrupted this agreement. Malays were dissatisfied with the persistent economic inequality in favour of the Chinese. Conversely, many Chinese resented their lower political and cultural standings. In the 1969 elections, many Malays expressed their discontent by migrating to the opposition Pan-Malaysian Islamic Party (Partai Islam Se-Malaysia, PAS). The Chinese shifted away from the MCA and voted in greater numbers for the Democratic Action Party (DAP) and other parties. As a result, the Alliance's share of votes declined markedly, leading to the loss of their usual control of two-thirds of parliamentary seats, while opposition parties won in two state assemblies (Case, 2004). After UMNO weakened in the 1969 elections, many Chinese who had voted for opposition political parties held "victory rallies", which inflamed Malays and led to the several days of rioting that began on 13 May.

This unprecedented violence between Malays and Chinese marked a turning point by which the government adopted new policies to prevent future ethnic violence and increase UMNO's control over political institutions. The government operated under emergency rule for the next two years, under the leadership of Tun Abdul Razak. Razak had been the deputy prime minister, and rose to the position of prime minister as Tunku Abdul Rahman was sidelined. A group of leaders within UMNO had concluded that the Tunku's policies had been too moderate and gradual. Instead, they supported a much stronger approach in favour of Malays.

When emergency rule was lifted, UMNO seized greater control over the administrative apparatus, and particularly economic ministries that the MCA had previously held. It also created state agencies to guide industrial deepening. Malays obtained even greater shares of public employment and, under a "New Economic Policy", benefited from a host of new measures to enhance their privileges (Case, 2004).

The New Economic Policy (NEP), and its successor the National Development Policy, constituted a massive pro-*bumiputra* ("sons of the soil", i.e. Malays) redistribution scheme, designed to raise the economic status of the Malays relative to the Chinese. In particular, it provided preferential quotas and differential admissions policies for access to higher education. It funded some graduates to study abroad. Government investment firms nurtured Malay-owned companies, the hiring guidelines imposed certain *bumiputra* quotas and government ministries awarded lucrative contracts to *bumiputra* firms. Large government-owned enterprises, such as oil-company Petronas and automobile firm Proton, provided large amounts of employment to Malays. Foreign investors also largely employed Malay factory workers. Even among the broader population, a scheme allowed ordinary Malays to purchase discounted stocks in *bumiputra*-owned firms. All these measures, particularly those benefiting the broader segment of Malays, sealed Malay support for the NEP (Case, 2004; Pepinsky, 2007).

In the aftermath of the 1969 riots, UMNO consolidated its power over the upper echelons of the government, and reinforced its hierarchical predominance over coalition partners. It more strongly curtailed opposition and civil liberties. With the implementation of the New Economic Policy, it created new state enterprises and business ventures that aligned state interests with a growing number of constituents in the business world. The government also distributed licences and other forms of patronage to loyal followers in the elite, thereby strengthening a network of clientelist relations tied to UMNO. The expansion of UMNO's reach greatly enhanced its power over the MCA and MIC. Furthermore, new partners were added to the coalition, including Gerakan, a mainly Chinese party, as well as small parties based in Sarawak and Sabah, the two remote states on the island of Borneo. For a few years, even PAS joined the electoral coalition that was now rebaptized BN. At the same time, the BN's rhetoric spelled out nation building objectives that appealed across ethnic lines to build a united Malaysia (Case, 2004).

Leadership styles began to shift away from the balancing approach that the Tunku had adopted towards greater pro-Malay politics. Tun Razak had distanced himself as the Tunku had lost increasing support among UMNO elites. Following his accession to the position of prime minister, he supported the rise of several politicians with more openly strong advocacy for Malay interests. Hussein Onn, the son of UMNO's founder Dato' Onn bin Ja'afar, eventually succeeded Razak as prime minister upon his death in 1976. Hussein Onn had not developed much of a power base within the party, as he had remained outside of UMNO for many years and only returned in 1969. He owed his rise in the party largely to Tun Razak and therefore struggled to establish his leadership. As a result, factionalism and criticism rose within UMNO, including from a group surrounding Tunku Abdul Rahman. Onn stepped down as prime minister in 1981.

The next prime minister, Mahathir bin Mohamad, had a much stronger style of leadership. Mahathir had been expelled from UMNO in 1969 for openly criticizing the Tunku's leadership and his lack of strong support for Malay interests. He returned to UMNO during Tun Razak's administration and quickly rose within the party, eventually acceding to the position of deputy prime minister under Hussein Onn. When the latter resigned, the once rebellious politician became leader of UMNO and prime minister in 1981. Mahathir strengthened UMNO's pro-Malay policies. He also developed grand projects and more than any of his predecessors used state incentives to stimulate economic growth. Under his leadership, Malaysia offered Vision 2020, a template for Malaysia to reach a status similar to the most developed countries in the world. He launched a made-in-Malaysia car, and announced the creation of a Multi-media Super Corridor to attract technological investment and innovation. He placed large emphasis on building Malaysia as an economic powerhouse while, in the political realm, strengthening policies that favoured the Malays. He was Malaysia's most influential prime minister, as he remained in power from 1981 to 2008. During his twenty-seven years, he managed to hold a very tight grip on power and to displace rising opponents within UMNO.

Regime persistence and its challenges

Leadership alone could not explain why the regime has remained so stable. Case looks at elite unity and disunity to understand and explain the longevity of the regime. He argues that Malaysia's elite has maintained a good degree of unity despite occasional disputes and factionalization. Certainly a new Malay business elite, built up during the 1980s and 1990s, depended largely on state contracts and close ties to the political structure. Chinese business elites have supported the regime as their businesses have flourished even though the New Economic Policy placed some constraints on their activities. They even supported Mahathir's government during the Asian financial crisis. They have been reluctant to advocate more democracy given their minority status and the prospects of PAS forming a government much less tolerant of the Chinese. As for the Malay elite more broadly, it has tended to close ranks after divisive disputes. For instance, even when a leadership challenge was launched against Mahathir in the 1980s or when Deputy Prime Minister Anwar Ibrahim and Mahathir competed against each other in the 1990s, purges occurred and even imprisonment but such divisiveness was usually followed by a period of reconciliation and rehabilitation (Case, 2009a).

UMNO has also used patronage not only to maintain elite cohesion but also to nurture its broader Malay constituency. It has provided Malay rural constituents with development projects and educational programmes. For its urban Malay constituents, it has provided managerial positions and shares in government-sponsored businesses. Islamization policies offered further benefits to both constituencies. Beyond the use of private resources, UMNO has maintained regime loyalty through extensive use of official state funds. This practice shows the depth of UMNO's penetration of the government, as officials use state budget allocations to maintain support, with clearly larger disbursements during electoral times (Pepinsky, 2007).

The government also used a number of measures to control social groups. It curtailed freedom of assembly through arbitrary registration and permit requirements for various organizations and group events. It controlled the print media through UMNO-linked ownership and licensing requirements. Nevertheless, some of these methods of control also had limits. In particular, after 2000 the print media began to report on political and business scandals even if they damaged the reputation of state officials. More importantly, the Internet became the site of vibrant, critical and free source of reporting. Various websites, blogs and online newspapers, such as *Malaysiakini*, openly criticized government policies and provided extensive reporting beyond state control.

Finally, it manipulated electoral rules to ensure favourable outcomes. Elections are competitive but distorted by strong gerrymandering and district apportionment largely favorable to Malays. UMNO, through its control of the government, also manipulates campaigning and voting rules. State resources and media are used also to promote the government party. Nevertheless, elections are not so distorted that they prevent opposition parties from making significant gains. They remain competitive within these constraints that favour the BN. The opposition has been able to gain 35–40 per cent of popular vote and to capture state governments (Case, 2004). In 2008, a complacent BN even ended up losing its two-thirds majority, with a large swing of popular support and seats going to opposition parties.

These mechanisms have been powerful means of maintaining UMNO's dominance. Political leaders, even with strong agendas and leadership skills as Mahathir, would not risk tinkering with these established sources of power. As Jason Brownlee has shown in a comparison with the Philippines under President Marcos, regime longevity in Malaysia can be partly explained by leaders' deference to UMNO and its capacity to attract and absorb opponents into its fold. Mahathir stayed in power in part because the party held some organizational control over him. In contrast to Marcos' ability to manipulate his party at will, Mahathir, despite his strong personal power, had to abide by some of UMNO's rules, which ultimately contributed to helping him stay in power and deflect some of the opposition (Brownlee, 2008).

Yet, it does not mean that challenges to UMNO's dominance have not been significant. The Malay elite has occasionally split and threatened UMNO's position although its ability to weather these crises has so far been strong. Successive challenges show that a split within the Malay governing elite will first precede a likely change in the regime.

The first major UMNO challenge shows the depth of its patronage resources to retain elite loyalty. When in 1986 a rift divided Prime Minister Mahathir and Tunku Razaleigh, a former finance minister, UMNO expelled Razaleigh who subsequently formed an alternative political party Semangat '46 (Spirit of '46). UMNO maintained its following by using its vast patronage resources. Many disgruntled members who supported Razaleigh in principle remained with UMNO to preserve their clientelist revenues. After Semangat '46 failed to garner sufficient numbers of Malays to defect, even Razaleigh quietly rejoined UMNO's ranks.

The 1999 election constituted a second setback for UMNO. Preceding the election, the 1997 Asian financial crisis had destabilized Malaysia and created a wedge between Mahathir and Deputy Prime Minister Anwar Ibrahim. Anwar had been the leader of ABIM (Angkatan Belia Islam Malaysia), the Malaysia Islamic Youth Movement, which promoted social issues and greater Islamization of Malaysia. Mahathir encouraged him to enter UMNO and run for election in 1982. Anwar quickly rose within the party and eventually became Mahathir's finance minister (1991) and Deputy Prime Minister (1993). Although he was groomed for succession, once he appeared to become more assertive, Mahathir responded by sidelining him and reaffirming his leadership. Anwar's proposed responses to the Asian financial crisis, for instance, openly challenged Mahathir's leadership.

In retaliation, Mahathir expelled him. Subsequently, Anwar was then ludicrously charged with sodomy and corruption to tarnish his reputation. He was arrested and convicted in an obvious ploy to thwart his leadership ambitions.

The sacking of Anwar Ibrahim, and growing disillusion with Mahathir's rule, provoked a mass protest movement known as *Reformasi*. Malaysians demonstrated over a period of several months against reports of Anwar's bad treatment and the obvious fabrication of the events for which he was being charged. Anwar had built up strong loyalty within UMNO and his expected succession to Mahathir enjoyed strong support. UMNO was consequently riddled with factional divisions as Anwar was sidelined and Mahathir reaffirmed his commanding position.

Following these events, UMNO was then punished at the polls in 1999 as many Malays chose to support the opposition PAS in protest against Mahathir's style of leadership, his handling of the crisis and Anwar's treatment. While the BN was able to compensate with greater support from the Chinese and Indian communities, this electoral defection nevertheless threatened its dominance. Furthermore, opposition parties began to craft an alliance in spite of ideological differences. Anwar's wife, Wan Azizah Wan Ismail, who enjoyed broad sympathy from the unjust treatment of her husband, formed an opposition movement, Adil (Pergerakan Keadilan Sosial, Movement for Social Justice). When she subsequently formed a political party, Partai Keadilan Nasional (National Justice Party, Keadilan), she then also created formal links to the PAS, the DAP and the Partai Rakyat Malaysia (PRM) by joining them in the creation of a broad coalition, the Barisan Alternatif, to compete against the BN in the 1999 elections (Weiss, 2006). This kind of coalition, while not unprecedented, showed a very strong commitment on the part of the opposition to join forces against the BN's electoral supremacy. Indeed, PAS and DAP were strange bedfellows as PAS traditionally stood for more Islamic law and promotion of Malay interests, while the DAP was officially a pan-ethnic party with its main base of support among the Chinese. PRM had strong secular and socialist inclinations and had built roots among poor Malays, therefore also oddly cooperating with PAS. In the elections that ensued, the Barisan Alternatif did not end up dislodging the BN but still provided a broadly based message of discontent with the government. At the state level, PAS gained the most by increasing its support across the north and winning elections in the state of Terengganu while solidifying its hold over Kelantan.

The 2008 election produced a greater challenge to UMNO's dominance, even prompting observers to speak of a transition to democracy. The BN lost its two-thirds majority for the first time since 1969. The popular vote declined from its usual 55–65 per cent range to 52 per cent. The BN share of seats dropped to only 63 per cent, thereby denying it the 75 per cent required to change the constitution. The DAP and PAS saw their seats rise from 19 to 51, while Keadilan (PKR, People's Justice Party) won 31 seats. The PKR was created in 2003 from a merger between Wan Azizah's former Keadilan party (PKN) and the PRM, who both shared similar commitments to reform and social justice. In addition to successes at the national level, opposition parties also won elections in five states, which was unprecedented.

Most analyses have attributed these results as protest votes against the ineffective government of Abdullah Ahmad Badawi, who succeeded Mahathir in October 2003. When he became prime minister, Abdullah first struggled to create his own path in the shadow of Mahathir. He first distanced himself from his predecessor by releasing Anwar Ibrahim from prison. Heading into the 2004 elections, he launched a reform campaign aimed at curbing corruption, reducing patronage appointments and improving the government's integrity. These efforts produced resounding success at the polls, as the BN won a record number of seats, and regained the state of Terengganu (which it had lost to PAS in 1999). PAS's number of seats dropped dramatically, while Wan Azizah's party Parti Keadilan Rakyat retained only one seat. The Barisan Alternatif opposition coalition had split in 2001, when the DAP could no longer agree on a joint strategy that included PAS. This coalition's dissolution did not help opposition results in the election. The BN was also helped by the strength of Malaysia's economy, which had bounced back since the previous elections and was then growing at an impressive rate of 7 per cent (Welsh, 2005). The election returned UMNO and the BN to a dominant position, while the Reformasi movement and its electoral incarnation in the Barisan Alternatif fizzled out.

It soon became clear, however, that Abdullah, a product of the UMNO establishment, was not an engine of change. His Cabinet remained filled with some of the notoriously corrupt insiders from the Mahathir era. Family connections to heavy UMNO stalwarts continued to ensure ascendency in government. Pro-Malay policies continued. In addition, Abdullah failed to establish promised agencies to monitor and crack down on corruption. By 2007, some independent NGOs successfully organized mass demonstrations to denounce electoral fraud and continued corruption. Other demonstrations combined with confidence from media outlets to report more liberally some of the opposition to the government.

The evidence of continued corruption, as well as fatigue with racially based policies explain the turn against Abdullah and the BN. It was in that context that the 2008 elections were held and returned unprecedented results in favour of opposition parties. With Anwar Ibrahim back in the political arena, the coalition was highly successful and created, for the first time, a strong parliamentary opposition (Case, 2009b). It was still short, however, of actually changing the regime.

After Abdullah's failure at the polls, his deputy Najib Tun Razak became prime minister in April 2009, with the expectation that he would undertake some political reforms. Yet, his first initiatives seemed quite mild. He introduced "One Malaysia" policies that preserved pro-Malay affirmative action polices but attempted to recreate more ethnic balance through more acceptance of ethnic and religious differences. He repeatedly emphasized the need for political reform but UMNO was more resistant to change than the prime minister's stated intentions. His government repealed the Internal Security Act but replaced it with a new law allowing detention without trial for twenty-eight days. Ethnically divisive issues continued to arise, for instance criticism of the national curriculum and reading materials that gave preponderance to Malays and downplayed the historical roles of Chinese and Indian populations. Najib announced a New Economic Model (NEM), intended to replace the NEP, yet he faced strong opposition from groups supporting Malay privileges. In the end, minor changes were made to redistributive schemes that favoured the Malays, rather than offering more balanced programmes.

Yet, 2008 marked a watershed year for Malaysian politics. With the BN having lost its two-thirds majority, opposition groups became increasingly confident that political change could happen. Many groups began to participate more actively in politics, while the Najib government attempted to readjust its policies to preserve support for the BN. In the aftermath of the 2008 election, the opposition formed a new coalition, the Pakatan Rakyat (People's Alliance, PR), which

Table 6 *Malaysia*

Population (rank)	Land area (rank)	Main ethnic groups (%)	Main religions (%)	Regime type (transition)	GDP per capita (rank)	GDP growth rate (%) (rank)
29 179 952 (43rd) (2011 est.)	328 657 sq km (66th)	Malay 50.4 Chinese 23.7 Indigenous 11 Indian 7.1 Others 7.8 (2004 est.)	Muslim 60.4 Buddhist 19.2 Christian 9.1 Hindu 6.3 Confucianist, Taoist, or other traditional Chinese religions 2.6 Other/unknown 1.5 None 0.8 (2000 census)	Semi-democracy Constitutional monarchy	$15 600 (77th) (2011 est.)	5.2 (66th) (2011 est.)

Source: CIA, *The World Factbook*; Polity IV Project, Polity IV Individual Country Regime Trends, 1946–2010.

included the DAP, PAS and the PKR. These parties attempted to continue the momentum from their electoral victory to keep up pressure in favour of political reform.

Many new groups seized the initiative to launch more public debates of various reform issues. For instance, a group called Perkasa mobilized in defence of special privileges for the Malays. The Malay Consultative Council (MPM), an umbrella organization representing seventy-six Malay NGOs, organized a large congress in 2010 warning Najib to change his policies and respect Malay interests. Conversely, in 2011, Bersih (the Coalition for Clean and Fair Elections) organized a large rally to demand democratic reforms. Although public demonstrations and deliberation have occurred in the past, they have been more prevalent since the 2008 elections and have created more intense pressure on the BN government, pitting reformists against those seeking to preserve the status quo.

This apparent increase in civil society activity has yet to produce political change. As Meredith Weiss argues, greater education, economic growth and more integration to global markets have gradually increased the extent to which Malaysians have been able to influence the government's orientation. Ever since independence, Malay associations have pressured the government for various privileges. Yet, the political space remained limited. The government welcomed civil society organizations that served some specific purposes and that did not adopt confrontational stances. Some of the larger, professional organizations were sometimes included in policy discussions. They have been able to participate in agenda-setting and discussions surrounding policies on issues such as Islamization, women's rights, environmental protection and health care. But overall these have not produced political change at the level of the regime (Weiss, 2005, 2006).

Singapore

The PAP's rise and dominance is based on Lee Kuan Yew's skilful consolidation of power and elimination of nascent working class mobilization. Elections for self-government were first organized in 1959 under British supervision. An English-speaking middle class, led by Lee Kuan Yew, had little support among the broader population so it created an alliance with left-leaning politicians who could attract votes from the Chinese-speaking working class. With this alliance, the People's Action Party (PAP) won the election with little opposition.

The PAP split in 1961, however, over the contentious issue of whether to join a Malaysian federation. Lee Kuan Yew's faction retained control over the party's Central Executive Committee and therefore wielded greater power over party policy than its left wing. The leadership of the party favoured the merger while the left wing faction opposed it out of fear that the federal government in Kuala Lumpur would represent an even greater challenge to the left, since Malaysia's communists had been eliminated during the Emergency. In 1961, the left wing broke off from the PAP and formed the Barisan Sosialis (Socialist Front). Lee Kuan Yew, with support from Malayan Prime Minister Tunku Abdul Rahman, under the Internal Security Act arrested 111 "pro-communist" agitators before the 1963 elections, mostly members of the Barisan Sosialis. The PAP's victory in these elections paved the way for joining Malaysia (Rodan, 2008).

The encounter with the Malaysian federation lasted only two years. In the run-up to federal elections in 1965, Lee Kuan Yew broke the understanding reached at the time of the merger: Singapore would retain its own government and autonomy in administrative affairs, as long as it did not interfere in the affairs of the Malaysian state. The Malaysian federation was dominated by UMNO, a Malay party that brokered an alliance with Chinese and Indian political parties and formed a winning coalition based on this alliance between ethnically based parties. In exchange for the acceptance of Malay dominance in politics, the large Chinese minority would continue to dominate economic sectors with the government's blessing. Lee Kuan Yew challenged this ethnic balance when the PAP ran a few candidates in the Malaysian election in 1964, in a challenge to the perceived weakness of the Chinese party. Also in 1964, riots broke out in Singapore when some UMNO leaders attacked the PAP on Malay rights. The PAP, in turn, had sponsored an alliance of political parties around the slogan "Malaysian Malaysia" to promote a federation with equal rights for Malays and Chinese, and the elimination of ethnically based politics. These tensions led the Malaysian government to expel Singapore from the federation (Mauzy & Milne, 2002).

The PAP found itself devoid of a political base and suddenly running an independent country. Rather than recreating its base, it chose instead to replace it with an organizational structure that would become increasingly dominant and paternalistic in its orientation.

Consolidating PAP rule

The PAP ruled by respecting certain institutional processes but curtailing opposition. It conducted regular parliamentary elections every five years. Electoral competition was genuine but districts were often gerrymandered so that PAP supporters dwarfed pockets of opposition. Over time, the government also threatened to withdraw government support to districts voting against the PAP. Once it established its electoral dominance, the PAP retained it with the opposition only making some limited gains in the 1980s and 1990s.

Three additional aspects helped to turn the PAP into a strong, dominant party: first, the extension of its network of control; second, the use of legal instruments to marginalize political opposition; and third, an ideology of survival to justify its dominance and to promote economic development.

Party and state became virtually merged. The PAP formed close relationships with the upper echelons of the civil service. The party's Central Executive Committee soon controlled appointments to most positions in the civil service's higher echelons. Yet, it did not use this power to fill positions with party loyalists but, conversely, used meritocratic criteria both to gain access to managerial and technocratic positions as well as to play a significant role in the PAP's leadership. Meritocracy and low corruption were essential to creating the bureaucratic capacity to engineer Singapore's development. In this respect, Singapore is distinct among authoritarian regimes, most of which fill the ranks of their civil service according to loyalty to the regime and opportunities for graft, rather than with highly skilled personnel. In Singapore, obtaining technocratic and managerial skills, as well as high positions in the civil service, eventually became crucial to gain access to political leadership.

By the 1980s, a structural change had occurred as state control also included a high degree of involvement in the economy. Singapore's development was largely state-led and Singapore's political executive has always played an important role in investment decisions. Government-led corporations (GLCs) became the hallmark of its model and continue to dominate Singapore's economy to this day. They operate according to market principles and, in this way, resemble private enterprises more than state-owned companies elsewhere. State control over large amounts of capital, both through GLCs and other sources of government funding, developed a quasi-state business class with high technocratic management skills. During the 1980s, these technocrats constituted Singapore's political and economic elite. An increasing number of them became MPs and controlled the highest levels of the state (Rodan, 2008).

The PAP also built strength by replacing grass-roots organizations with its own. Various organizations, reporting to the prime minister's office, provided linkages to the party and the state. They ranged from the People's Association's Community Clubs and Citizens' Consultative Committees to the important National Trade Union Congress (NTUC), which constituted a single trade union organization under PAP control and which displaced the previously active network of trade unions that had backed the Barisan Sosialis. The PAP also organized youth and women's wings, and even established a network of kindergartens. In the 1980s, the government also created "self-help" organizations for the major ethnic groups. Initially, PAP Malay MPs and Lee Kuan Yew established Mendaki, a Malay organization to raise the educational performance of the Malays. It was placed under PAP control and funded through a scheme of mandatory contributions from every Malay worker. Indian and Chinese similar organizations (SINDA and CDAC respectively) were established subsequently to promote education and welfare, although the Chinese CDAC also benefited from very strong private financial backing. These organizations created state tentacles into every aspect of Singaporean society and greatly increased the PAP's power.

Some state policies and programmes also served the dual purpose of enhancing development while increasing the regime's political control. The government established a form of social contract by which Singaporeans were willing to accept less political freedom in exchange for rapid socio-economic development. It invested massive amounts into education and public housing. Housing became an important instrument of political support and control, as the percentage of Singaporeans dependent on public housing rose steadily (Rodan, 2008). Most Singaporeans live in public housing, which the Housing and Development Board (HDB) manages. The HDB controls access to waiting lists, supply and choices of housing units, as well as the level and frequency of maintenance. All of these can be manipulated for political purposes. The Central Provident Fund (CPF) constitutes a second good example. The British initially set up the CPF as a superannuation fund for retirement but Lee's government expanded its use. In addition to retirement, the CPF became a saving instrument for such other uses as a mortgage deposit, paying off a mortgage or borrowing for children's education (Barr, 2003). Although the government promoted a "self-help" welfare system, it used a paternalistic approach including mandatory contributions. Such dependence on the government created additional incentives to remain loyal to the PAP.

The regime also uses legal instruments to suppress opposition. The Internal Security Act, a remnant of British colonial rule, is the most draconian of these laws. It allows for arrest without warrant and detention without trial. The Societies Act was amended in 1967 to specify that no organization could engage in "political" activities without registration with the Registrar of Societies. Under these regulations, the PAP was able to eliminate the political significance of independent organizations and also of opposition parties. In order to control the press, the government's legislation included provisions for discretionary licensing but also softened the repressive aspects of the law by creating more sophisticated methods of control. For instance, it required newspaper companies to be publicly listed with a cap of 3 per cent shares that ordinary shareholders could posses. It created a class of managerial shares that were allocated through government nominations. The government therefore retained some editorial control through its influence over management, rather than through threats of repression or closure in case of violations to its publication norms (George, 2007). In 1986, the government amended the Newspapers and Printing Press Act to restrict the circulation of newspapers that engaged in domestic politics. Armed with this new instrument, it curtailed some prominent international newspapers and magazines such as *Time*, the *Far Eastern Economic Review* and *Asiaweek*.

During the 1980s, the state increasingly used the courts to control and repress opponents. Armed with allies throughout the legal system, Lee and PAP members routinely sued opposition members for libel. The courts, often staffed with career civil servants or even PAP cadres, most often awarded lofty damages to PAP members in the 1990s. Libel suits bankrupted some prominent members of the opposition, such as the Workers' Party MP J. B. Jeyaretnam and the Singapore Democratic Party's leader Chee Soon Juan.

Finally, ideology provided the rationale to sustain authoritarian rule. Lee built a political structure that reflected his vision to turn Singapore into a modern city-state. With Singapore's expulsion from Malaysia, Lee relied on an "ideology of survival" to justify PAP dominance in the national interest, so that it could build a viable political entity through development and in order to build a city-state capable of development and defending itself. This ideology was later supplemented with a developmentalist imperative and the special circumstances of Singapore's multiculturalism. The "myth of meritocracy" was elevated to a quasi-ideological level. As Michael Barr argues, even though personal networks and privilege are present among Singapore's ruling elite, nevertheless there is sufficient truth to its claims to maintain Singapore's prosperity and growth, and therefore make it highly believable (Barr, 2006). Whether Singaporeans actually believed the ideology, they nevertheless gained benefits from its promise. With strong state control came the delivery of rapidly increasing living standards, which made its justification widely acceptable.

Multiracialism has been another key ideological instrument. Although difficult to argue that it was intentional, nevertheless multiracialism provided the government with an effective means of dividing the population to better control it. It has been able to deny individual rights by claiming the primacy of group rights, for instance by denying individuals political expression and channelling it instead through representatives of their racial group. Conversely, the government appeals to the level of individuals when advancing its meritocratic system, and denying any group an advantage. At the same time, the government upholds racial harmony. By appealing to multiracialism and racial harmony, the government justifies its intervention to prevent ethnic clashes such as riots in the 1960s. It created instruments such as the Ministry of Muslim Affairs, through which the government retains oversight over the practice of Islam, as well as educational standards in Islamic religious schools (*madrasah*). At the same time, it prohibited racial and religious appeals for electoral purposes. It therefore institutionalized racial differences while denying the ability to use these references to mobilize politically.

Multiracialism later justified the creation of a new type of electoral constituency to further increase PAP control: Group Representation Constituencies (GRCs). GRCs group several electoral constituencies into one larger unit. The political party that wins the greatest aggregate number of votes from all constituencies in the GRC obtains all the seats. Some candidates had to be non-Chinese, with the objective of securing representation for ethnic minorities. It does not however challenge Chinese dominance in parliament and has had the added pernicious effect of reducing democratic representation by erasing the possibility of voting for single candidates and diluting one's vote by a proportion equal to the number of candidates running in a GRC (Beng Huat, 2007).

The rise of opposition and the PAP's institutional adjustments

Political opposition has had little chance of any electoral breakthrough in this system. From independence until 1981, the PAP controlled all of the seats of parliament. Only in 1981 did the opposition Workers'

Party win a first seat, held by J. B. Jeyaretnam. When in 1984, the opposition gained much stronger support than in the past and won two seats – Jeyaretnam's re-election as well as an additional seat gained by the opposition Singapore Democratic Party – the PAP realized the potential rise of political pressure resulting from decades of tightly controlled economic development. Furthermore, the PAP was aware of democratic transitions occurring in South Korea and Taiwan as a result of decades of rapid socio-economic change.

To address this perceived threat, the PAP sought ways to weaken opposition leaders. Lee Kuan Yew won a defamation lawsuit against Jeyaretnam, who was forced to resign from parliament in 1986. Later in the 1990s, Goh Chok Tong also sued him and forced him into bankruptcy while he was still the Workers' Party leader. Francis Seow, a strong critic of the government, won a seat in the 1988 elections but was barred from parliament as the government promptly sued him for tax evasion and fined him enough to prevent him from taking up his seat. Four opposition candidates nevertheless won seats in 1991, and electoral support for opposition parties rose to an unprecedented 39 per cent that year, from a much lower 24.5 per cent in 1980 (Means, 1996).

At the same time, the government modified its approach by introducing a number of consultative mechanisms to increase citizen participation in the political process, without feeding political opposition. For instance, in 1985, the government created Feedback Units to allow the public to express its concerns over policy issues. In 2006, these units were renamed REACH (Reaching Everyone for Active Citizenry @ Home). In 1987, it launched the Government Parliamentary Committees (GPCs). Other reforms continued to broaden the spectrum of participation to include even independent organizations. The Nominated Members of Parliament (NMP) scheme, introduced in 1989, constitutes such an innovative mode of participation. NMPs are appointed as members of parliament who are chosen for their expertise in particular fields. They are intended to represent the perspectives of social groups with specific expertise such as professionals, commerce or industry but also that are absent or under-represented within the parliament, such as women. Appointees have ranged from professionals in the medical and academic field, to the private sector and even some members from the NTUC and independent social groups. It has served to increase representation of particular social groups while attempting to elevate parliamentary debate to a greater technocratic level (Rodan, 2009). These and other similar mechanisms used participation to increase administrative efficiency in the delivery of public policy without actually increasing representation.

Finally, Lee orchestrated a leadership succession. Goh Chok Tong became prime minister in 1990, through an orderly succession. A new generation of leaders had been appointed to Cabinet in 1984 with few clear indications of Lee's successor. Although the Cabinet favoured Goh, Lee Kuan Yew expressed some doubts. Goh also faced a significant challenge from Lee's older son Lee Hsien Loong, who was a rising star with leadership ambitions. Nevertheless, the Cabinet reconfirmed Goh as the successor prime minister in 1988 and he formally acceded to the position in 1990. After failing to gain a strong victory in the 1991 election, which he had declared to strengthen his leadership, Goh initially appeared as a transitional leader under Lee's shadow, with the expectation that Lee Hsien Loong would eventually replace him. However, as Lee Hsien Loong became ill, the PAP fully backed Goh, allowing him to consolidate his leadership (Mauzy, 1993). Goh subsequently remained prime minister for 14 years.

Goh Chok Tong's style was more open and more greatly concerned with public consultation. He gained some popularity for his different leadership approach. The government left space for some independent organizations to operate more freely than they had before. Organizations such as the Association of Malay Professionals (AMP), the Association of Women for Action and Research (AWARE) and the Nature Society of Singapore (NSS) could operate under slightly less restrictions than they had before. Goh also sponsored the creation of a "Speakers' Corner" to allow citizens to voice their concerns. Looser licensing also allowed some diversification of media outlets.

Nevertheless, these reforms were clouded by an obvious continuity in the repressive nature of the Singaporean state. Despite giving the impression of being more open, it remained clear that the Goh government maintained a strong hold over political debate and did not allow much opposition or criticism of government policy. The Speakers' Corner still operated under government scrutiny and new media licences were only issued to newspapers and the media under government control.

Whether in media content or generally in public policy discussions, the government maintained a system of self-censorship by the use of "out-of-bound" (OB) markers. The unwritten norms refer to issues that are deemed too sensitive to be discussed in public, as they can threaten stability and order. Racial and religious issues are considered out-of-bounds because of race riots in the 1950s and 1960s. In 1995, a controversy arose after a journalist published an article in the Singapore *Straits Times* seeking clarification over the limits and content that OB markers involved. Prime Minister Goh Chok Tong again reminded the Singaporean public to remain responsible and to respect these markers, but failed to provide more clarity. Instead, the sense was the boundaries of "out-of-bound" issues had expanded beyond religious and racial issues, and included many political issues that could stir controversy (Leong, 2000).

Overall, Goh maintained the basic structures of the regime by favoring elite control, reinforced by the myth of meritocracy and implemented through strict hierarchical control of society and politics.

Prime Minister Lee Hsien Loong, who succeeded Goh Chok Tong in 2004, continued to give Singapore an air of renewal, without moving towards more liberal democracy. In his first year, he tolerated NGOs' protests against the introduction of casinos, which were meant to enhance Singapore's attraction as an exciting destination. It could be argued that criticism was tolerated as some of the greatest opponents of the bill included socially conservative supporters of the PAP as well as many Malays on the basis that Islam forbids gaming. The government also showed greater openness to public debate by lifting in 2008 the need to obtain a police permit to use the Speakers' Corner, a space designed to allow public debate.

Yet, such evidence of openness was counterbalanced by more repressive actions. In the 2006 elections, the government continued to explicitly tie public housing upgrades to PAP support. In the first years after Lee Hsien Loong became Prime Minister, the government took forceful measures against bloggers critical of its policy. It also censured the Singapore short film festival to prevent the showing of a documentary on opposition leader Chee Soon Juan. In 2008, Lee Hsien Loong and Lee Kuan Yew filed defamation charges against Chee Soon Juan and other opposition leaders. In 2009, the government took new measures to appoint more opposition members to parliament, through nominated MPs and non-constituency MPs, but while giving more representation these mechanisms also continued to divert from electoral competition to espouse a more co-optive approach. Even the Speakers'

Table 7 *Singapore*

Population (rank)	Land area (rank)	Main ethnic groups (%)	Main religions (%)	Regime type (transition)	GDP per capita (rank)	GDP growth rate (%) (rank)
5 353 494 (113th) (2011 est.)	697 sq km (191st)	Chinese 76.8 Malay 13.9 Indian 7.9 Other 1.4 (2000 census)	Buddhist 42.5 Muslim 14.9 Taoist 8.5 Hindu 4 Catholic 4.8 Other Christian 9.8 Other 0.7 None 14.8 (2000 census)	Semi-democracy Parliamentary republic	$59 900 (5th) (2011 est.)	4.9 (78th) (2011 est.)

Source: CIA, *The World Factbook*; Polity IV Project, Polity IV Individual Country Regime Trends, 1946–2010.

Corner, which supposedly allowed for more public debate, remained monitored and was closed down during the 2011 elections. Such examples represent only a few of the mechanisms that continued to curtail free expression and opposition, in spite of superficial commitments tomore openness.

In the 2011 elections, there were some significant gains for the opposition. Only 60 per cent supported the PAP, which obtained 81 out of 87 seats. Prior to the election, the government had taken the initiative to reduce the number and size of GRCs ostensibly to increase opposition representation in parliament. Nevertheless, it was the first time that the opposition gained as many seats. A five-member team from the Workers' Party won the Aljunied GRC where the PAP team included two high-profile senior PAP politicians. Although opposition parties had won some seats in previous elections, such a large gain was unprecedented. The popular results also showed the steady erosion of support for the PAP, and popular desire for reform. At the same time, the results showed continuing, strong governmental control over the electoral process. Its ability to redraw districts and tinker with a variety of electoral mechanisms continue to highly skew how popular votes translate into number of seats. With only 60 per cent of the vote, the PAP, with its 81 seats, still held 93 per cent of parliamentary seats.

Singapore, as with the case of Malaysia, defies the expectation that the middle class will seek greater democratization. Instead, a strong dominant party, elite unity, sustained economic development and "performance legitimacy" have been key factors in maintaining soft authoritarian regimes in both countries. In addition, some unique features have reinforced the regime: the relative "softness" of authoritarianism by using sophisticated manipulation of institutional rules, legal measures and relatively open elections instead of more outward repression; the particular configuration and institutionalization of ethnic diversity; and some more idiosyncratic features.

Economic development in both countries has created much prosperity. Singapore's small size has ensured a rapid rise in GDP per capita. In this respect, it is well ahead of other Southeast Asian countries and a large proportion of the population enjoy living standards that are comparable to those in Europe and North America. Although Malaysia is well behind, with roughly a quarter of Singapore's GDP per capita, it is nevertheless by this measure well ahead of other Southeast Asian countries. Such high levels of economic development have transformed the economies and societies of both countries, rapidly increased rates of urbanization and developed a middle class employed in a range of sectors. We should expect democratization to occur in these countries rather than elsewhere in the region, yet no change has occurred.

At another level, it can be argued that greater pressures for some reforms and change have arisen. In recent years, the increasingly divided Malay constituency that has migrated away from UMNO clearly seeks such change. So have a number of Chinese who have supported the Barisan Alternatif. In Singapore, recent support for the Workers' Party offers small signs that more Singaporeans seek reform. Yet, we must be careful to attribute such desire for change on the development and rise of the middle class that has been relatively large for many years. While a segment of the middle class might now be seeking change, it is by no means shared across the board. Furthermore, the working class and the poor might as well be drivers of some of these shifts, especially the greater support for PAS in Malaysia and the Workers' Party in Singapore. At the state level in Malaysia, states that have elected PAS governments are not those with a highly developed middle class.

In part, the middle class has been dependent on the state and has enjoyed the proceeds of development. In both cases, high levels of economic development and steady improvements in living standards provided performance legitimacy to the regime, and therefore cushioned the effects of less political expression. At the same time, the state created some dependence through a variety of mechanisms. State patronage and rewards for supporting UMNO kept many well-off Malaysians loyal. Even when members of the elite split from UMNO, several returned to the fold after being lured back. In Singapore, the PAP-led government maintained even greater leverage by providing career opportunities but also by making the middle class dependent on housing, pension funds and other schemes tied to the state.

Ethnic politics have also cut across class alliances. Tensions between Chinese and Malays in particular in both countries have prevented class alliances between ethnic groups and therefore weakened the possibility of strong reformist movements to emerge. Some parties and organizations in Malaysia, as well as the Reformasi movement, created some cross-ethnic alliances but not to dislodge UMNO and the BN's dominance. With strong parties institutionalizing ethnicity, as well as the New Economic Policy and other pro-Malay measures, the Malaysian government has maintained ethnicity as a key political factor. While less institutionalized in Singapore, nevertheless the ideology of multiracialism as well as a number of official ethnically based associations have provided the state with the ability to maintain ethnicity as a divisive force while also using tensions and the potential threat of violence to justify some of its mechanisms of control.

Institutional and legal mechanisms helped to sustain support and reduce opposition. Both countries used repressive laws that allowed detention without trial, censorship, reduced freedom of assembly and prevented public discussions of topics deemed sensitive. Singapore's government has used lawsuits to quell dissent. "Gerrymandering", the redrawing of electoral district boundaries, has allowed dominant parties to win a greater number of seats. Malaysia's government frequently used its two-thirds majority to implement constitutional changes favourable to maintain UMNO's dominance.

At the same time, governments have not intervened in elections as much as other authoritarian countries that held elections. In both

Malaysia and Singapore, votes count and shifts in the electorate are reflected in results. Instead, governments use other means of ensuring a reproduction of the dominant party dominance but less intervention in elections has allowed opposition parties to make some inroads in both cases. It does not provide the legitimacy that democracies enjoy but does soften the effects of authoritarian rule.

Under these conditions, there has only been a thin space for civil society to expand into and become a significant force. In Malaysia, greater space allowed students, women and a number of other groups to form organizations that have successfully influenced aspects of government policy without gaining sufficient momentum for a change in the regime. In Singapore, such space and potential for change has been more narrow and circumscribed. As a result, political stability and continuity, with some pressures for change, remain the norm in both countries.

5 | Thailand

The case of Thailand is the most complex in some respects. In contrast to Malaysia and Singapore, political instability has been its hallmark. Under authoritarian rule, from 1932 to 1973, internecine disputes within the armed forces triggered changes in government but maintained the same regime. In 1973, Thailand began a brief period of democracy before the armed forces launched a coup and regained power in 1976. They intervened again with military coups in 1991 and 2006 but both times remained in power only briefly. Civilian governments ruled Thailand starting in the early 1980s. For most of that decade, however, the armed forces kept control over the appointment of the prime minister and their influence on the government was still very strong. They remained influential but, after 1992, democratically elected governments played a central role. Democratic rule was no less unstable as fragile coalitions frequently collapsed until a constitutional change in 1997 that paved the way for a majority government under the Thai Rak Thai party. Looming in the background, a popular monarch provided decades of continuity as the Thai people not only revered him but also appreciated his occasional interference in political disputes. In more recent years, a deep-seated crisis divided supporters of the former Thai Rak Thai party and the coalition of military, business, bureaucrats and politicians that had dominated Thailand's politics for several decades. In sum, Thai politics have been marked by frequent changes of government, looming military intervention and fragile democracy.

Yet, Thailand seems to represent an almost textbook case of modernization theory. Fuelled by decades of economic growth, it was poised for a transition to democratic politics. If we abstract from the short democratic hiatus of 1973–6, Thailand was authoritarian from 1932 until the early 1980s. Most of the decade of the 1980s was a softer, more open authoritarian regime where parties and parliament were active. After 1988, with the exception of the 1991 and 2006 coups that brought the armed forces to power for one year or less each time, democratic politics prevailed. Electoral democracy became the norm until today.

These broad periods of authoritarianism and democracy correlate quite well with broad transformations in economic development. After a period of economic growth in the 1960s, Thailand's economic boom ran mostly from the late 1970s until the Asian financial crisis of 1997. Per capita GDP rose from an average of $353 in the 1970s to $864 in the 1980s and $2,175 in the 1990s. This wealth contributed to the creation of a rapidly growing, urban-based middle class. An extensive entrepreneurial class also developed alongside the more long-standing Bangkok-based conglomerates that mostly contributed to the high growth rates of the late 1960s. From this perspective, the pressures for democratization that began with large-scale demonstrations in Bangkok in 1973 and that contributed to the downfall of the authoritarian regime are direct consequences of a stronger and more demanding middle class (Bunbongkarn, 1999).

There are reasons, however, to be somewhat sceptical that the middle class is the main driver of democratization in Thailand. Although they have played an important role, the mass movements that contributed to the collapse of military-led governments in 1973 and 1992 were broader. They involved labour unions, workers and even some rural poor. Instead of a purely middle-class movement, it is better to see pro-democratic demonstrations as involving the working class and other segments of society. Furthermore, the middle class in Thailand has also been supportive of authoritarianism. In 1991, by some accounts, the middle class welcomed the coup that removed the highly corrupt Chatichai government. Certainly, a good portion of the middle class supported the 2006 coup that removed the democratically elected government of Thaksin Shinawatra.

Elite disunity has been dominant in Thai politics but its repercussions have varied. The Thai army and police were long divided along factional lines, with ties to particular allies in the bureaucracy. Later, they extended these ties to business partners as well. Competition among factions led to unstable politics. Yet, under the leadership of Field Marshals Sarit and Thanom, although factions were still apparent, the regime remained solidified and united until 1973. Many of the subsequent political crises can be seen as a persistent inability to reproduce a consolidated elite and divisions that were sufficiently deep to even threaten regime stability. Electoral democracy absorbed some of this competition during the 1980s and 1990s, and allowed the rise of alternative elites particularly from the rural provinces. The coups of 1991 and 2006 showed that beneath the veneer of democracy, factions that included the military continued to compete for power and were ready to remove elected governments when their interests were threatened.

Duncan McCargo has offered an insightful explanation for one of the strong lines of division within the elite. He argues that a dominant elite group, which he calls "network monarchy", was formed around the current King Bhumibol and particularly the Privy Council. This dominant group, which formed strong allies within the armed forces and among middle-class politicians in the Democrat Party in particular, ruled Thailand for most of the period between 1973 and 2001. Divisions in recent years arose mainly from Prime Minister Thaksin and the Thai Rak Thai's challenge to this network, which has exercised its power through proxies in the armed forces or in the political system. Thaksin came to represent an alternative elite primarily composed of provincial businessmen, some middle-class activists and politicians outside Bangkok, who gained support among the rural poor. These divisions severely weakened the stability of democratic politics, and created several crises that even led to the temporary suspension of democracy (McCargo, 2005b).

From another perspective, Thailand also shares some measure of continuity similar to that in Indonesia and the Philippines. As in these other countries, patrimonialism and "bossism" permeate Thai society. In particular, provincial-based businessmen became more important in politics in the 1980s. They created support through money politics that became rampant across the electoral system. Vote-buying was widespread so the quality of elections and of the democratic process was very low (King & LoGerfo, 1997). By some accounts, the democratic arena simply became another arena for alliances of politicians and business people to compete for wealth.

Against some of these continuities, nevertheless periods of authoritarian rule were very different from periods of electoral democracy, despite its weaknesses. At least democracy has allowed more public debate, freedom to organize political parties, a freer media and freedom of association.

Mass mobilization has mostly blocked a return to authoritarian rule. Despite the 1991 and 2006 coups, it became increasingly difficult for the armed forces to sustain itself in power as society became more complex, new business elites and the middle class grew rapidly and yearned for their place in politics. Student protests, middle-class demonstrations and mass demonstrations involving workers and the rural poor have demonstrated the ability of large-scale protests to introduce some change in Thailand.

What does it mean for civil society? As in other cases, although these mass movements were key in bringing down authoritarian regimes or, in recent years, blocking their return, it would be exaggerated to view the emergence of a more permanent electoral democracy as a result of the growth of civil society. Nevertheless, the greater freedom since the late 1980s has allowed many organizations to develop and to assist the rural poor and the marginalized. They have been primarily middle-class and elite-led organizations, which have not always been at the forefront of deep political reform (Ockey, 2002).

The classic "bureaucratic polity"

For several decades, scholars viewed Thailand as a classic "bureaucratic polity." As Fred Riggs (1966) has argued, the bureaucratic polity is a political system characterized by the dominance of civilian and military bureaucrats, to the exclusion of meaningful participation of social forces. For several decades after the 1932 coup, civil servants and military officers occupied major positions in the Cabinet, bureaucracy and parliament. They formed cliques that competed against one another for influence and power. While they created linkages to the business sectors to yield revenue, their business partners, mainly among the Chinese entrepreneurial elite, remained subordinate (Riggs, 1966).

The bureaucratic polity was a particular form of authoritarian rule that had its roots in Thailand's early efforts to form a modern polity. King Chulalongkorn's reforms to modernize Thailand in the nineteenth century had led to the creation of a relatively strong military and a state bureaucracy designed to turn Thailand into a modern state able to resist European colonial powers. By the 1930s, when the armed forces launched a coup against absolute monarchy, Thailand already had a well-functioning military and civil service while the country remained essentially agrarian. With few other forms of political or social organization, they enjoyed a virtual monopoly of power, which they retained for the following decades. Influenced as well by fascist ideologies spreading through Europe and Asia, Thailand's leaders consolidated and justified their authoritarian model.

Authoritarian dominance reached its peak under the leaderships of Field Marshals Sarit Thanarat and Thanom Kittikachorn. After years of factional struggles among military elites, Sarit Thanarat seized power in 1958 and gradually consolidated power. He was able to overcome, at least temporarily, the divisions that had plagued the military and bureaucracy. He used this power to increase authoritarian control while launching a vast industrialization program. He closed down parliament, banned political parties and eliminated trade unions. Yet, his government's policies also fuelled rapid economic growth. In previous years, inefficient state enterprises linked to the governing elite dominated the economy. Sarit mandated the National Economic Development Board (later renamed the National Economic and Social Development Board) to implement necessary reforms to boost economic growth. Highly skilled technocrats, with Sarit's backing, placed a new emphasis on private businesses to boost production and economic growth. They promoted a vast infrastructural development programme that included the building of roads and a steady power supply. They crafted new policies to boost education and human resource development. They also designed incentive schemes to attract foreign investment. As a result, the economy grew at an unprecedented pace of 8 per cent in the 1960s and maintained a growth rate above 7 per cent throughout the 1970s, in spite of the oil crisis that led to high oil prices and a cut in private sector profits (Bunbongkarn, 1999; Case, 2002). Upon Sarit's death in 1963, Field Marshal Thanom Kittikachorn was appointed Prime Minister. Thanom essentially continued his predecessor's policies until he was forced to resign in 1973.

Democratic interlude and soft authoritarianism: the erosion of the bureaucratic polity

A brief democratic interlude between 1973 and 1976 signalled early consequences of political and social changes resulting from economic growth. Democracy had little chance of settling in, however, amid a growing international economic crisis and the unravelling of the Vietnam War next door. The middle class had begun to expand and the student body had grown considerably as a result of Sarit's push for higher education. Factionalization in the military and bureaucracy had re-emerged, and protests grew in response to perceived corruption and economic mismanagement. As the high oil prices began to affect Thailand's economic climate, so the protests rose. In October 1973, more than 500,000 people demonstrated against the regime. Mobilized by student groups, the protests forced Thanom to resign and elections to be called. The new democratic government was, however, short-lived as the economic crisis deepened. A fragile coalition failed to organize a stable government. At the same time, the armed forces became uneasy as the end of the Vietnam War in 1975 triggered the fall of Vietnam, Cambodia and Laos to communism. With King Bhumibol Adulyadej's nod of approval, the armed forces returned to power.

The return to authoritarian rule had different aspects. No longer could the Thai military close off demands for political representation. The brief democratic interlude had shown that a growing Thai middle class rejected a return to military dominance in the model of Field Marshals Sarit and Thanom. Furthermore, business groups had begun to demand a greater role in the political arena. As a result, although the military remained predominant, it allowed a much greater role for civilians and reinstated democratic-style political institutions. The armed forces retained control over the Senate, as well as Cabinet portfolios important to their interests. When General Chavalit Yongchaiyudh became armed forces commander in the mid 1980s, he resurrected the armed forces' role in development projects, under the Internal Security Operations Council (ISOC). By involving the military in development projects, it could legitimize its greater presence in rural areas (Neher, 1988). At the same time, the government allowed political parties to organize and operate relatively freely, and elections were held. The prime minister, however, came from the armed forces and not from elected politicians. When General Prem Tinsulanond was made prime minister in 1981, he managed to stabilize the political system and orchestrate an economic boom. He appointed professionals and technocrats to direct key economic portfolios and to sit in Cabinet as non-party ministers. With control over key economic ministries, they created conditions for double-digit growth in the late 1980s. Furthermore, Prem created new institutional mechanisms by which business groups could interact with state bureaucrats and Cabinet ministers. Through the National Defence College, the military also created closer links with business interests, as they invited leaders from different sectors to participate in special programmes designed for them (Samudavanija & Chotiya, 1998).

Yet, this semi-democratic system came under pressure in the late 1980s. Elections in 1986 produced an unstable government. The coalition led by the Democrat Party was mired in political squabbles. Prem's authority was quickly declining in the face of this internecine fighting and criticism rose over corrupt ministers (Neher, 1988). In an attempt to preserve his leadership, he twice sought to dissolve parliament to placate the opposition. When elections in 1988 returned inconclusive results, Prem announced that he would no longer remain as Premier. His replacement, General Chatichai Choonhavan was also an elected member of parliament. As a result, politicians began to play a much greater role in the government, especially after Chatichai's government curbed the power of the Senate, and thereby reduced the influence of military appointees. At the same time, corruption and graft rose rapidly as politicians acquired new access to state resources (Samudavanija & Chotiya, 1998).

The 1991 coup and unstable democracy

A faction of the armed forces launched a coup in February 1991. The military, bureaucrats and the rising business elite welcomed the coup led by General Suchinda Kraprayoon, as they rejected the growing power of politicians and political parties that hurt their business interests. The junta appointed as prime minister a respected former diplomat and businessman, Anand Panyarachun. Instead of being a puppet leader, Anand ended up restoring economic stability and a measure of public confidence.

The authoritarian government was short-lived but not without a controversial attempt to remain in power. After the coup, the armed forces had promised a quick return to democratic rule. Elections were scheduled for March 1992 but it soon became apparent that the military sought to retain power. The new constitution created a senate whose members the junta would appoint. Furthermore, the prime minister was not required to be an elected member of parliament. Friends of the coup leader Suchinda launched a political party, the Samakkhi Tham Party (STP) which won the elections and formed a new coalition government. Soon after, however, demonstrators protested for weeks to denounce the junta's attempts to remain in power, as Suchinda presented himself as a candidate for prime minister after the leader of the STP, Narong Wongwan, was discredited by suspicions of links to drug traffickers (King & LoGerfo, 1997; Maisrikrod, 1994).

Repression in May 1992 was a crucial turning point. An estimated half a million people demonstrated to demand Suchinda's resignation. Instead of doing so, Suchinda ordered the armed forces to crack down. Dozens of people were killed and hundreds were injured. King Bhumibol only intervened to stop the repression when it became sufficiently apparent that a number of factions within the armed forces also opposed the crackdown. Nevertheless, in a show of his influence, he summoned to the palace General Suchinda and Chamlong Srimuang, the leader of the Palang Dharma (Righteous Force) Party, and asked that they resolve the crisis peacefully. A few days later Suchinda decided to resign. Anand Panyarachun was again asked to form a government. This time, he purged the armed forces of officers deemed responsible for the brutal repression. As he organized elections for September 1992, the armed forces retreated into a lesser political role (Bunbongkarn, 1993).

In the following years, democracy seemed to become more routinized but it was also fraught with important sources of instability. Thailand's oldest political party, the Democrats, won the election by a slim margin. The party leader, Chuan Leekpai, became prime minister and the first in more than twenty years without a military background. Yet, the Democrats could not rule without a coalition with several other parties in order to form a majority in parliament. In subsequent years, no party was able to obtain a large number of seats. It became difficult for any government to finish its mandate as they depended on the support of one or more parties, which often left the government coalition over a number of different issues. The Democrats were able to retain support for almost three years in spite of having to modify the coalition. They fell when Palang Dharma withdrew over a scandal linked to the government's land-reform programme (King & LoGerfo, 1997).

The next two governments were very short-lived. Again, they were formed only through the cobbling together of fragile coalitions. The 1995 election led to a coalition under the leadership of the Chart Thai Party. Chart Thai's victory confirmed two growing trends. First, voting-buying was developed into a systematic mechanism to obtain support from poor, marginalized voters, particularly in rural areas where Chart Thai had an advantage. Second, it showed that political parties were divided along regional lines. Chart Thai gained more votes in central Thailand but increased its support among the poorest regions of the North and Northeast. The Democrats were strongest in the South. Palang Dharma, which had been most popular for its leader Chamlong's role in ousting the junta in 1991 retained strong support in Bangkok. The New Aspiration Party (NAP) of General Chavalit, the former armed forces commander, gained some strength in the Northeast. Chart Thai's government, under Prime Minister Banharn Silpa-Archa, fell only one year later, as it was quickly marred with corruption and internal divisions. Elections in 1996 allowed the NAP to gain power. Under General Chavalit, the NAP was only in power for a few months when the Asian financial crisis of 1997, which started in Thailand, sent the economy in a tailspin under the collapse of the financial system.

This unstable political and economic period opened up opportunities for reformists. During the 1990s, a group of academics, NGOs and reform-minded politicians had been meeting to discuss and draft a new constitution. They were mostly concerned with the endemic vote-buying and money-politics that eroded the credibility of electoral democracy. They also wanted to reduce corruption and unstable coalitions. They succeeded in making constitutional reform a public issue that gained media attention and widespread support. The coalition included unlikely partners such as some business people and reformist politicians, alongside NGO activists and academics. Yet, some political parties and businesses that benefited from established networks of patronage strongly opposed constitutional reform. As the proposal for a reformed constitution had been drafted and even presented to parliament, the Asian financial crisis of 1997 shook the fragile government of General Chavalit. Protests over the pain of the economic crisis combined with calls for political reform. After failing to lobby successfully for some amendments, the government capitulated and the parliament passed the new constitution. Soon after, the Chavalit government was removed and replaced with the Democrats who were able to cobble together a new coalition. It is likely that the king, operating through his proxy General Prem Tinsulanond, played a role in the removal of Chavalit's government and the subsequent palace support for the Democrats (McCargo, 2005b). The Democrats offered a more stable government and managed to hold onto power until new elections were due to be held in 2001, benefiting from the support of "network monarchy". They also launched a number of reforms in response to the financial crisis and in the hopes of recreating favorable conditions to resume high growth rates (Connors, 1999).

Thai Rak Thai and Thaksin Shinawatra

The election of Thai Rak Thai (TRT) in 2001 marked a new direction for Thai democracy. The Constitution of 1997 fixed some of the problems that had plagued the Thai political system and allowed a single party to gain a majority. At the same time, it created the opportunity for the marginalized to ally with segments of a new political elite that could strongly challenge the establishment. In the following years, it became increasingly clear that Thaksin and TRT intended to displace the influence and political role that the monarchy and its network of political allies held over Thailand's political system (McCargo, 2005b). While the Constitution of 1997 appeared to be a hallmark of democracy, its unintended consequence was to allow political divisions to resurface.

The 1997 Constitution introduced significant modifications. Notable features included a host of oversight institutions, such as the Constitutional Court to oversee the judiciary, an independent Election Commission to replace the Interior Ministry's previous control over the electoral process, and expanded powers for the National Anti-Corruption Commission (NACC). The electoral system was also replaced with one in which most seats were allocated through a single-district member system, which favours party consolidation. There were other measures intended to strengthen the party system and stabilize elected governments to prevent the previous problems associated with frequent threats of coalitional collapse. The Constitution was also progressive on many fronts, including human rights, welfare, health and education.

Thaksin Shinawatra built up a new type of party and politics that partly succeeded because of its broad appeal but also because of constitutional changes. Thaksin built up vast wealth namely through his acquisition of government concessions in the telecommunications industry. In 1998, he founded Thai Rak Thai (Thais Love Thai). Initially the party catered to urban-based business groups whose interests were threatened by the Democrats' economic reforms. Furthermore,

Thaksin and other Bangkok-based businessmen resented the growing political involvement and influence of provincial businessmen through their extensive patronage-based machinery in rural areas. As the campaign neared, Thaksin broadened his appeal to provincial business through promises for small and medium-sized businesses. He also orchestrated party defections in favour of TRT, ahead of the ban on party switching mandated by the Constitution. Having sealed vast support among parliamentary representatives, Thakin adopted a populist platform to reach out to the vast constituency of rural poor. As the Democrats pleaded for austerity to recover from the economic crisis, Thaksin promised inexpensive health care, agrarian debt relief and more funding for villages (Case, 2001; Phongpaichit & Baker, 2008).

Thai Rak Thai obtained a near majority for the first time in Thai politics. The Democrats had been discredited for the austerity programme that dictated their response to the financial crisis, while other parties had been financially weakened. Backed by Thaksin's vast wealth, TRT appeared relatively strong and attractive for politicians who abandoned smaller parties and joined TRT's ranks. As the Constitution favoured fewer and larger parties, the incentives to join winning parties were even greater. Thaksin himself was an attractive leader because of his wealth and different style of political leadership. These factors combined to give TRT initially a thin majority that was lost only after the electoral commission disqualified a few of the elected TRT representatives because of violations to the electoral law. Nevertheless, short of only a few seats, TRT formed a coalition with the NAP and Chart Thai but these junior partners held little power, given their marginal role (Phongpaichit & Baker, 2008).

Thaksin himself was also subjected to scrutiny under the now stronger power of independent agencies. In December, the NACC indicted him for failing to report some of his assets during a brief period when he served as minister during the 1990s. The investigation and trial hung over him during the electoral campaign and during the first few months of tenure as prime minister. In response, Thaksin used the opportunity to bolster his popular appeal. He hosted his own weekly radio show and made regular appearances on TV to discuss his case and his government. He attempted to discredit the NACC and used the opportunity instead to promote his alternative style of government and his policies. He blamed the "old elite" for attempting to remove him while he sought to address the problems of the poor. His public presence and rhetoric gained a favourable audience among the Thai public and contributed to increasing his popularity (Phongpaichit & Baker, 2008).

Either as a ploy to enhance his popularity in spite of charges against him, or because he wanted to show efficient government, Thaksin proceeded to implement quickly the three main promises of his platform. His health scheme promised cheap rates for hospital and clinic visits. Each village was allocated a fund to promote economic "diversification". Finally, he quickly adopted a debt relief scheme in rural areas.

At the same time, Thaksin showed early signs of rejecting democratic values. He threatened to expel foreign correspondents for the *Far Eastern Economic Review* when they published a report of his relations with the monarchy. He also showed impatience and intolerance towards criticism when *Time* magazine and the *Economist* published unflattering reports in 2000. He showed similar contempt for criticism in the domestic media as he used his power to have journalists fired for attacking him and managed to significantly silence the press under such threats of retaliation (McCargo, 2002).

As the next election neared, many middle-class, educated Thais grew increasingly disillusioned with Thaksin's style of rule. In 2003, he declared a "war on drugs" and gave the police the authority to take any measures deemed necessary to eliminate the problem. In three months, they had killed around 2,500 alleged drug dealers (Phongpaichit & Baker, 2008). One of his most important blunders contributed to growing insecurity in the Malay-Muslim provinces of southern Thailand. Over the last few decades, several groups have mounted secessionist movements against the Thai state. For over a decade, the region had been relatively quiet after the monarchy and previous governments had provided targeted resources for education and some job opportunities. After 2000, however, new groups launched attacks against government targets but remained underground. Thaksin reacted strongly by declaring that criminal gangs were responsible for the attacks and force should be used to repress them. Violence then escalated in 2004. Troops stormed the Kru-ze mosque and killed 32 Muslim men whom they suspected of being involved in attacks. Later that year, soldiers round up hundreds of Muslim demonstrators and loaded them into the back of several trucks. Some were apparently shot during the process but, even more shockingly, seventy-eight suffocated in the back of the trucks (McCargo, 2005b).

In spite of these issues, Thaksin' popularity grew as the 2005 elections approached. He toured villages and doled out funds for projects under a large central fund that he controlled. He held some Cabinet meetings in rural areas. These initiatives were well publicized to enhance his image. Only a month before the election, he expanded his promises to include additional village funds, more debt relief, cheaper school fees, free cows, a nationwide irrigation scheme, care centres for the elderly and more (Phongpaichit & Baker, 2008).

The 2005 election gave TRT an unprecedented victory. It won by a very large margin having obtained 377 out of 500 seats. By comparison, the main opposition party, the Democrats, obtained only ninety-six seats. This feat was unprecedented in Thai political history. TRT had delivered concrete welfare programmes for the poor in rural areas and, beyond the populist rhetoric, offered to expand these schemes through concrete measures. Opposition parties instead campaigned on vague themes such as the need for more honesty and transparency, but with few tangible promises. The urban middle class and intellectuals most disenchanted with Thaksin's style of rule, his increasing disregard for the media, for parliament and for several other democratic institutions, were powerless in the face of TRT's strong support in rural areas across Thailand. Part of the TRT's success was a direct effect of the 1997 constitutional reforms that encouraged party consolidation. The 2005 election confirmed this trend as many of the smaller parties simply disappeared, and only four parties obtained any seats at all (Albritton, 2006).

The 2006 coup and return to semi-democracy

Thailand's democracy ended abruptly when, in September 2006, the armed forces seized control of the government with no opposition. Tensions had been rising steadily between the mainly Bangkok-based urban middle class and Thaksin's government. A few events surrounding Thaksin's business interests provided the immediate justification for intervention, but it represented a longer-term power struggle between this urban-based middle class and the vast majority of rural poor then mobilized by TRT and Thaksin.

Only one year after the election, Thaksin faced mounting opposition. In early 2006, the media revealed that Thaksin's family had sold their assets in Shin corporation (the Shinawatra family's main business) to Singapore's Temasek corporation for $1.9 billion without any taxes being paid. The scandal provided a catalyst for the formation of the People's Alliance for Democracy (PAD). The PAD staged mass demonstrations that called for Thaksin to be ousted on the basis of alleged corruption, undermining of democracy and growing threat to the institution of the monarchy (Ockey, 2007).

In response, Thaksin called a snap election for April 2006, in order to reaffirm his popular support. Opposition parties denounced the ploy and decided to boycott the election altogether. TRT emerged with lots of support but many voters chose the "no vote" option available on the ballot. Plagued by accusations of irregularities, many of the seats also remained unfilled while the Electoral Commission investigated the voting in those constituencies. Parliament could not be convened without a resolution of this crisis, and Thaksin was then appointed caretaker prime minister until a new parliament could be convened. By April, the courts had annulled the election after reviewing the Electoral Commission's conduct of the election and declaring irregularities (Ockey, 2007).

It was clear by then that two major political forces, backed by two prominent personalities, openly struggled for control over the Thai polity. The PAD pursued its mass demonstrations with the support of the urban middle class mainly in Bangkok, monarchists and politicians from the Democrat party in particular. Prem Tinsulanond, the President of the Privy Council, the king's main advisory body, appeared to play a central role in the growing alliance against Thaksin. Conversely, Thaksin's supporters, mainly based in rural areas, had yet to gain momentum in Bangkok.

The armed forces intervened before a new election could be conducted. Coup leaders quickly obtained the approval of the president of the Privy Council and the palace. They appointed as prime minister the former army commander Surayud Chulanont, who was at that time a member of the Privy Council. Surayud appointed mainly technocrats to the Cabinet. The new government suspended the Constitution as well as parliament and created, instead, a legislative council whose members were mainly bureaucrats and technocrats (Ockey, 2007). TRT was dissolved and Thaksin left the country.

Coup leaders did not intend to remain in power for a prolonged period. They were aware that Thailand's middle class had long rejected military government, as the demonstrations and bloody outcomes of

1992 had shown. The Bangkok middle class, academics and politicians supported the coup but would have been reluctant to give its leaders an unlimited term. Consequently, coup leaders announced an election within one year, and they held their promise. Under their guidance, a committee drafted a new constitution that sought to prevent the concentration of power enjoyed by the TRT yet it also meant that it introduced anti-democratic elements, such as a return to a partially appointed senate, and a marginalization of politicians and political parties (Pongsudhirak, 2008).

The junta held elections in December 2007, as promised, but the outcome was different from what they had initially hoped. Results returned a strong victory for the PPP (Palang Prachachon Party), essentially TRT under a new name. The new government of Prime Minister Samak quickly restored Thaksin's populist programme while the armed forces returned to their barracks. The junta had failed to solve the problems they had promised to address, most significantly the violence in the Malay-Muslim south that actually escalated during its short time in power. They had also failed to restore to power the monarchy-based establishment that they supported. Consequently, the armed forces retreated for the time being (Pongsudhirak, 2008).

Disappointed with this outcome, the PAD returned to the streets. This time, it escalated its efforts to destabilize the government by first occupying Government House (the seat of the executive) in August 2008 and later by closing down Bangkok airport for several days. It aimed at creating sufficient instability for a new extra-constitutional intervention to remove the PPP from power (Pongsudhirak, 2008). As it had done with TRT, the Constitutional Court dissolved the PPP in December 2008 when it ruled that it had violated electoral laws in 2007. Two other parties were also dissolved. In a scramble to retain power, the PPP soon reinvented itself as the Puea Thai Party but failed to secure a stable coalition. With backing from the military and the palace, the Democrats, under the leadership of Abhisit Vejja-jiva, returned to power in a coalition with smaller parties, whereas Puea Thai formed the main parliamentary opposition (Prasirtsuk, 2009).

Far from restoring stability, the Democrats faced renewed escalation of violence for the following two years. This time, the "red shirts", the United Front for Democracy against Dictatorship (UDD), occupied the streets of Bangkok in protest against the Democrats. Puea Thai remained the largest party in parliament so the pro-Thaksin UDD considered illegitimate the Democrats' control of government. Furthermore, they viewed the Constitutional Court's rulings against TRT and PPP as suspiciously favourable to the anti-Thaksin traditional ruling elite. On several occasions, the UDD blocked off portions of the capital city. Thaksin frequently joined protesters by phone or by live video connection. His huge popularity continued to galvanize protesters. The UDD became bolder in its efforts to dislodge the Abhisit government as Thai security forces failed to disperse them. In April 2010, they seized the Ratchaprasong area one of Bangkok's prime commercial districts. After a month of occupation, as well as further provocation, Abhisit declared a state of emergency. The armed forces cracked down on the protesters who nevertheless burned down several buildings and damaged many others. Over the period of the crisis, security forces killed ninety-one people (Prasirtsuk, 2010).

Although the violence subsided, the crisis remained deep. Supporters of Thaksin, which included most rural areas and even some portions of the middle class, recognized the benefits they reaped during his administration. For the first time, a Thai political leader provided some relief for the poorest. The established elite, however, could not accept Thaksin's encroachment on its interests, his attempts to gain greater control at the expense of the oversight mechanisms that the 1997 Constitution had established, as well as his challenges to the monarchy. The crisis became deeper after the coup, as former TRT supporters and the "red shirts" continued to denounce what they perceived as the unlawful removal of Thaksin and the TRT, as well as their successors.

Abhisit maintained the state of emergency for most of 2010. Yet, occasional skirmishes with UDD supporters still occurred. The government created several bodies to foster reconciliation and constitutional reform, in the hopes of finding an acceptable compromise to end the crisis. As the state of emergency was lifted by the end of 2010, prospects improved for such a reconciliation.

Elections in 2011 appeared to confirm an end to confrontation and an acceptance of the changing political landscape. Puea Thai secured a landslide victory with 265 seats, while its major opponent, the Democrat Party, won only 159. Puea Thai's leader, Yingluck Shinawatra, the sister of the discredited Thaksin, became prime minister. The armed forces, and the previous "yellow shirt" camp accepted the results in the face of repeated confirmation of Thaksin and his party's popularity. At the same time, Yingluck also softened her party's stance and adopted a more conciliatory approach to address the opposition's concerns.

Thailand represents in many ways the classic modernization case by which high levels of economic development are associated with democratization. Certainly over the long run, several decades of high growth, a fair amount of redistribution and the expansion of the middle class have produced pressures to establish and maintain democratic politics. Although interrupted and imperfect, since the 1980s electoral democracy has been dominant. In addition, a rising rural-based business class challenged the more established one based around Bangkok and close to its growing middle class. With these groups entering politics, the business class has been divided and found the democratic framework useful as a competitive ground. While the armed forces have not completely withdrawn from political intervention, they have retreated from seeking to directly control the polity.

Elite divisions within the security apparatus and in the political class provided some support for democracy. Yet, they have also been a source of democracy's fragility when those divisions have been too deep. When Thailand was a bureaucratic polity, factions of security forces and bureaucrats competed for resources and power but the regime remained. Coups marked occasional rotations of power until the regime became more stable under Sarit and Thanom. The rise of new divisions within security forces in the early 1970s allowed for a brief democratic interlude and set the stage for a more permanent installation of electoral democracy in the 1980s. Business groups, as well as the rise of provincial business people diversified the elite and further prevented a return to consolidated authoritarian rule. Electoral democracy became the new competitive arena among diverse elites that sought to advance their business interests and access to state power. Frequent coalition changes reflected this competition while a deeper division eventually threatened democracy. The wedge between pro- and anti-Thaksin forces in the last decade revealed the limits of Thailand's democratic framework. For the Bangkok-based middle and upper classes favourable to the status quo and supportive of the monarchy, Thaksin's bold policies to empower the poorest segments of Thailand and challenge the power of the monarchy as well as the establishment defied their sense of the established rules of the game. Conversely, for pro-Thaksin forces, especially the newly empowered rural poor, Thailand's previous democracy had repeatedly failed to address their plight. In this context, deepening divisions struck at the heart of regime legitimacy and became serious challenges to Thailand's democracy.

The preservation of the monarchy is a unique factor that must be addressed when analyzing Thailand's regime changes. King Bhumibol Adulyadej's great popularity among the Thai people provided a key role at times of instability. More than just a constitutional figurehead, the king yielded respect and influence over the elite and the masses. Nods of approval were influential at key transition periods. Yet, a challenge from Thaksin and TRT struck at the heart of deep-seated loyalty among elements of the armed forces and a network of monarchists associated with the Democrat Party and Bangkok's elite. It was a unique way in which the elite divided, although it also reflected structural conditions pitting poor and marginalized rural areas against the wealthier urban ones.

During periods of change, mass mobilization was an important feature. Student-led mobilization was key to the fall of authoritarian rule in 1973. During the Black May events in 1992, mass mobilization provided a block against attempts by the ruling junta to remain in control of a new democratic system. Large demonstrations also characterized the opposition between Pro-Thaksin "red shirts" and anti-Thaksin "yellow shirts" after 2005. Since the 1970s, demonstrations added important pressures on the armed forces and their allies who intended to maintain authoritarian rule. Yet, they were effective only against the backdrop of elite division and the rising middle class mentioned above. These factors were crucial in making civil society pressures effective. While the development of a larger middle class also marked the rise of student movements and greater numbers of organizations, it is also clear that civil society organizations were not the primary leaders of mass mobilization in the last few years. Thaksin and his allies on the one side, and supporters of the monarchy on the other were elite drivers of mass mobilization and to some extent manipulated and directed civil society organizations that joined them.

Finally, there is some continuity that permeates both authoritarian and democratic regimes. Aside from some of its unique features, Thai democracy in many ways resembles other weak democracies in the region. Patrimonial features dominated not only close ties between armed forces personnel and bureaucrats under the bureaucratic polity but migrated as well to the democratic context where provincial

Table 8 *Thailand*

Population (rank)	Land area (rank)	Main ethnic groups (%)	Main religions (%)	Regime type (transition)	GDP per capita (rank)	GDP growth rate (%) (rank)
67 091 089 (20th) (2012 est.)	510 890 sq km (50th)	Thai 75 Chinese 14 Other 11 (2000 census)	Buddhist 94.6 Muslim 4.6 Christian 0.7 Other 0.1 (2000 census)	Semi-democracy (–2007)[a] Constitutional monarchy	$9 700 (112th) (2011 est.)	0.1 (197th) (2011 est.)

Source: CIA, *The World Factbook*; Polity IV Project, Polity IV Individual Country Regime Trends, 1946–2010.

[a] The year indicates the most recent transition; (+) means a transition towards democracy and (–) denotes a transition towards authoritarianism.

business people gave resources in exchange for political support. Vote-buying was perhaps its most blatant form. Furthermore, in some cases, businesspeople turned politicians have come to dominate areas and use tactics resembling political bosses to maintain power. While Thailand therefore maintains an electoral democracy, its low quality is comparable in many respects to that of Indonesia or even the Philippines.

PART II

State-socialist countries and authoritarian stability

State-socialist countries often maintain stable authoritarian systems. In Southeast Asia, Vietnam and Laos are officially communist. Cambodia and Burma departed from a socialist path while maintaining strongly authoritarian regimes. All four countries experimented with state centralization and management of the economy. Subsequently, they introduced market-friendly policies, reforms to attract foreign investments and allowed more private property. In the political realm, moving away from socialist economic policies generally did not produce more political openness.

These countries all began with similar socio-economic profiles. They were agrarian economies with a large majority of their populations living off subsistence agriculture, particularly rice production. The earliest comparable figures available are the 1970s, where the average GDP per capita was $90 for Vietnam, $85 for Cambodia, $63 for Laos and slightly higher for Burma ($124) (see Table 1). They were the four poorest countries in the region during the 1970s.

War was one of the factors that undermined growth, particularly in Vietnam and Cambodia. Vietnam in particular was divided by war against the returning French colonial rulers. A communist movement developed and expanded militarily in North Vietnam, while the French regained control over the South. While a communist regime was in place as soon as the 1950s in North Vietnam, it took until 1975 to expand to the South. During most of the 1960s and early 1970s, as the French had abandoned their colonial ambitions in the region in 1954, Vietnam then fought the United States, which was concerned about the spread of communism. Cambodia was similarly caught in the struggle against the French and later the Americans, although most of the war occurred in Vietnam. Cambodia became destabilized primarily in the early 1970s, with the rise of the communist Khmer Rouge that succeeded in undermining the long-standing authoritarian regime of King Norodom Sihanouk. Laos was very similar, with a king at the head of an authoritarian regime that the French had controlled. Yet, as soon as the French left in 1954, competing forces were more equal and the regime less able to rule alone. Successive attempts were made to rule in a coalition with the communist Pathet Lao but they repeatedly failed. The country remained divided territorially, with the Pathet Lao in control of some areas, while the royalists maintained weak control over the capital and surrounding areas until 1975, when the victory of communist forces in Vietnam spilled over to Laos and the Pathet Lao was able to seize control. Finally, Burma, for its part, was mainly affected by ethnic minority rebellions, as well as troops from Republican China that spilled over the border when the Red Army succeeded in establishing the People's Republic of China in 1949. Although liberal democracy was adopted when the British departed, rebellions and violence destabilized it throughout the 1950s, eventually leading to the establishment of a caretaker government under military leadership, a precursor to full military control only a couple of years later. War resulted from some of the region's decolonization, from Cold War competition between the United States and communist regimes and in some countries from internal rebellion. Countries most affected by destruction and chaos not surprisingly failed to develop strong economies.

All state-socialist countries remained quite poor for several decades after independence. They relied primarily on rice production and some cash crops, which are sold onto world markets via middlemen tradespeople. Some regions had fared comparatively better. Once a poor, subsistence-rice producing economy, in the late 1850s Burma's rice production for export boomed, as the British gained control over the country and invested heavily in agriculture. Exports grew by a factor of twelve between 1885 and 1906 so that Burma became the world's largest rice exporter, a status that it maintained well into the mid twentieth century. The French had engaged in similar investments in agriculture in the south of Vietnam (Cochinchina), where rice production increased dramatically in the same period and propelled Vietnam to the status of the world's third largest rice exporter. The north of Vietnam, and the kingdoms of Cambodia and Laos however remained relatively unaffected by the rise in international commerce that transformed some parts of Southeast Asia in the early nineteenth century (Elson, 1992). Up until the mid twentieth century, rich agricultural land provided a substantial source of wealth, particularly in Burma and parts of Vietnam.

After independence, Burma, Vietnam, Cambodia and Laos struggled to maintain strong economic growth. Rice exporting areas in Burma and Vietnam continued to thrive while poorer regions remained relatively unchanged. While Burma showed great promise with its rich resource base and strong agricultural economy, its future was severely compromised after the military took over in 1962 and established a state-socialist system. In the south of Vietnam, Saigon was the site of increased industrial production and urbanization during the 1950s and 1960s, and was stimulated further with the large presence of American troops in the 1960s. Otherwise, other regions remained poor and primarily subsistence-based economies. When socialist regimes gained power in North Vietnam, and later in Cambodia and Laos, poor rural areas initially welcomed socialist policies. Collectivization and the pooling of farmers' means of production promised a safety net that would be guaranteed but incentives to maximize production were low. As a result, farmers ended up producing less, many of them became poorer and consequently agricultural collectivization was eventually abandoned.

None of these countries, therefore, developed much of a middle class. South Vietnam was the exception, particularly around Saigon, but many successful business entrepreneurs were ethnic Chinese. When the communist North won the war, many of these entrepreneurs and professionals left the country as the regime began to repress them. Burma's economy had been relatively strong at the end of colonial rule and had a small middle class tied to the colonial administration and economy. It had few chances of growing significantly before the regime imposed its "Burmese Way to Socialism". The state seized the assets of the small industrial sector and turned them into state-run companies, while changes in rural areas destroyed previously strong markets that gave incentives to produce more. Cambodia and Laos had very little industrial infrastructure and urbanization.

Table 1 and Figure 2 illustrate part of the economic picture. GDP per capita shows the extent of initial poverty in all these countries. As explained above, Cambodia and Laos were the poorest, followed closely by Vietnam and then Burma. While some data is missing for the 1960s, Table 2 shows that Cambodia had negative growth rates during the 1970s, which corresponded to a period of the strongly closed socialist system of the Khmer Rouge. It therefore became even more impoverished before recovering some slow growth in the early

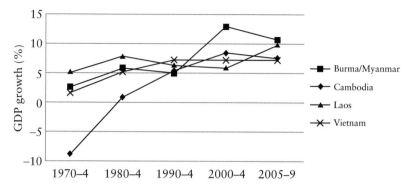

Figure 2 GDP growth in Burma/Myanmar, Cambodia, Laos and Vietnam

1980s and then steadily positive growth by the late 1980s. Cambodia was mainly catching up to wealth levels of the 1960s during this period. Laos, starting at very high poverty levels, grew at 5.2 per cent in the early 1970s but then only at 1.3 per cent in the late 1970s, after the imposition of state socialism. Vietnam had low growth (1.7 per cent) during the Vietnam War, although even this figure can be doubted given the disruption and destruction of the war. It fared better in the late 1970s in spite of collectivization but growth was more modest throughout the 1980s. Burma similarly maintained very low growth rates during the whole period of the 1960s and early 1970s (close to 3 per cent), during the height of its state-socialist experiment.

This survey of growth and development shows three trends. First, countries that followed state-socialist policies were mostly the poorest in the region at the time they followed this path. With the exception of Burma, all three other countries were among the poorest. Second, at the peak of state-socialist experiments, all countries showed negative or very low growth rates. Consequently, although it might have been more broadly distributed, total wealth remained sufficiently low that all countries remained quite poor. Third, both war and some of the policies of state-socialism contributed to further impoverishment. War certainly left deep scars in Cambodia and Vietnam. State socialism turned Burma from a relatively wealthy agrarian economy with a promising future to one of the least developed economies in the region.

All four countries therefore did not undergo transformation to an industrial and non-agricultural base that would have created a large middle class. Few pressures or opposition movements were capable of displacing the existing authoritarian regimes or creating stable democratic rule. Such an outcome at first glance is consistent with the key role of the middle class (or its absence).

From the late 1980s to the present, this has begun to change as all four countries adopted significant economic reforms. Vietnam, since the launch of *Doi Moi* ("renovation") in 1986 dramatically expanded its foreign investments and market friendly policies, as it relaxed state controls over ownership, prices and production quotas for instance. It maintained growth rates above 7 per cent on average after 1990. Cambodia emulated Vietnam's path after the Hun Sen regime succeeded the Khmer Rouge in 1979. Initially, however, the regime was under Vietnamese tutelage and subsequently divided by civil war. Laos in the 1990s also followed reform policies similar to Vietnam's. Burma mostly stayed away from deep economic reforms. It eventually allowed some foreign investment, which attracted mostly Chinese and Thai investors. Meanwhile the United States and European countries began to impose economic sanctions against the country when the regime cracked down on peaceful protests in the late 1980s. It continued and even expanded these sanctions during the following two decades. In addition, the Burmese military continued to own or control most firms, and therefore left little space for private entrepreneurship. Growth rates were higher in the last decade mainly because of a rise in exports of natural gas and other resources but much of the profits went to strengthening the military's revenue. With little investment in health or education, Burma remained far behind other countries in terms of developing a significantly large middle class.

For countries having pushed ahead with reform, such policies in themselves are not necessarily sufficient to produce political change. Economic growth must occur over a good period of time, and with a certain amount of redistribution, before levels of education rise and the middle class expands, including professionals, office workers and students. Vietnam has continued to expand in this direction, but Burma, Cambodia and Laos have done so much more slowly.

State-socialist regimes in Southeast Asia, furthermore, have created strong incentives to preserve elite unity. In Vietnam and Laos, where communist parties still officially rule, the structure, hierarchy and benefits allow them to retain their top status. Many communist regimes remained stable and strong for long periods of time because of a highly structured party organization. They are hierarchically organized, from villages up to the central government. Party cadres implement central directives, recruit members and keep tight control at the local level. At the top, the Political Bureau (Politburo) typically defines policies and controls the regime. It also acts as a mechanism to regulate the top leadership and constitutes a pool of candidates for leadership succession. Members of the Politburo are long-standing party members with demonstrated loyalty who have risen through the party's ranks. The party then maintains strong control over state institutions, and provides few outlets for organized opposition. Such systems have been in place both in Vietnam and Laos, and the benefits of reform have continued to give strong incentives for the party elite to perpetuate the system. Burma has its origins in a similar system. Organized around the Burmese Socialist Programme Party (BSPP), the military regime that took power in 1962 emulated many of the policies and practices of communist regimes, while defining its own unique ideology and path. By the late 1980s, the BSPP had been abolished and the military more openly dominated the regime. It expanded its control over all sectors of the economy. When crises arose, it introduced some limited reforms but did not compromise its own status. Its numbers expanded and provided substantial benefits to its members. Meanwhile it allowed some young Burmese to seek education abroad. Slow growth and some educational opportunities began to create a larger middle class, although still far smaller than in fast growing Southeast Asian countries. This rising but still weak middle class participated in protests and riots against the regime, which erupted most intensely in the "Saffron revolution" of 2007. The regime began to introduce significant political change in 2011, after it passed a new constitution and organized elections that led to the first civilian government in several decades. Nevertheless, many of the Cabinet members remained former military generals from the previous regime, so the established political elite controlled the pace and extent of reforms.

Cambodia has been different. The political elite has mostly been divided. Why then have we not seen more democratization? Prior to 1975, King Norodom Sihanouk held tight control over Cambodia. Many Cambodians held the monarchy in high respect, which contributed not only to its stability at the time but also to the continued relevance of Sihanouk and his son for several more decades. The Khmer Rouge, in 1975 established a brutal regime with goals of rapid and deep transformation but essentially failed and left destruction behind it when the Vietnamese interfered in 1979. Subsequently, Hun Sen established a communist regime similar to Vietnam's but could not eliminate opponents. Royalists around Sihanouk and his sons opposed the regime. The Khmer Rouge maintained sufficient military capacity to wage a civil war. The United Nations intervened and brokered a coalition government that replaced the UN Transitional Authority in 1993. Elections have been held but the externally imposed democratic process failed to deepen. Hun Sen maintained stronger control, since his party, the Cambodian People's Party, continued to benefit from stronger structure and organization from its days as the dominant state party. Elite divisions in this case sustain alternative parties but fail to stabilize democratic politics given the uneven strength of various groups.

Under such regimes, it is difficult to identify any trace of civil society. Since civil society refers to independent organizations occupying a space that is autonomous from the state, the lack of freedom to organize, the high capacity of communist regimes to repress and monitor opposition groups, as well as tight linkages of most sectors to the communist party, this makes it quite difficult for any independent organizations to be formed. Mass mobilization has been possible in some cases but civil society has been absent or very weak and small.

6 | Vietnam

Vietnam's regime has been stable and strong since 1975. After the country was split and mostly at war for three decades, it was reunified as the Socialist Republic of Vietnam at the end of the Vietnam War. While the regime has been officially communist, it gradually reformed its economy in favour of open markets, private property and capitalist investment. Its economy shows few remnants of its communist past. Its political institutions, however, retain the main features of communist regimes. Political reform has occurred but has been much slower. Overall, the regime has transformed itself since 1975 but has remained stable and firmly entrenched.

Prior to 1975, Vietnam constitutes a somewhat exceptional case. Not only was it divided into two, but also North and South Vietnam were almost continually at war with each other. The international context of the Cold War played a crucial role in determining the types of political regimes and their sustainability. In the South, successive governments were highly dependent on French and then American support. They failed to gain strong local support among the population. They were consequently vulnerable to the ideological appeal and promises of the communist North. In the meantime, the communist regime in the North used anti-colonial nationalist ideology as well as promises of a more egalitarian society to gain widespread support among the rural masses. Similarly this appeal grew in the South as war ravaged the countryside and its regime showed few attempts to address the population's needs.

Why has Vietnam's regime been stable? Mostly because the Communist Party was able to create an elite that has remained united and committed to maintaining the regime. Much of the South's political elite was eliminated after 1975. Meanwhile the regime benefited from the initial wave of sympathy and ideological strengthening that came with the North's victory over the United States and its allies in the South. Few communist regimes have benefited from the ability to merge their agenda with the strong emotions that can be raised through a war of national liberation. Nationalism, as an expression of resistance to French and American powers, created a powerful source of legitimacy, combined with promises of a stable, reunified Vietnam. Although this appeal diminished over time, it allowed the Vietnamese leadership to create a very solid institutional basis after 1975.

Economic development transformed Vietnam in the last few decades but little political change has occurred. Much of the initial growth after the Vietnam War was devoted to reconstruction. Economic reforms since the mid 1980s have loosened the state's control over the economy and allowed a modest middle class to rise but the latter remains tied to the state and the party. Cadres and supporters of the party have been some of the main beneficiaries. As a result, it can be argued that the middle class has been too small or too weak to develop pressure for political change.

Nevertheless, some more specific factors explain the weak opposition and virtual absence of a civil society. Vietnam's communist system developed strong institutional links to various groups across society. As a classic communist regime, the party has organized and channelled opportunities for advancement, and therefore funnelled elite groups into the state's structures. Furthermore, the state sanctioned official functional groups to represent women, farmers and other interests groups, while tying them to the party. With the armed forces playing a central role in the evolution of Vietnam's regime, this institutionalization combined with strong repressive capacity has prevented the emergence of opposition. Instead, gradual changes within the party have allowed more space for debate and disagreement, thereby absorbing some of the pressures from economic development and transformation without introducing more significant political change.

Divided Vietnam: effects of the Cold War

After the end of the Second World War, the French returned in an attempt to regain control over its former colony. During the War, the Japanese had struck an agreement with the Vichy regime – the government created after the German invasion of France and that sided with the Axis powers of Germany and Italy. The agreement provided for joint sovereignty over the colony. In effect, the Vichy regime allowed the Japanese to seize control of Indochina. The armed wing of the

Communist Party, the Vietminh (the Independence League of Vietnam), was created in 1941 and managed to organize strong resistance to the Japanese within a few years. The Japanese occupation was very harsh, and famines in the South were partly caused by Japanese policies to extract food and resources for its war effort. The Vietminh mobilized poor peasants to raid rice depots. The success of these attacks increased their legitimacy in rural areas. Once the Japanese had surrendered in 1945, the Vietminh, who already controlled large areas of the North, seized power without opposition and proclaimed the Democratic Republic of Vietnam.

The French however refused to recognize the new independent government. The leader of the Communist Party, Ho Chi Minh, had allowed the French to enter parts of the North under Vietminh control. He needed their support to push back Chinese troops of the Kuomintang forces who entered the country to disarm Japanese troops. Ho Chi Minh bargained with the French that, with permission to enter Vietminh-controlled areas, they would support general elections and the independence of Vietnam. The French reneged on their commitment and, instead, launched a fierce campaign to regain control over all of Vietnam. The First Indochina War lasted almost a decade but the French never succeeded. Instead, the Geneva Agreement officially split the country in 1954. President Ngo Dinh Diem led the newly created Republic of Vietnam in the south.

The regime in the South was never able to consolidate its power. From the outset, communist supporters were already present. Several people had actively participated in the Vietminh's resistance against the French. Others had strong ties to the Communist Party. The Diem regime attempted to eradicate the communist presence by repressing, detaining and executing its supporters. Promised elections in 1956 of a united Vietnam never materialized as violence and conflict between the North and the South escalated.

As the French retreated, the Americans became more heavily involved. With escalating resistance, the Diem regime declared emergency powers to clamp down more forcefully on opposition and weed out communists. The United States provided large amounts of aid that was meant for economic and social reforms. Instead, the regime diverted increasing amounts to the armed forces.

Meanwhile, communists in the north sought allies in the south to topple Diem and gain control. They sponsored the creation of

the National Liberation Front (NLF), which was an alliance of anti-
communist parties opposed to Diem as well as communist supporters.
The NLF strategically targeted villages where they organized peasants
and mobilized them on issues of land inequality and ownership. Their
penetration of rural areas formed a grassroots movement upon which
the resistance to the regime and the American presence grew.

The Vietnam War escalated after 1963 and remained intense for the
following decade. Although neither side made strong territorial gains,
the war nevertheless led to massive destruction and death. US troops
were unprepared for guerilla warfare in which its enemy could not
easily be identified. They lost large numbers of soldiers in skirmishes
and surprise attacks. Vietminh troops would attack American soldiers
and swiftly disappear among villagers. They also used a vast network
of underground tunnels to disappear. The Americans and their allies
in power in South Vietnam grew suspicious of civilians who could
be sheltering the enemy and even be soldiers in disguise. The scale of
destruction was massive when the United States used bombing campaigns after 1965 against villages and rural areas to flush out communist soldiers and sympathizers. In the end, the violence and scale
of destruction contributed to increasing peasant support for the communist North. Faced with increasing losses and failures to seize the
upper hand in the war, the United States began to disengage after
1973. Shortly thereafter troops from the North gained control over all
of Vietnam.

The Socialist Republic of Vietnam: institutionalization of the communist regime

The communist regime proclaimed a new Socialist Republic of Vietnam
and extended its structures over all of Vietnam. For the following
decade, the regime progressively replaced economic arrangements in
the South with its own brand of agricultural production. It extended
the reach of the Communist Party into rural areas. Scars from the
war and a strong military influence remained even though the regime
attempted to homogenize and normalize governmental structures in
an attempt to unify the country and build its socialist future.

"Reunification" was not straightforward. The socio-economic landscape of South Vietnam differed substantially from that of the North.
Most significantly, an entrepreneurial class had developed around

Saigon and it had grown substantially from proceeds of the war economy. Although some remained, a very large number of entrepreneurs fled the country after the communist victory. They left a commercial infrastructure that was more developed than in Hanoi but with a decimated entrepreneurial class. In the North, most industrial production had been placed under state ownership. In the South, the state seized control over private industry but did not fully convert factories to collective ownership. Many remained under a public/private partnership of state-private enterprises, although factory owners received very little overall compensation. Nevertheless, they remained much more productive than the fully state-owned sectors that were dominant in the North.

In rural areas, the SRV encountered strong resistance after "reunification". During the years preceding the war, the state had successfully collectivized rural areas in the North, by which it replaced family owned farms with large state-owned estates. Yet, it had difficulty shaping the collective farms to perform as desired. Benedict Kerkvliet has shown that peasants in the North already in the 1970s were undermining collective farming by using a number of strategies. Frustrated at the lack of benefits from state imposed collectivization, peasants only worked minimally to achieve requirements for compensation. They were neglectful in their farming practices, they hid parts of their harvest or seized some of the collectivized land for their own private use. They resented the declining living standards that came with collectivization and mistrusted state officials as well as other farmers. In the end, collective farms performed very poorly and by the early 1980s, several were abandoned and reconverted to family farming. In the South, where Vietnam's richest agricultural land is located, peasants strongly resisted the state's attempt to transform or seize their farms after 1975. In the following decade, only a quarter of households joined collective farms (Kerkvliet, 2005, 2006).

Political structures were much more easily converted. Down to the village level, the Vietnamese Communist Party (VCP) replaced existing institutions with its own socialist organizations. As with other communist states, the Political Bureau and Central Committee of the Vietnamese Communist Party constituted the central ruling organs of the party but also of the state. Since the VCP controlled the state at all levels, the party's ruling elite effectively decided on state policies and actions. The National Party Congress of the VCP held official representative functions designed to approve party policies every four or five years and officially select the party's leadership. At the lowest level, villages were ruled by party officials and organized as communes under party rule. Other administrative levels were granted powers devolved from the central organs of the VCP and the state. In the end, as with other communist states, a small party elite sits at the apex of a highly structured pyramid through which power is exercised in a top-down fashion.

State institutions in Vietnam, as well as in other communist states, run parallel to the structures of the Communist Party but are also sub-sumed under its authority. Real power is vested in the ruling organs of the Communist Party. Although the National Assembly, Vietnam's leg-islature, was vested with powers to elect key officials in all state organs (such as the Council of State and Council of Ministers), it mainly rubber-stamped the VCP's decisions. The State Council is formally most powerful after the National Assembly. It exercises all powers of the National Assembly between its meetings, including the ability to abrogate the Council of Ministers' decrees. Nevertheless, the Council of Ministers, with a higher number of Political Bureau members, has been the most important state institution. It is responsible for decrees and orders, as well as the state's policy directions (Porter, 1993).

The Vietnam People's Army (VPA) has been particularly central to the regime. Stretching back to the First Indochina War (1945–54), the armed forces were crucial to the communists' revolutionary effort. In the Vietnam War, their continued strength against US troops elevated even more their prestige in the eyes of the Vietnamese. After independence, the VPA emerged as a large, well-organized entity that was intrinsically tied to the Communist Party. In the 1980s, it had more than 1.1 million regular troops and 3 million trained reserves. Nevertheless, it has not constituted an alternative source of power to the Communist Party but rather one of its pillars. Top generals were integrated into the Communist Party leadership and credentials within the party have often been preconditions for advancement and leadership in the VPA. In sum, the military plays a central role that reinforces rather than competes with the civilian power vested in the Communist Party (Porter, 1993).

In communist systems, the Secretary General of the Communist Party holds the greatest amount of power. Vietnam has followed other communist states, with some minor differences. During the 1950s and

1960s, Ho Chi Minh clearly held most power by virtue not only of his formal leadership of the Communist Party but also as the leader who resisted colonial occupation, led Vietnamese troops to defeat the French, and conducted a successful revolution. Although his influence and power declined by the early 1960s, in recognition of his special historical role, he was named "chairman" of the VCP. It was exclusively attributed to Ho Chi Minh so that, after his death in 1969, no other Vietnamese leader was ever given that title. Instead, the secretary-general retained most power under more collective leadership than in the past. Le Duan occupied the position of secretary-general from 1960–86.

Under Le Duan's leadership, Vietnam followed the Soviet path towards industrialization. The government placed strong emphasis on heavy industrialization. It established state-owned enterprises, and invested in the construction of new plants. The government determined output levels, prices, input supplies, retail trade and goods targeted for export. It attempted to keep tight control over every step in the production process. Output was channelled to the governmental agencies which then redistributed products according to the plan. Such tight control required huge amounts of coordination and planning (Beresford, 2006).

Central planning created a number of problems. Most significantly, the production system suffered chronic shortages of raw materials as it used limited aid from the Soviet Union to import capital equipment to build factories and supply them. With persistent shortages, plants failed to produce at satisfactory levels and to attain production targets. In the 1970s, when debates over reform already began, believers in central planning argued in favour of retaining the approach but more realistically assessing the economy's real financial and resources capacity. Others blamed the attempt to set prices and resource requirements through administrative means. A flourishing black market created even more problems, as goods were often diverted to it (Beresford, 2006).

Many party members also benefited from central planning, and were therefore reluctant to modify it. With control over resources and their allocation came political powers. If they allowed the market to operate more freely, they would lose the ability to leverage compliance and reap benefits from their control over production. Political battles divided various interests within the central planning system. Bureaucrats in central government ministries negotiated prices and resource allocations with enterprise managers and local authorities, who sought to retain greater shares at the local level. The negotiated outcomes did not tend to reflect an efficient allocation of resources that would close the gap between demand and supply (Beresford, 2006).

In rural areas, the government intensified collectivization. The North had already collectivized agriculture beginning in the late 1950s. Under a vast programme of land reform, Ho's government had already given 810,000 hectares to poor peasants between 1954–6, but some of the poorest pushed further for collectivization as their plots were too small and poorly irrigated. They benefited from a guaranteed minimum level of income and standard of health and education. By the mid 1960s, almost all of the rural population was organized in cooperatives, in which all income was pooled and redistributed according to a system of points. After 1976, collectivization was extended to the South but met with greater resistance, in particular among middle peasants who had benefited from substantial land reforms in the 1960s and 1970s and who were likely to lose from collectivization (Beresford, 2006).

As it was spreading, collectivization also revealed its weaknesses. While poor peasants enjoyed guaranteed minimum living standards, collectives' overall productivity stagnated. Cooperatives failed to produce incentives to increase agricultural output. The government set prices for agricultural products at low levels so that it could supply urban areas at relatively low cost, keep urban wages low and thereby ensure greater profits at state-owned enterprises. Within cooperatives, income distribution contributed to stagnation. As the government increased pressure to supply greater output to urban areas, the remaining income for redistribution among cooperative members dwindled. The poorest peasants benefited but the wealthier and more productive peasants resented the meagre incomes that were obtained through cooperative production (Beresford, 2006).

As a result, privately owned plots persistently outgrew the productivity of the vast collectivized areas. As in other socialist systems, Vietnam allowed peasants to retain very small plots to supplement their family needs. Although capped at 5 per cent, in many regions greater areas of land were diverted to private production. Furthermore, since market prices were generally higher than government-imposed ones, peasants devoted greater energy to their household plots and sold their goods on the black markets. They also diverted produce from collectivized areas on the black market. Beresford estimates that by the late 1970s peasants earned 60–70 per cent of their income from household plots (Beresford, 2006). In particular, party members and officials were most likely to profit from these sideline activities and became increasingly wealthy relative to other peasants.

As the system was eroded, pressure mounted for reform. Peasants lobbied provincial party bosses, particularly in the south, to abandon or modify collectivization in their favour. These provincial party officials emerged as a strong constituency for change.

Doi Moi: economic reform and political continuity

Rising economic problems triggered a momentum for reform. Leading up to the Sixth Party Congress in 1986, reformers within the Vietnamese Communist Party argued that the path forward required a new direction in order to avert more decline in the economy and potentially costly political instability. During the Sixth Party Congress in 1986, reformers successfully gained control of the party with the election of Nguyen Van Linh as secretary-general.

As with other communist political systems, Vietnam's is quite closed and opaque. While political observers were unable to trace the origins of the Doi Moi movement, since the Communist Party strives to present a unified front, nevertheless the selection of the new, younger generation of leaders suggested a new division between reformists and more conservative supporters of central planning and orthodox communist ideas. While this split constituted a measure of division among the political elite, it was not sufficiently deep to trigger vast political change, as reformers and conservatives continued to share the common objective of maintaining the Communist Party's dominance.

Overall, Vietnam's Communist Party appeared to have few staunch ideologues and many more pragmatists willing to shift alliances within the party in the support of more successful policies. Such a shift accompanied the alignment of new interests in favour of reform. With the death of Le Duan in July 1986, the long-standing party leader who represented the first-generation leaders most committed to the ideological tenets of Communism, reformers could more forcefully take centre stage. They were supported furthermore by a similar shift in orientation in the Soviet Union under Mikhail Gorbachev's leadership. Gorbachev had signalled in early 1986 the need to accept market forces as part of building a stronger socialist system.

By the early 1980s, signs were already apparent that central planning was eroding. The regime had allowed limited markets to expand in some rural areas and, even in the state-owned enterprise sector, many firms sold their products at market prices rather than at subsidized prices according to the central plan. In the south, peasants and officials had never really accepted Hanoi's attempts to collectivize agriculture and impose central planning. Their continued resistance ensured that some market processes continued to operate and largely undermine the increasingly stagnant command economy. Reforms in the cooperative agricultural sector had given individual households more options to increase their wealth as they were permitted to sell at market prices and for their own profit any surpluses beyond contracted outputs. As these initial reforms succeeded in raising the productivity of the cooperative sector, ironically it encouraged the party to intensify in 1983 the campaign for collectivization in the South. They also raised taxes on the private sector to prevent the development of wealthier classes. Combined with a currency reform in 1985, these policies contributed to more discontent and further economic crisis (Beresford, 1993).

The set of policies that were implemented in the subsequent decade were collectively known as "Doi Moi" ("renovation"). The Eight Party Plenum in 1985 was a crucial turning point. At the meeting, reformers succeeded in convincing the party that the system of strict state control over prices, production and supply had failed to produce expected results. Instead, they proposed to move steadily towards espousing market forces to determine price levels, and to stabilize supply and production (Porter, 1993).

The most important reforms began after 1988. A new foreign investment law, passed in December 1987, gave wide access to foreign investors and allowed them 100 per cent ownership. The law also included generous tax incentives. A few months later, the party effectively abolished collectivization of agriculture by giving back to households the power to set their own production goals and market their produce. In 1989, it eliminated official prices and allowed all prices to set according to market forces (Beresford, 2006).

By all accounts, these reforms and the transition to a market economy yielded considerable success. Throughout the 1990s, Vietnam enjoyed high GDP growth rates, reaching more than 8 per cent per year between 1992–7, and declining only slightly after the Asian financial crisis. By 1990, it had increased agricultural production to the point of being the world's third largest exporter of rice. By 2005, it was ranked the world's second largest exporter, while in 2010 it threatened Thailand's position as the world's top exporter of rice. With this increased wealth, poverty declined from 58 per cent of the population in 1993 to 23 per cent in 2004 (Beresford, 2008). While it abandoned central planning, the Vietnamese government retained an important commitment to the state's leadership role. It created long-term, and significant structural changes to stimulate industrialization. Foreign investment played a key role and constituted almost 30 per cent of total investment by 1995. Yet, because it grew in the context of a large "bubble" in Asian investment, after the Asian financial crisis of 1997 it declined steadily to 15 per cent by 2004. Much of this investment was made through joint ventures with state-owned enterprises, which were seen as a more secure sector for investment (Beresford, 2008).

As part of its continued commitment to socialism, the government retained state enterprises but their role changed over time. For most of the 1960–90 period, state enterprises received very little support after they had been established. In the earlier periods, Soviet aid provided initial capital to purchase machinery and build plants. Priority was given to the establishment of new enterprises rather than updating existing ones. As a result, over time many enterprises could not fully produce their target outputs because they depended on old equipment that often dated back to the 1960s. During the 1990s, the government used partnerships with foreign investors partly to upgrade state enterprises' equipment and technology (Beresford, 2008).

Economic reforms have created new wealth but also rising inequalities. The Vietnamese government has pursued the objective of an "equitable society". Certainly, many Vietnamese have benefited from a more privatized economy. Employment across different industrial sectors, for instance, has grown considerably. In 2005, firms established mainly through foreign investment employed a million workers, which represented a 156 per cent increase from employment levels reached in 2000. Domestic non-state firms employed 2.5 million – a 137 per cent increase from 2000 – while state enterprises employed 2.2 million workers. During the decade of the 2000s, the role of state enterprises appeared to decline relative to the non-state and foreign-invested sectors. Employment in state enterprises rose by only 8 per cent during the same period (Beresford, 2008).

Despite its rapid rise, employment in these industrial sectors was highly skewed. Since most of these firms are situated in two growth poles around Hanoi and Ho Chi Minh City, the urban/rural divide has been growing. In some areas, such as the Mekong Delta, more farmers have become landless. Among the elite, there are clear winners among party officials and well-connected entrepreneurs, whether they are in the state or non-state sectors. Yet, a large number of Vietnamese with no connections to these growth networks have been left behind. Reform, then, is transforming the class configuration of Vietnamese society and increasing inequality, thereby making the government's objective of an "equitable society" increasingly difficult to achieve.

Political changes have also been part of the Doi Moi reforms. During the 1980s, many reformers focused on the need to increase political openness and representation. They attributed many of the Vietnamese economic bottlenecks and rising socio-economic problems to its rigid political system. Some even suggested the introduction of multi-partyism although the Vietnamese Community Party promptly warned against taking this direction.

A number of reforms have increased transparency, participation and political debate. In the 1990s, the government codified and reorganized laws and regulations to make them more coherent and consistent. It aimed at increasing transparency and reducing corruption, partly to increase foreign investors' confidence. Within the party, the leadership allowed more dialogue and criticism of main policy issues. Within state institutions, the National Assembly was permitted to debate more freely and even to criticize the government. Under changes made to the constitution in 1992, the party allowed candidates to run in elections without as much close scrutiny and formal approval from its central organs. The National Assembly's committees were permitted to amend legislation, although they were still prevented from initiating it. In effect, the National Assembly gained greater oversight rather than simply rubber-stamping the government's legal agenda. Later changes to the constitution went even further to increase formally the National Assembly's role. In 2001, the assembly obtained the right to hold non-confidence votes against leaders (Beresford, 2008; Fforde, 2005).

These changes on paper disguise the VCP's continued hold on power. The party retains very strong influence over the selection of candidates running for the National Assembly. In effect, because the VCP is the only political party authorized to field candidates, elections for the

National Assembly could be seen as some kind of popularity contest between party members. The VCP uses elections to gage the relative popularity of central committee members in particular and election results can modify someone's standing in the party. Only candidates who are nominated by the highest organs of the party are likely to assume leadership roles in the National Assembly. Even those expected to play leadership roles at the provincial or local levels need support centrally. Candidates who are nominated locally tend to play lesser roles after their election (Malesky & Schuler, 2009).

The National Assembly's overall power still falls short of expectations set in the 1992 Constitution. Given the VCP's continued control over candidates and legislation, the National Assembly cannot exercise much autonomy in introducing legislation or perform a genuine oversight role. Members can introduce amendments to legislation. Question time has become more active and some members have even been challenged in the Assembly over sensitive issues such as suspected corruption. But overall, the National Assembly remains weak (Malesky & Schuler, 2009).

Nevertheless, changes since the early 1990s placed some constraints on the one-party state in Vietnam, and the pursuit of economic growth through integration to world markets was a key motivation. As Mark Sidel argues, the Vietnamese government has consistently used the constitution to increase its legitimacy, while also using it to maintain state dominance (Sidel, 1995). As a consequence, a vast array of organizations, ranging from government-owned media to public interest groups has appealed to the constitutional process to pressure the state into compromise. The Vietnamese state after Doi Moi increasingly used the law and constitutional reform to provide a framework conducive to foreign investment and economic growth, while also responding to demands from foreign donors. While the state's dominance remains, various groups have increasingly been able to place some limits on its reach.

Outside the formal political realm, Doi Moi has given more space for organizational autonomy, within limits. The dismantling of state cooperatives and the elimination of collectivized agriculture, for instance, led to the formation of credit groups and community-based organizations tailored to the needs of local communities. After widespread peasant disturbances in 1998, the party allowed more participation at the local level and increased transparency in terms of its policies and budgets. In 2003, under a "Grassroots Democracy" directive, it further encouraged the participation of locally based organizations in development activities. They have come to play increasing roles in environmental protection, farmers cooperatives, health and welfare support, even the cultural realm in some areas. At the same time, as Mark Sidel and Carlyle Thayer argue, they fall short of our common understanding of non-governmental organizations as they remain under the party's control and the state even sponsors many of them. They occupy a semi-independent space in which they complement the state's role in delivering services to local communities (Sidel, 1995; Thayer, 2009). Nevertheless, they constitute an important source of autonomous space to influence policy and to negotiate concessions from the state. As Thaveeporn Vasavakul has observed, these organizations have developed new methods of advancing their interests. They create vertical linkages to various party-state organs to obtain political resources, while nurturing horizontal ties to networks of other popular organizations. This model creates new forms of pluralism that depart from the top-down, tight control usually maintained under state socialism (Vasavakul, 2003).

Economic reforms have not been sufficiently deep and sustained to create a strong middle class outside of the Communist Party's circle. The political elite tied to the Communist Party has been the primary beneficiary of these reforms. Much of the emerging middle class has therefore been tied to the Communist Party and the state. With relatively slower economic development, certainly up until the 1990s, Vietnam has developed a smaller middle class than in other Southeast Asian countries. More importantly, this middle class has not enjoyed the independence of its peers in other countries.

Ideology, strong institutions, pragmatism, as well as economic development helped to sustain the regime's longevity. The Cold War was a key factor in the creation of Vietnam's regime and an early source of political and material support. The Soviet Union helped Ho Chi Minh develop strong resistance to the French and later the United States. A victorious North in the Vietnam War reunified the whole country under the Socialist Republic that, again, benefited from financial and political support from its communist allies. At an ideological level, communism promised a more egalitarian society among Vietnamese who were very poor. While such principles appealed to poor

Table 9 *Vietnam*

Population (rank)	Land area (rank)	Main ethnic groups (%)	Main religions (%)	Regime type (transition)	GDP per capita (rank)	GDP growth rate (%) (rank)
91 519 289 (14th) (2011 est.)	310 070 sq km (65th)	Kinh (Viet) 85.7 Tay 1.9 Thai 1.8 Muong 1.5 Khmer 1.5 Mong 1.2 Nung 1.1 Others 5.3 (1999 census)	Buddhist 9.3 Catholic 6.7 Hoa Hao 1.5 Cao Dai 1.1 Protestant 0.5 Muslim 0.1 None 80.8 (1999 census)	Authoritarian Communist state	$3 300 (167th) (2011 est.)	5.8 (49th) (2011 est.)

Source: CIA, *The World Factbook*; Polity IV Project, Polity IV Individual Country Regime Trends, 1946–2010.

Vietnamese peasants, nationalism strengthened even more the support for the regime. Much of the North's successful mobilization among a broad segment of the Vietnamese population was based on the nationalist, anti-colonial appeal of the communist movement. Resistance to French colonial rule was subsequently channeled into even stronger motivation to fight the United States during the 1960s and 1970s. Nationalism and anti-colonial liberation therefore provided ideological support, as the Communist Party consolidated its regime with the rhetorical help of its victory over the United States.

As with other communist systems, its primary strength was the strong institutionalization of the party. Single-party dominance provides a strong incentive to maintain elite unity. In spite of rising divisions between conservative factions and reformists committed to deepening economic transformation, they shared an interest in preserving the unity of the party and the regime. Furthermore, the party was strongly present among Vietnamese at all levels of society. Cadres recruited and mobilized supporters. They have led and sponsored organizations representing different interests. As a result, the regime has been able to monitor and control society, thereby aiding to prevent the effective rise of opposition.

At the same time, the strong role of the armed forces has been important. The armed forces gained strength and respect for their role in the Vietnam War. In comparative terms, they play a stronger role in Vietnam than in other countries. Combined with party strength, the key presence of the armed forces has given the state a strong repressive arm that also contributed to weak opposition.

Finally, economic reforms support regime stability by increasing living standards and private benefits among the elite. Over time, economic benefits replaced the previous ideological and nationalist strength that the regime enjoyed in the 1970s. With the decline of the Soviet Union and less credible communist ideology as socio-economic inequality increased, the regime became more pragmatic and more strongly rooted in generating economic benefits for its political elite.

7 | Cambodia and Laos

Political trends in Vietnam have shaped political trajectories in Cambodia and Laos. During French colonial rule, Vietnam was the colony's epicentre. The French recruited from and trained their administrators among the Vietnamese, and sent them out across Indochina. After Cambodia obtained its independence in 1953, the Khmer Rouge, a communist movement with ties to the Vietnamese communists, had already challenged the fragile regime. It was an alternative nationalist movement with its own brand of communist project, and largely rose in opposition to Vietnamese influence. It gained power for a few years but subsequently the Vietnamese army dislodged and replaced it with a government under its control. Although the government eventually gained more autonomy, Vietnamese influence has remained present, although to a much lesser degree. In Laos, political division was deep after independence, and no political force was able to exercise sufficient power to establish a stable government. Laos was drawn into the Vietnam War, as was Cambodia, and suffered casualties and destruction as well. The end of the war provided the opportunity for the communist Pathet Lao to establish its dominance, with Vietnamese support. The Vietnamese government maintained strong influence over the communist regime in Laos for the following decades.

Communist regimes in both countries, however, were never able to establish the stability and continuity that characterized the Vietnamese regime. While they shared some of the institutional strength of communist regimes, other factors intervened to create much more unstable and even chaotic political histories.

External factors as well as some unique features best explain the messiness of political change in these countries. Cold War politics defined dividing lines, with Vietnam providing support for communists, and after the Vietnam War political regimes in both countries, except for the few years of the Khmer Rouge regime in Cambodia from 1975–9. The United States supported anti-communist groups but these

were severely weakened after the United States lost the war and left
the region in 1975.

Relatively even but deeply divided political groups created conditions for civil war in both countries but in different time periods.
During the 1950s, communists fought anti-communist supporters of
the Lao king, establishing their control over different parts of the territory. Only after 1975 was the communist Pathet Lao able to defeat
its opponents and consolidate a regime that would remain stable for
the following decades. In Cambodia, periods of instability and war
were more common than periods of stable governance. The authoritarian regime of King Norodom Sihanouk after independence in 1954
was soon vulnerable when faced with challenges from pro-Vietnamese
communists, the Khmer Issarak (later Khmer Rouge) and the escalation
of the Vietnam War in the 1960s. The main dividing line after 1975
was between the Khmer Rouge and pro-Vietnamese communists who,
with Vietnam's military intervention, created a more stable regime
after 1979. Nevertheless the Khmer Rouge continued to pose significant military challenges, as did the pro-royalist opposition. Only in
the last decade has the successor to the Vietnamese communist regime,
the Cambodian People's Party (CPP), been able to tip the balance and
solidify its rule. Deep ideological division prevented not only elite unity
in Cambodia and Laos but also the ability for a single regime to contain
and manage these divisions.

These conditions were not conducive to economic development.
Among the poorest countries in Southeast Asia, Cambodia's and Laos'
economies also deteriorated during the Vietnam War and, in Cambodia's case, the following civil war. With poor economic development,
there was a relatively small and politically insignificant middle class.
While economic growth has been higher in the last decade, with more
stability in Cambodia and reforms in Laos, nevertheless it has been too
soon to offset past trends and create an independent middle class that
could propose a political alternative.

Cambodia

Since its independence, Cambodia's politics have been marked by violence, war and authoritarian dominance. There is no socio-economic or
institutional reason why Cambodia should have followed such a dramatic path. Originally a fairly peaceful kingdom with a strong sense of

its Khmer history and identity, it was caught in the radical transformations brought about by Cold War politics, and particularly the Vietnam
War. Its communist movement, the Khmer Rouge, gained strength in
the chaos of the war and succeeded in seizing power at its end. Its
radical ideology and transformational programme destroyed Cambodia's society, and scarred it for decades afterwards. Vietnam's political
intervention determined much of Cambodia's future after 1979. When
the United Nations attempted to reconstruct the country and build a
stable democracy, it was faced with a deeply divided and suspicious
society. Hopes for a stable democratic regime quickly faded. Since
then, an authoritarian regime has maintained control while following
some democratic procedures.

Some specialists argue that Cambodia's political culture prevents it
from developing stable, democratic politics. They argue that the Khmer
Empire nurtured a culture of suspicion, authoritarianism and pursuit
of private gain among power holders that has persisted through time
(Chandler, 1998).

The cultural argument, however, fails to consider the immense
changes that have occurred in the country, including cultural ones
that have dramatically transformed Cambodian society. Much evidence suggests that elites intent on preserving their power transformed
and manipulated notions of Khmer culture and tradition, in particular
in the revival of tradition following the destructive years of Khmer
Rouge rule. While the monarchy has remained present, it has transformed itself. King Sihanouk and Prince Ranariddh both became modern politicians who appeared little different to their counterparts.

In comparative terms, a small middle class and deeply divided elite
have been a hindrance to democratic institutions. As previously discussed, the absence of a middle class or its small size tends to prevent
democratic politics since it allows an elite to control a polity with
little resistance. When elites are divided, we often see democratic politics emerge even in the absence of a strong middle class, because of
the inability of the elites to consolidate power. Democratic politics
then acts as a forum for elite competition. At minimum, however, it
requires that elites accept a framework for such political competition
to occur. When it is deeply divided, elites are unable to agree on rules
of political competition and, instead, often choose violence or war
to seize political control. The ability to develop stronger military and
institutional power to either defeat or sideline other groups tends to

underpin the level of stability and consolidation of authoritarian rule. Such dynamics have marred Cambodia's political landscape.

Finally, regional and international factors contributed to shaping much of Cambodia's political path. Khmer nationalism at the outset developed in the shadow of French policies in Indochina (Goscha, 1995). The French used Vietnamese as colonial bureaucrats in all areas of Indochina. Inflows of Vietnamese into regional cities of today's Cambodia and Laos were compounded by their strong involvement in various small-scale businesses. French colonial policies encouraged Vietnamese migration. In 1921, Vietnamese constituted 61 per cent of the population of Phnom Penh, Cambodia's largest urban centre. By 1936, there were 191,000 Vietnamese in a total Cambodian population of 3 million (Goscha, 2009, p. 1193). Vietnamese presence and their key role in the colonial bureaucracy contributed to solidifying modern Khmer nationalism that adopted an anti-Vietnamese dimension. After independence, Cambodia remained tied to political changes in Vietnam. The communist movement gained a strong ally in the Vietnamese communist party that eventually controlled not only the north but all of Vietnam. At the same time, the Khmer Rouge, which eventually seized control of Cambodia at the end of the Vietnam War in 1975 was driven, in part, by the strong anti-Vietnamese Khmer nationalism that had evolved in various forms in preceding decades. Vietnam's military intervention to topple the Khmer Rouge regime in 1979 set a new course of Vietnamese dominance that lasted for a decade. Cambodia's fate once again changed as the Cold War ended in 1989 and opened up opportunities for a negotiated settlement under United Nations auspices. Yet, by then, the strongest power remained the previously Vietnamese supported government that, under the rubric of the CPP, maintained its dominance for the following decades, albeit with more autonomy from its former patron.

An authoritarian, monarchical regime first dominated Cambodia largely because the French were relatively uninterested in dislodging it. Had the monarchy been removed and replaced by a set of parliamentary institutions as in Malaysia or the Philippines, Cambodia's path may well have been different. Instead, the tranquil kingdom, largely unpenetrated by colonial economic ventures, remained largely parcelled into family owned agricultural land. It exported few of its agricultural commodities and was hardly integrated into world markets.

The strength of the Khmer majority, and its historical importance, did give birth to a strong sense of Khmer identity and pride that was often mobilized to counter foreign intrusion. Although Cambodia was a quiet corner of French Indochina during colonial times, in previous centuries the Khmer Empire had extensive power in the region. Furthermore, Khmers constituted the vast majority, with 80 per cent of the population, while Vietnamese, Chinese and Chams constituted significant but small minority groups. As in other parts of Southeast Asia, these minorities mainly controlled trade networks while some were employed in rubber plantations.

On the eve of French defeat in 1954, Cambodia obtained its independence in 1953 under the leadership of King Norodom Sihanouk. During the period of French colonial occupation from 1863 onwards, the monarchy had been re-established and nurtured as the embodiment of a glorious past. The French froze Cambodia's institutions to create a stable monarchy under its control. When the French returned, they attempted to establish a parliament, while maintaining King Sihanouk as a figurehead. When parliament became more assertive, Sihanook staged a coup that was supported by French troops. The French nevertheless faced increased resistance from communist insurgents and nationalists seeking independence. Sihanouk seized the opportunity and organized a Crusade for Independence, turning against his former colonial supporters. Faced with increased losses in Vietnam and growing pressure in Cambodia, the French relented and allowed independence to be declared in 1953. Sihanook had managed in a few years to turn himself from a pliant monarch under the French, to an authoritarian ruler intent on crushing opposition. Nevertheless, he had gained popularity for his ability to force the French into granting independence (Chandler, 1991; Kiernan, 2002).

French attempts to re-impose their dominance over Indochina after the Second World War marked the rise of resistance movements across the former colony. In neighbouring Vietnam, the Indochinese communist movement launched the Viet Minh that successfully rebuked French attempts to regain control over the North. The defeat at Dien Bien Phu in 1954 ended the French colonial adventure. In Cambodia, the communist movement was an embryonic off-shoot of the Vietnamese resistance. The Khmer Issarak, as it was then called, was a very small group with few grassroots links to the peasantry. They were completely dependent on their Vietnamese counterparts in the broader Indochinese Communist Party. In 1951, they created the Khmer People's Revolutionary Party (KPRP). Meanwhile, Khmer students in Paris formed an alternative left-wing group. They were highly influenced by communist ideas in France and elsewhere in Europe. When they returned to Cambodia, they joined the communist movement but remained relatively unknown. They rose in the KPRP's ranks and eventually formed a faction that sought to break away from Vietnamese influence (Chandler, 1991; Kiernan, 2002).

Deep elite division and war

For the following decade, Sihanouk managed these challenges. He remained a ceremonial head of state just after independence but then abdicated and ran in the 1955 elections at the head of a royalist party. After a resounding victory, partially due to voter intimidation, he increased his command over power and created, in effect, a one-party kingdom. He imprisoned and sidelined opponents while promoting a policy of peace and neutrality with respect to Cold War politics. His leftist tendencies and relatively low level of repression compared to other authoritarian states contributed to his ability to maintain broad support and prevent the communists from becoming popular (Chandler, 1991).

Yet, escalation of the nearby Vietnam War destabilized the country throughout the 1960s. As violence intensified, Khmer refugees left Vietnam and sought refuge in Cambodia. Cross-border smuggling increased and had devastating consequences on the country's finances. The regime's tightening grip alienated in particular the French-educated, extremist group of communists who had returned to Cambodia and had assumed the leadership of the communist movement. Saloth Sar (later to rename himself Pol Pot), Ieng Sary and Son Sen fled to the jungle to organize mass resistance against the regime. They attracted increasingly disgruntled unemployed, educated youth as well as leftists whom the regime considered to be a growing threat. In 1967, civil war broke out as the renamed Communist Party of Kampuchea (CPK) mounted an insurgency that rapidly escalated. Furthermore, the economy was faltering. Sihanouk was generally disinterested in economic management and so failed to adequately address rising economic problems. Government agricultural credits were insufficient to alleviate farmers' rising debt and available resources failed to help increase yields. Cambodia's main export, rubber, suffered from declining world prices. Light industry rose but remained too small to offset the decline in other sectors. As a result, the economy was in poor shape by the late 1960s. In 1969, the United States began bombing areas of Cambodia where communist Vietnamese troops were hiding (Chandler, 1991; Kiernan, 2002).

Faced with severe threats externally and internally, Sihanouk stepped aside and allowed the head of the armed forces, General Lon Nol, to rule Cambodia. Only a year later, in 1970, opposition to Sihanouk had grown so strong that Lon Nol was forced to stage a coup. The new government suspended a number of civil rights and gradually eliminated parliament and all opposition. Lon Nol's government became deeply imbedded in the Vietnam War that now spilled into Cambodia. It was unable to contain the continuing incursions from across the border. US and South Vietnamese troops provided some support. Yet, Vietnamese communists and the CPK gained increasing control over rural areas. Sihanouk, in the meantime, sided with the communists from his exile in Beijing. The CPK accepted his claims to leadership because of his symbolic appeal but, in reality, he wielded no influence. The CPK needed the Vietnamese communists to make significant advances but a large faction resented Vietnamese control. In Phnom Penh, many Cambodians targeted Vietnamese and forced several thousands to return to Vietnam. As the war reached its final stages, in 1973 Vietnamese troops from both sides withdrew. The CPK intensified its insurgency amid the vacuum of the withdrawal, targeting ethnic Vietnamese, Khmer communists returning from Hanoi and other allies who had collaborated with the Vietnamese. These actions against former allies surprised Vietnamese communists but they had little chance to intervene given their own efforts to gain control over all of Vietnam. The armed wing of the CPK, the Khmer Rouge, seized power amidst the instability on 17 April, 1975 (Chandler, 1991; Kiernan, 2002).

The Khmer Rouge's radical alternative

The Khmer Rouge regime was one of the most brutal authoritarian regimes to have ruled any country in the twentieth century. Motivated by an extremely radical ideology, it sought to destroy Cambodia's past and engineer a new society through repressive means. Upon assuming power, it had emptied the cities of their people and sent them to do forced work in rural areas. Within a few months, it seized land in a massive effort to collectivize agriculture. In the Cambodian context, however, this meant mainly taking away family owned small plots without compensation, which greatly alienated a large portion of the population. Once land had been turned into vast, state-collective farms, the Khmer Rouge regime exported rice to finance itself despite the increasing starvation of hundreds of thousands of people who were relocated to various areas under their forced labour scheme. The regime then closed itself off from the outside world and refused humanitarian aid despite failures to feed its population. By 1979, more than 1.2 million people had died of starvation, disease, overwork or outright execution (Kiernan, 2002).

Its ideology was inspired by Marxist-Leninist principles interpreted through its own assessment of revolutionary experiences elsewhere. For instance, it borrowed from mass mobilization and experiments to purify and renew the population during the Great Leap Forward and the Cultural Revolution in China. It suspended the market economy and adopted the idea of agricultural collectivization that was implemented on a massive scale under Stalin's rule in the Soviet Union. Dubbed the "Super Great Leap Forward", the effort aimed at increasing revenues to create the basis for industrialization but it was done within an incredibly short period of time, and with massive disruption to existing productive systems. Intensive revolutionary fervour inspired the regime's actions, rather than any rational assessment of preconditions for such a revolution to succeed. For instance, it scrapped the use of rice varieties that were adapted to local conditions in favour of uniformity of a single variety for a particular region. It abandoned money, abolished salaried employment and closed down markets. Whole segments of the population that were neither poor peasants nor factory workers were sent to rural areas for re-education and a new beginning (Chandler, 1991).

On the cultural side, the regime regulated all forms of behaviour. It prodded into the details of people's lives to force conformity to its revolutionary objectives and to eliminate those it saw as threats. The regime regulated haircuts, clothing, vocabulary and even leisure. In order to prevent external influences, it severed international connections, including flights and phone calls.

Violence reached a scale that is difficult to fathom. Executions and torture were performed on a large scale in an apparent zeal to purify Cambodia of its enemies. The regime preyed especially on young, influential children from the poorest families who were more easily persuaded to abandon their families and be heavily indoctrinated. These youths were often the most easily manipulated into using extensive violence against the population. At the village level, many of these youths were given much autonomy to interpret the regime's command and punish by death those who disobeyed. When the Vietnamese invaded in 1979, they found few political prisoners. Hundreds of the regime's opponents had been killed rather than imprisoned.

Promises of a new, strong Cambodia inspired thousands of youth, but alienated most of the population. The regime was self-consciously trying a revolutionary experiment that was novel and that would give Cambodia a new status by getting it out of decades of poverty and overcoming its past humiliation at the hands of occupying foreigners. The regime was imbued with a sense of returning to some glorious and pure Cambodian past, while creating a novel society.

The Khmer Rouge's leadership remained mostly hidden. Originally, Prince Sihanouk retained in exile some form of recognized leadership role, although it was only symbolic. He had supported the revolution and had close ties to the communist regimes in China and North Korea, which therefore protected him against Khmer Rouge temptations to eliminate him altogether. When he returned to Cambodia in 1975, he was soon eclipsed. For the following years, he remained mostly confined to his residence and was not seen in public. As for the true leadership of the regime, it maintained an aura of mystery and secrecy by issuing commands through various channels but not revealing themselves. Pol Pot (Saloth Sar), the Khmer Rouge leader who held a despotic command over the Communist Party and the country, remained known only as "Brother Number One" as part of what was called "the Organization" (Chandler, 1991).

Vietnamese-supported regime, civil war and United Nations intervention

In 1979, the Vietnamese invaded Cambodia and removed the Khmer Rouge from power. The Khmer Rouge had targeted ethnic Vietnamese and other minorities in particular as it sought to purge the country of foreign influences. Its staunch anti-Vietnamese stance created tensions with its powerful neighbour. As the genocide against Cambodians persisted, the Vietnamese toppled the Khmer Rouge government and seized control of the country.

Surprisingly, despite its horrible treatment of Cambodians, the Khmer Rouge was supported externally. China had supported the Khmer Rouge, in part for ideological reasons and in part because Sihanouk had created links to the Chinese regime while supporting the Khmer Rouge revolution. China also had developed significant tensions with the communist regime in Vietnam so it was inclined to support the Khmer Rouge as the latter distanced themselves from Vietnam and even proceeded to purge Vietnamese from Cambodian territory. The United States supported the Khmer Rouge as well because of its own suspicion and acrimony directed at communist Vietnam. Countries of the Association of Southeast Asian Nations (ASEAN) sided with the United States and could not condone the invasion of a sovereign country in Southeast Asia, as it might create a dangerous precedent in the region. As a result, these powers continued to recognize the Khmer Rouge as the official regime. Its representatives continued to sit at the United Nations for the following twelve years (Kiernan, 2002).

The Vietnamese-controlled regime renamed the country the People's Republic of Kampuchea. The leadership was Cambodian but Vietnamese troops remained until 1989. Heng Samrin led the government until 1985 when Hun Sen, previously foreign minister, succeeded him as prime minister. Although it largely contributed to restoring stability and reconstructing the economy, the regime was discredited as a Vietnamese puppet.

In the meantime, Cambodian exiles and the Khmer Rouge attempted to gain support to dislodge the Vietnamese-supported regime. Sihanouk had supported the Khmer Rouge from his exile in Beijing after Lon Nol ousted him in 1970. He had kept his distance during its years in power but then resumed his cooperation after 1982. He formed a new coalition government in exile called the "Coalition Government of Democratic Kampuchea (CGDK)". The Khmer Rouge dominated the coalition, while Sihanouk and anti-communist parties were junior partners. Sihanouk nevertheless was the CGDK's leader and gave legitimacy to the continued presence of the Khmer Rouge at the United Nations (Kiernan, 2002).

The Vietnamese-led government was not sustainable, and pressure mounted for an internationally brokered agreement to orchestrate a withdrawal and the establishment of a new government in Cambodia. International negotiations began in 1988 under an initiative involving Southeast Asian governments but were expanded and moved to Paris in 1989 as major powers became involved. With China's support, the Khmer Rouge could not be sidelined. Pol Pot used the opportunity to reorganize his military force and regain a strong presence in the countryside, as Vietnamese forces began to withdraw. A successful agreement depended, then, on Khmer Rouge cooperation to be effective. As a result, attempts repeatedly failed to bring the Khmer Rouge to justice, to condemn the genocide in UN bodies, or even to include its mention or adherence to the UN Convention on the Prevention and Punishment of Crimes of Genocide in the final agreement that was reached in October 1991. It would take almost two more decades before any Khmer Rouge member was taken to trial for crimes committed during its brutal regime (Kiernan, 2002).

The United Nations Transitional Authority in Cambodia (UNTAC) supervised the organization of elections and the formation of a new government. It stayed from November 1991 to September 1993. The elections, and the formation of the new government, were fraught with potential instability. Civil war continued as the Khmer Rouge refused to participate in the process or to demobilize its troops. It rejected the UN cease-fire despite benefiting from protections under the Paris agreement on Cambodia. It continued to expand its control over rural areas and boycotted the 1993 elections. Nevertheless, an election was organized and a new, power-sharing arrangement was crafted. In spite of the fact that the royalist FUNCINPEC party won 45 per cent of the vote against the Cambodian People's Party (CPP) who won 38 per cent, the new government formed a power-sharing coalition that included two prime ministers as well as equal representation within the ministries. FUNCINPEC agreed to the arrangement.

Fragile power-sharing: CPP dominance under unstable coalition

The new government was never able to stabilize. Most importantly, Hun Sen's CPP continued to control large portions of the state's institutions. Hun Sen had been the prime minister of the

Vietnamese-controlled government until 1991. FUNCINPEC agreed to power sharing under the CPP's threat of withholding its needed support for the adoption of a new constitution and under the threat of being destabilized by disgruntled soldiers loyal to the CPP. When forty top military and police offers arrived at the palace to convince Sihanouk of the need for reconciliation and unity, there seemed to be little choice (Roberts, 2007).

The rewards and spoils of power were part of the problem. The CPP, which had previously dominated the single-party state, now was expected to share state resources with coalition partners. Members of FUNCINPEC jockeyed for positions and favour with party leader Norodom Ranariddh, King Sihanouk's son. Bribes to obtain these posts and gain access to patronage funds were rampant (Roberts, 2007).

FUNCINPEC sought to integrate a large number of its supporters to the state's apparatus, while the CPP was reluctant to give up its positions. As a result, rather than create an efficient state apparatus, the state instead grew larger to absorb FUNCINPEC representatives into the civil service, police and military, while the CPP preserved its clientelist base. There was no clear logic in the allocation of state positions and resources other than political support and corruption (Roberts, 2007).

The CPP was a much better organized party than FUNCINPEC or any other opposition party. During its years in power, it had built up a strong network and its influence was deep in rural areas. FUNCINPEC was never able to build strong linkages to the rural population, as its leaders were essentially self-interested and incapable of reaching out to the masses.

The façade of stable relations between the main players hinged largely on the two top leaders, Ranariddh and Hun Sen. By 1996, they were openly confrontational as Ranariddh accused Hun Sen of various misdeeds, while the latter threatened to bring down the power-sharing arrangement. In the following year, tensions escalated further as Ranariddh sought support from the now outlawed Khmer Rouge, and recreated the alliance of the 1980s. Ranariddh also smuggled weapons in an attempt to build a sufficiently strong army to confront Hun Sen's well-organized forces (Roberts, 2007).

It became evident that the reality of the "peaceful" transition was that there had been no transition at all. Hun Sen and the CPP remained in control of Cambodia while they essentially paid lip-service to the shared government with FUNCINPEC. Hun Sen launched an internal coup and seized formal power in 1997 as tensions remained high (McCargo, 2005a).

Elections thereafter simply reaffirmed Hun Sen's grip on power with no actual transfer of power to FUNCINPEC or other parties. The 1998 elections as well as the 2003 elections were essentially "political theater", as Duncan McCargo (2005a) writes, designed to give Hun Sen and the CPP legitimacy. At the ballot box, the CPP improved its performance largely because of intimidation in rural areas. In 2003, it took more than a year before a new government was formed. Opposition parties seriously attempted to form a coalition that could prevent the CPP from remaining in power but they failed. Opposition parties remained more loosely organized than the CPP, and lacked strong leadership. Sihanouk, who had created FUNCINPEC, often ended up supporting the CPP and Hun Sen after he was given a ceremonial position as head of state after 1993. In the end, the weakness of the opposition continued to ensure that the CPP still remained dominant. FUNCINPEC had decided to join a two-party coalition reportedly with an agreement that gave its leader, Ranariddh, substantial rewards. The effect was to further divide opposition parties, now that some of its members chose to side with the CPP government (McCargo, 2005a).

The 2008 election consequently saw an even greater consolidation of the CPP's power. The CPP won 58 per cent of the popular vote, which translated into 90 of the 123 seats in Cambodia's parliament. No longer did it suffer delays in forming a government, as it had for over a year in 2003 and at least six months in 1998. Instead, it formed a government with two deputies of FUNCINPEC but now controlled all ministerial positions, committees of the National Assembly and other key positions. FUNCINPEC and other opposition parties were decimated. During the years preceding the election, the government had launched defamation lawsuits against FUNCINPEC and the Sam Rainsy Party, another opposition party. Individuals from these parties, as well as the media and trade union, were imprisoned. FUNCINPEC lost much of its support as it split into two rival parties. Together, they won only four seats. Other opposition parties did better. The Sam Rainsy Party gained two more seats from its twenty-four in 2003 and some new parties also made some gains. Even their combined victories, however, paled in comparison to the CPP's dominance (Hughes, 2009).

Table 10 *Cambodia*

Population (rank)	Land area (rank)	Main ethnic groups (%)	Main religions (%)	Regime type (transition)	GDP per capita (rank)	GDP growth rate (%) (rank)
14 952 665 (67th) (July 2012 est.)	176 515 sq km (89th)	Khmer 90 Vietnamese 5 Chinese 1 Other 4	Buddhist (official) 96.4 Muslim 2.1 Other 1.3 Unspecified 0.2 (1998 census)	Authoritarian Multiparty Competitive authoritarian regime under a constitutional monarchy	$2 300 (185th) (2011 est.)	6.7 (30th) (2011 est.)

Source: CIA, *The World Factbook*; Polity IV Project, Polity IV Individual Country Regime Trends, 1946–2010.

The CPP has increased its power by strengthening its leverage over local governments and by overseeing a booming economy. It organized elections for common chiefs and councils (local level government) in which the CPP had a strong advantage over less well organized parties. As a result, the CPP built up a massive network at the local level that could be used as leverage at the time of the national election. Local officials transformed patronage and administrative control into a successful electoral machine for the CPP in the 2008 elections. Furthermore, the Cambodian economy grew by an average of 11 per cent annually after 2005 and until the global financial crisis of 2008. The boom came in part from the rapid expansion of the private banking sector, increased investment from Cambodian sources and foreign direct investment mainly from China, South Korea and Thailand. Growth was primarily concentrated in the agricultural and mining sectors. The ability of the regime to divert some of this new wealth into the electoral machine also served to strengthen the CPP's success at the polls (Hughes, 2009).

It is too early for the recent economic growth to have had any impact on middle-class formation. Where some benefits have accrued to the large population, they have served to give the regime some additional support. The regime has also been able to finance some of its patronage and thereby strengthen loyalty to the CPP. Given the CPP's institutional strength, and network established during the previous communist period, it has been able to consolidate the pro-CCP elite's power against the competing royalist elite around FUNCINPEC. In theory, such division should be conducive at least to maintaining electoral competition but the CPP's power has largely overrun FUNCINPEC and other opponents, giving it the upper hand and allowing the maintenance of the authoritarian regime.

Laos

Laos has remained authoritarian throughout its modern history. After independence in 1953, Laos' politics were very divided but became more stable after 1975 when, at the end of the Vietnam War, the Communist Party of Laos overthrew the ruling government. Since then, the Lao People's Revolutionary Party (LPRP) has officially governed the state under a communist regime. Beginning in 1986, some reforms were introduced along the same lines as Vietnam. Economic reforms allowed for more private sector investment but there has still been very little political change.

Laos resembles Cambodia's path as the elite became deeply divided between royalist and communist groups. It differs as both parties attempted and briefly agreed to form coalition governments, as their forces were fairly equal after independence. Yet, instead of providing a democratic framework for competition, coalition building involved authoritarian power-sharing and agreement on each side to control different parts of Laos' territory. After the Vietnam War, however, power tipped in favour of the communist Pathet Lao, supported by communist Vietnam. Since then, the communist government has maintained tight control over Laos.

By doing so, the communist regime eventually created a unified elite. It followed the Vietnamese path in institutionalizing party rule and extending its presence at all levels of society. The armed forces also played a central role. In fact, top military officers have occupied the highest position in the state in the last decade or so. As a result, party dominance is backed up by strong unity of purpose among the armed forces.

As a poor country, mainly agrarian and with little industrialization, urbanization or sustained high levels of economic growth, Laos has not developed a significant middle class or alternative power groups that could challenge communist party dominance. Economic reforms since the mid 1980s have allowed the regime to maintain some degree of well-being for its broader population but not to the extent of creating a wealthy class that could challenge the existing regime. Instead, the ruling elite with ties to the party have reaped most of the benefits from reform. Consequently, economic reforms have strengthened elite unity rather than stimulated greater opposition.

As with Cambodia, Laos' political status has been influenced by regional and international trends. From 1945–54, the Lao government remained under French influence. After 1954, no single party was able to establish its dominance. The country was divided between competing forces that drew their respective strength from Cold War foes. The communist Pathet Lao remained very close to the Vietnamese communist party that sponsored its creation. Anti-communist groups and the Lao Royal Army benefited from US backing. This chaotic period resulted as much from internal divisions as from Cold War competition among communist powers and the United States for influence in the region. This tension was only resolved with the US retreat after its defeat in the Vietnam War. The Pathet Lao, sponsored by the victorious Vietnamese Communist Party, could then establish full control. For the following decades, Laos' government remained closely tied to the Vietnamese communists. Its decision to introduce market reforms emulated Vietnam's own Doi Moi, and resulted in part from Vietnamese influence.

The rise of deep elite divisions

The modern state of Laos was born out of the ashes of the French colonial empire. The Lao people were divided after the French-Siamese treaty of 1893, which gave French control of Laotian territory east of the Mekong River but left territories west of the river to the Siamese. The much-reduced territory of Laos was then integrated into the broader French colony of Indochina. Independence was achieved when the French abandoned their Southeast Asian journey and left behind a French-appointed, newly independent government.

Nationalist and communist movements were slow to emerge. Despite very active ones in other parts of Indochina, namely in Vietnam, a Lao nationalist movement did not emerge until the 1940s. Similarly, before the Second World War, virtually no Lao were members of the Indochinese Communist Party. Interest in communism only grew, along with nationalist objectives, when the French attempted to reimpose their colonial order after the War (Stuart-Fox, 1986).

In support of the French, the king initially proclaimed the re-establishment of the protectorate, and organized a provisional government, but the latter failed to impose its authority. Instead, the territory and its governance became divided between competing forces without a clear winner. The king had maintained some status under French colonial occupation, although he had been stripped of much real power. Yet, the new government formed a provisional constitution, eventually reinstated the king as a constitutional monarch and formed a government known as the Lao Issara (Free Laos). The Lao Issara was only briefly in power, but it laid the basis for resistance organizations to be formed. When the French regained their dominance over Laos in 1946, the Lao Issara forces retreated and the government fled in exile in Thailand. From its base in Thailand, Lao Issara leaders attempted to negotiate independence but failed repeatedly to find a solution. One of them, Souphanouvong, instead advocated for closer relations with the communist Viet Minh, and their efforts to remove the French from Vietnam. In 1950, he organized with Ho Chi Minh and the Viet Minh's help the first Congress of People's Representation of the "Lao Resistance Front". This Congress created a Lao resistance government which it named *Pathet Lao* (of the Land of the Lao). Pathet Lao became the common name for the communist movement. Souphanouvong was made prime minister of this government, which organized a broad resistance front against the French, in collaboration with the Vietnamese communists. Between 1950 and 1953, the Viet Minh coordinated the resistance front in all of Indochina, leading to French defeat in 1954. By the end of French colonial rule, therefore, Laos was already divided among royalist and communist groups.

The 1954 Conference on Indochina met in Geneva to negotiate the post-colonial order but opposing forces only temporarily agreed to form a coalition. The Pathet Lao, in control of large areas of northern Laos, demanded a role in the new government. The Royal Lao government, which had been reconstituted from former allies of the king, reluctantly accepted to form a coalition with the Pathet Lao in 1957.

With the Cold War in full swing, the alliance was short lived. The United States supported more anti-communist factions with the ruling group, which turned against the Pathet Lao shortly after the 1958 elections. The Pathet Lao had run in elections under the banner of the Lao Patriotic Front (LPF). By 1959, the Royal Lao Army had banned the LPF's newspapers and arrested its representatives in the National Assembly. The Pathet Lao subsequently continued to operate clandestinely. As Martin Stuart-Fox notes, ironically the Democratic Republic of Vietnam (DRV), China and the Soviet Union had been ready to accept a neutral Laos with the communist Pathet Lao as part of a broader coalition, but with American and anti-communist Lao forces unwilling to accept this compromise the subsequent years became confrontational. Elections in 1960, rigged with the help of the American CIA, confirmed the rightists' seizure of power. The Committee for Defence of National Interests (CDNI), which the Lao Royal Army backed, formed the new government (Stuart-Fox, 1986).

For the following decade, Laos was part of the battleground against the spread of communism in the Southeast Asian peninsula, which continued to divide the Laotian political elite. The competing forces were sufficiently equal in strength that they continued to replace each other in brief, unstable governments. The CDNI government was short-lived. Kong Le, a young captain, launched a successful coup, and reinstated a more moderate government. Former Prime Minister Souvanna Phouma accepted the top position once again and reopened talks with the Pathet Lao. Shortly thereafter, the right-wing CDNI again gained power, sending Kong Le and Phouma's government into retreat. The latter obtained support from the communist bloc while the United States and its allies backed the return of the CDNI. While more attempts were made to broker a new coalition government, the Vietnam War reduced the neutralists' influence and deepened the gulf separating communist and non-communist powers. By 1965, the country was effectively divided into two separate zones: the Pathet Lao ran its own government in areas under its control, while the Royal Lao Government controlled the capital, with US support.

Laos was subjected to intense bombing campaigns and heavy involvement of the Democratic Republic of Vietnam and the United States. When the United States began in 1972 to negotiate a withdrawal from Vietnam, negotiations were broadened to include Laos. For the next few years, a new broad coalition appeared feasible. Yet, with communist parties seizing full control of Vietnam and Cambodia, the Pathet Lao was increasingly in a position of strength. Eager to consolidate its power and strengthen relations with Vietnam, in December 1975 the Pathet Lao abandoned compromise, forced the abdication of King Savang Vathana, abolished the six-century old monarchy, and replaced it instead with the Lao People's Democratic Republic (LPDR).

The consolidation of the LPDR regime

The new regime quickly moved to consolidate its power. The Lao People's Revolutionary Party (LPRP), which had operated underground until then, created new structures across Laos, while officials and security personnel of the former Royal Lao government were sent to re-education camps. Armed with new slogans and with the party's support, young cadres ran in village elections and displaced village elders. Although there were few security threats from opposition groups, the LPRP imposed strict measures to control freedom and movement.

In the economic realm, the implementation of communist policies was elusive. Eager to resolve the crisis left behind by the war's massive destruction and displacement, the LPRP swiftly implemented state controls. It regulated prices, nationalized industries, eliminated markets and replaced them with state-run stores and marketing cooperatives. By 1978, the regime decided to implement rapidly a programme of collectivization of agriculture. Yet, these reforms deepened rather than resolved Laos' economic problems. Peasants refused to cooperate with the planned collectivization so yields decreased markedly. Thousands of Laotian refugees crossed the border into Thailand. In 1976–7 around 38,000 people had left, mainly Laos' technocratic and professional middle class. In 1978, 50,000 Lao peasants also left. In 1979, the crisis was sufficiently bad that both the Soviet and Vietnamese communist governments advised Laos' leaders to abandon collectivization and its stringent economic policies.

The LPRP dramatically shifted its strategy. Collectivization was abandoned, markets were re-established. Private production was encouraged, as was productivity and profit to increase state enterprises' efficiency. By the end of 1980, rice production had already risen. Ambitious new targets were set for agriculture, industrialization and infrastructure. Yet, these targets were difficult to achieve. In the end, growth rates varied considerably during the 1980s, and production targets failed to reach their published levels. Some of the problems were generic to communist systems, even with the increased liberalization of various economic sectors. But Laos also had some significant deficiencies: it had lost much of its skilled workforce, had little technical expertise and remained dependent on the Vietnamese economy. Most of the government's budget for large development projects depended on aid from the Soviet Union and Vietnam (Stuart-Fox, 1986).

When the French left in 1953, Laos was an agrarian economy. The French had developed very little industry or even infrastructure, except for 5,000 kilometres of bad roads. Ninety per cent of Laos' population worked in subsistence farming. In comparison to other Southeast Asian countries, it was one of the poorest and least developed. Three decades later, industry still represented only 7 per cent of Laos' economy. Periods of development had been interrupted by political instability and war. The communist regime after 1975 had failed to improve conditions. In the mid 1980s, therefore, Laos' economy still remained primarily agricultural, with 85 per cent of its population practicing subsistence farming, with few modern fertilizers or new technologies for rice production.

Economic reform and regime stability

Economic reforms were deepened after 1986 but the political system remained unchanged. The same year, Vietnam had launched its "Doi Moi" (renovation) system and Laos followed in its steps. It began to introduce a market economy and to attract foreign investment. As a result, urban areas began to grow much more rapidly. Foreign investment led to rapid urbanization and a growing gap between urban and rural areas. Prior to 1999, the main source of household income was foreign remittances (28 per cent compared to only 22 per cent from agriculture), as the large number of Laotians who left after 1975 sent money home to support relatives. After 2000, however, these remittances diminished rapidly as relatives became more concerned about sending money back to Laos, and wealth increased. Urban areas have continued to profit from foreign investments but rural areas remain behind. At the same time, they are poorly equipped for population growth, with still limited and poor infrastructure. Finally, unemployment is high as many people migrate from rural areas (Lintner, 2008).

Despite a new direction in economic policy after 1986, the political system has remained relatively intact. As in other communist systems, the Politburo of the Communist Party (the LPRP) remains most powerful and, at the apex, the Communist Party leader. For most of the post-independence period, Kaysone Phomvihane was the paramount leader, holding the positions of general secretary of the LPRP and prime minister until 1991, and then president after the introduction that year of a new constitution. The 1991 Constitution introduced new political institutions, such as a National Assembly. Yet, the LPRP clearly remained in control. Only members of the LPRP could run in the elections, and party organizations screened all candidates before they were allowed to participate. After Kaysone's death in 1992, Khamtai Siphandone acceded to the position of party chairman and prime minister. Khamtai was a former commander-in-chief of the Pathet Lao. Under his leadership, a greater number of generals began to accede to the top positions in government and the party. For instance, Senior

Table 11 *Laos*

Population (rank)	Land area (rank)	Main ethnic groups (%)	Main religions	Regime type (transition)	GDP per capita (rank)	GDP growth rate (%) (rank)
6 586 266 (102nd) (2011 est.)	230 800 sq km (83rd)	Lao 55˙ Khmou 11 Hmong 8 Other 26 (over 100 minor ethnic groups) (2005 census)	Buddhist 67 Christian 1.5 Other/unspecified 31.5 (2005 census)	Authoritarian (−1974)[a] Communist state	$2 700 (175th) (2011 est.)	8.3 (9th) (2011 est.)

Source: CIA, *The World Factbook*; Polity IV Project, Polity IV Individual Country Regime Trends, 1946–2010.
[a] The year indicates the most recent transition; (+) means a transition towards democracy and (−) denotes a transition towards authoritarianism.

Lieutenant General Choummali Saignason became minister of national defence and also chairman of the LPRP in 2006. Overall, the LPRP remained firmly in control of all levels of decision making (Dommen, 1994).

Nevertheless, the party has also had internal divisions. The LPRP maintained tight relations with the Vietnamese Communist Party from the days of the Pathet Laos' close relations to Ho Chi Minh, and the Vietnamese fight against the French and the Americans. Some members of the LPRP had been critical of Kaysone's promotion of closer relations with the West, Japan and Thailand. They preferred Laos to be more closed. Although its role was not entirely clear, the VCP appeared to play a key role in helping the LPRP to maintain its unity. Certainly, the presence of Vietnamese troops until 1989 and subsequent reaffirmation of the close friendship between both countries suggested an important Vietnamese influence in Laos' internal affairs (Dommen, 1994).

The group of mostly military men who have controlled Laos since 1996 has proceeded cautiously. They have been reluctant to push much faster the economic reforms that have already been implemented. In the political realm, they have preferred the status quo. When Khamtai and other older, top party members stepped down in 2006, power remained firmly in the hands of military leaders, many of whom were still part of the revolutionary generation. General Choummali Saignason obtained the position of party chairman as well as president of the LPDR. Opposition has been limited as the LPDR has maintained strong control over the whole political system.

International and regional factors strongly affected Cambodia's and Laos' political trajectories. The Vietnam War was one of the Cold War's key battlegrounds, as the United States feared the victory of communist forces in Vietnam might create a domino effect throughout Southeast Asia. They were right in both Laos and Cambodia but with a more complicated twist in the latter. The Pathet Lao won against its opponents and consolidated their regime in 1975 with support from Vietnamese communists. In Cambodia, external support for the communist movement had fuelled a nationalist reaction, as anti-Vietnamese sentiments inspired the Khmer Rouge's xenophobic rhetoric and ideological programme. They could capitalize on chaos from the end of the War and the void of the US retreat to seize power. In the end, however, Vietnam's influence was determinant once it forcibly removed the Khmer Rouge regime and replaced it with its own. Finally, external factors again played a decisive role when the United Nations brokered an end to the civil war that pitted the Vietnamese-backed communist government against pro-Sihanouk royalists and the ousted but still strong Khmer Rouge.

Elites in both countries were deeply divided along ideological lines after independence. While common during the Cold War, its impact was most significant where divisions created groups with relatively equal strength. In Cambodia, groups splintered among royalists, Khmer Rouge and pro-Vietnamese communist forces. Every government faced powerful opponents who used armed resistance and destabilized existing regimes. Only in recent years, with the demise of the Khmer Rouge, has the current regime been able to extend its dominance. Royalists remained opposed to the Hun Sen government but the depth of the divisions is less since the regime has been less tied to the Vietnamese government, royalists have been weaker, yet have benefited from some of the spoils of power from remaining in a coalition with Hun Sen's Cambodian People's Party. In Laos, elites were deeply divided between the communist Pathet Lao and royalist forces, and even thwarted the ability of any group to control all of the territory until 1975. With the victory of the Pathet Lao, however, and the elimination of the pro-royalist group, the current elite consolidated within the current communist regime. Deep division was conducive to instability and war, while this recent consolidation solidified the Laotian communist regime. In Cambodia, however, elite unity is significantly weak and maintained primarily through the greater organizational strength of the communist-like CPP regime and sharing of spoils with its opponents. Although elections are held, they are highly skewed and liberties associated with democracy remain limited.

Economic development and growth have progressed in both countries but not sufficiently to stimulate political change. The persistence of communist and authoritarian regimes in Cambodia and Laos are consistent with theoretical propositions regarding the effects of economic development and its impact on the middle class. Both countries are poorer than most other countries in the region. While economic reforms have stimulated greater growth rates in the last decade, living standards remain well below those of other Southeast Asian countries. Similarly, while the middle class has begun to grow more significantly, it has yet to reach the size or breadth found elsewhere. Finally, as with the case of Vietnam, to the extent that the existing middle class owes its wealth and status to the regime in power, as clearly is the case in Laos and to a lesser extent in Cambodia, it is unlikely to become a powerful force for change in the near future.

8 | *Burma/Myanmar*

Since 1962, a military regime has dominated Burma. It has used repression extensively, while attempting to reinvent itself a few times to gain some legitimacy. The stability of authoritarian rule requires explanation. More often than not, it is very difficult for authoritarian regimes to justify their rule and maintain control by force. Instead, they seek to justify their existence by appealing to exceptional circumstances, to promises of a better society, or to the need to defend the state against internal or external threats. Burma's military regime, under the Burmese Socialist Programme Party (BSPP) sought to create its own vision of a Burmese road to socialism. After failing to reach its goals, and after a crisis in 1988 that nearly led to its collapse, it reinvented itself as the State Law and Order Restoration Council (SLORC), which began a period of much more unapologetic military rule designed to forestall and prevent a reoccurrence of political instability. With only a minor change in its designation in 1997 as the State Peace and Development Council (SPDC), the regime essentially maintained its iron-first approach to political opposition until 2010. Under a new constitution, the junta has ceded control to a civilian government but the pace and extent of change remains uncertain.

Prior to 1962, Burma enjoyed almost ten years of democratic politics. At the outset, it was a promising country, given its vibrant political system and relatively rich economic base. Yet, instability and political crisis eroded its potential. The democratic regime never managed to consolidate itself. Despite promising economic development, low levels of urbanization and not much of a middle class provided little structural support for the fragile democracy. At the same time, divisions were deep along ethnic lines, as minority areas had been kept completely separate under British colonial rule. Their sudden inclusion in a state strongly dominated by the majority Burman group proved difficult. Furthermore, regional instability contributed to the new democracy's demise. The new government had difficulties protecting its territorial integrity as pro-Republic Chinese soldiers fled China after the 1949 victory of the Communist Party, and flowed into Burma. This instability set the stage for the 1962 coup.

Why was the military-dominated regime so resilient? First, Burma's authoritarian regime lasted longer than other military-led regimes in part because its foundations also lay on a dominant party. Initially, the military created the BSPP, adopted an ideological programme and strongly repressed opponents. It built up the military's strength while attempting to expand the BSPP's network. Once the BSPP was later dissolved in the late 1980s, the military had become sufficiently powerful and its network sufficiently broad to keep strong control. Second, elite unity became very strong as the military nurtured loyalty through its expansion, benefits to soldiers and patrimonial linkages. Privileges flowed to officers and businesses tied to the regime. Its institutions were solidified in the early years of the regime and therefore maintained their strength even through periods of crisis.

Low economic growth and a relatively small middle class prevented the rise of effective challengers. As in other cases, low economic growth and economic development can severely weaken a regime but it also prevents the development of a larger middle class. In Burma's case, the regime's initial policies based on autarchy and its own brand of socialism destroyed the economy's foundations and bred crisis. The regime made some minor adjustments but not sufficient to prevent further economic and financial crisis that threatened regime stability by the mid 1980s. After the 1988 demonstrations and political instability that ensued, the regime abandoned some of its dogmatic economic policies and attempted to reap benefits from some foreign investment and exposure to foreign markets. Successive economic crises threatened the regime but did not result in its collapse. A small middle class did arise, in spite of slow economic growth, and its role became very important during the 1988 demonstrations and their aftermath. Yet, it lacked sufficient strength and sustained allies among the broader population to exert sufficient pressure for political change, especially given the elite unity and institutional strength of the regime.

Nevertheless, the regime proceeded with some unilateral change in 2010. It moved away from a clearly military regime to a civilian one, a new constitution and attempts to broaden participation. Elections allowed the opposition National League for Democracy to obtain some seats. Most of new government's leaders were from the previous regime but they left their military positions and ruled as civilians. Sustained pressure from the opposition, particularly of its popular Nobel Peace Prize Laureate Daw Aung San Suu Kyi, could in the end have yielded some effect. More importantly, external factors were probably most significant. Because of its poor human rights record, the United States, European countries and several other countries maintained economic sanctions for several years, which began to place a strain on the economy. It is likely that to prevent the rise of another crisis, the regime chose to introduce some minor changes while maintaining full control of the pace of change and its wealth of privileges.

Democratic rule, 1948–1962

Burma's new democracy was vibrant but faced many challenges. Its constitution established a British-style parliamentary democracy. Elections led to the formation of a strong, popular government. Yet, internal and external challenges soon emerged. Burma's quest to create a strong, unified nation clashed with ethnic minorities' aspirations for recognition of their identities and accommodation of their desire for self-rule. These problems were compounded by external shocks related to Cold War politics.

Parliament was composed of two chambers: the Chamber of Deputies and the Chamber of Nationalities. Legislative power resided primarily in the former. The latter departed somewhat from British-style parliamentary institutions as it was designed to represent ethnic groups and the class structure of society, while formally representing Burma's states. Burma was named a Union, based on the objective of creating one united Burmese nation. At the same time, the constitution espoused some federalist principles. Each state except Burma Proper[1] was governed by a head of state and a state council, but members of the council were also required to be members of the Union parliament.

One party, the Anti-Fascist People's Freedom League (AFPFL), dominated Burma's political landscape during the first decade. It was formed originally as a resistance movement against the Japanese occupation. After the Second World War, under the leadership of Aung

[1] "Burma Proper" was the region known as Burma during British colonial rule, and primarily populated by Burmans. "Outer Burma" comprised mainly highland areas populated by ethnic minorities. They were administered separately.

San, the AFPFL organized against the returning British and sought independence. When Aung San was assassinated at the eve of independence in 1947, he was hailed as a martyr and remained hugely popular. In the first elections held in 1951–2, the AFPFL won overwhelmingly as it still enjoyed strong support for leading Burma to independence. While it retained such a following in the 1956 elections, its cohesion and popularity declined thereafter.

In spite of its strength, the AFPFL eventually split over personal conflicts as well as strains caused by rising threats to Burma's stability. U Nu had succeeded Aung San as leader of the AFPFL and became prime minister after independence. His role was dominant as he took part in every major Cabinet decision and maintained strong oversight over his Cabinet ministers. The latter were generally weak as key members of the AFPFL's executive often played more influential roles than Cabinet ministers. Factionalism divided the party and eventually caused a split in 1958 as the strains became untenable. U Nu maintained control over one part, which became the Clean AFPFL, while his rivals Ba Swe (who held briefly the position of prime minister in 1956–7) and Kyaw Nyein established the Stable AFPFL.

External threats and internal instability exacerbated tensions. Burma's borders were relatively porous and vulnerable. After communist forces established China's People's Republic in 1949, some republican troops of the Kuomintang fled into Burma's northern territory. Muslim insurgents also created instability along the border with East Pakistan. Some ethnic minorities also rebelled to obtain their own state and right to secession.

Ethnic rebellion was one of Burma's most significant challenges. The 1947 Constitution did not assign equal rights to different states and ethnic groups. It conferred upon the Kayah and Shan states a right to secession that could be exercised after 1958. The Kachin state was denied such right. The Chin were given a Special Division so therefore could not claim to be a state, while the Karen were denied any special status. The Karen organized armed resistance as early as 1949. While they obtained a state under the constitutional amendment of 1951, they failed to obtain a similar right to secession and continued the rebellion. Finally, the Arakanese and Mon also wanted their own state but their request fuelled further tensions.

Combined with the AFPFL split, these threats prompted Prime Minister U Nu in 1958 to ask the military for help. The two factions disagreed over the appropriate approach to ethnic minorities and to the security crisis. Once the AFPLF split, parliament was strongly divided. U Nu faced an impasse as he expected parliament to defeat his budget. He fuelled further criticism with his attempt to overstep his powers by asking the Union president to promulgate the budget without a parliamentary vote. Rather than face defeat, U Nu turned to General Ne Win, the armed forces commander, and asked him to form a caretaker government.

The caretaker government began to play a more significant role than anticipated, so U Nu became increasingly critical of its policies. Ne Win named a Cabinet of members that were not affiliated with the political parties, in order to establish a more neutral government. At the same time, however, he adopted a national ideology that gave the military a key role. The government hailed the goals of a socialist economy, law and order, as well as democracy. In minority areas, it reneged on the Panglong Agreement of 1947, which had allowed minority ethnic groups to continue governing themselves through traditional institutions. The caretaker government pressured local chiefs and princes to give up power in favour of elected leaders, particularly in the Shan and Kayah states. Some minority areas were placed under the authority of a special administrative body to maintain stability. These policies contributed to restoring security but created controversy.

As the end of the caretaker government's six-month term approached, Ne Win began to request an extension of its mandate. Yet, U Nu was highly critical of its policies. He was also irritated by its support for the rival Stable AFPFL. Elections were therefore called in 1960 to form a new, democratic government. U Nu campaigned on making Buddhism a religion of state. He also promised states for ethnic minorities who did not yet have one. His party won very comfortably as the Stable AFPFL was decimated. U Nu returned to power victoriously but problems were far from resolved (Silverstein, 1977).

The 1962 coup and the military regime

The 1962 military coup ended democracy in Burma, and began one of the longest lasting authoritarian regimes in the world. The caretaker government's brief term gave the military the taste of power and a glimpse of its abilities to rule alone. Burma's problems, in the meantime, were not resolved so the elected government continued to face instability.

The military justified its coup as deepening the revolutionary impulse begun at independence. Coup leaders in many countries justify their actions as temporary responses to particular crises. While the Burmese armed forces did cite continued instability, it then shifted its rhetoric to announce more concrete ideological objectives and institutional transformations. Socialism had been one of the AFPFL's objectives. The military, which cast itself as a defender of the Union and an important actor leading up to independence, then proposed a plan to implement socialism and transform Burmese society.

The path to Burma's transformation was spelled out in "The Burmese Way to Socialism". The military's socialist ideologues defined its ideology as distinctive to Burma's conditions. Although Marxism provided some inspiration, other sources also did, including Buddhism. The ideological foundations sought to build on Burma's anti-colonial movement and traditions, rather than reject and replace them. The military claimed to represent all Burmese people, rather than only the working class or peasants as other communist regimes did. At the same time, it spelled out a plan for deep transformations. Political institutions were to be replaced in order to implement a socialist democracy. Almost all sectors of the economy, including agriculture, industrial production, distribution and external trade would be nationalized. The regime's approach resembled in many aspects some of the deep, ideologically driven projects occurring elsewhere in the communist world but remained on its own path.

Political power resided in the Revolutionary Council and the Burmese Socialist Programme Party (BSPP). Ne Win dominated the small Revolutionary Council composed of top military officers. Council members had close personal ties to Ne Win, who swiftly dismissed or sidelined allies when disputes arose. The Revolutionary Council ruled with few restrictions. Yet, in order to bolster its legitimacy, the regime created the BSPP in 1962. The BSPP was tasked with implementing "The Burmese Way to Socialism". In its first decade, it was structured as a cadre party. It recruited members along functional lines (in factories, administrative units, military units etc.). Members were trained to assist the government in implementing its programme and ideology. During this phase, BSPP membership remained very small and composed of carefully selected people who were highly supportive of the regime and committed to pursuing its goals.

The implementation of the regime's economic policies resulted in chaos, confusion and decline. Firms in several sectors were nationalized in the first few years of the regime. Military personnel replaced private managers, assets were seized and partnerships between the government and the private sector were abolished. As a result, prices rose, shortages abounded and a black market for basic commodities rapidly grew. The government fixed wages, tried to manage supplies and prices but ultimately urban areas suffered from high inflation and confusion. In rural areas, the state seized ownership of the land and forced peasants to sell their harvest at low prices in order to subsidize urban areas. Peasants' welfare suffered and they lacked incentives to increase production. They tended instead to produce only what was sufficient to meet their family's needs. As a result, the economy steadily declined and Burma became increasingly impoverished (Silverstein, 1977).

The regime virtually closed off Burma from the outside world. Not only were foreign firms seized and nationalized but even foreign missionaries and aid organizations were asked to leave. The regime expelled thousands of Indians most of whom were descendants of migrants that came to Burma under British colonial rule. Very few Burmese citizens were given the opportunity to travel abroad, while foreigners were restricted initially to one and later six days. Finally, the government controlled access to information and prevented outside news from reaching the population (Steinberg, 1999).

In 1974, the regime adopted a new constitution, in an attempt to formalize its socialist system. It enshrined the one-party state dominated by the BSPP. It created a new legislature, with only one chamber, the People's Assembly (Pyithu Hluttaw), replacing the old bicameral system that included a Chamber of Nationalities – representing ethnic minorities – in addition to the Chamber of Deputies. The constitution created four levels of government, organized hierarchically: at the top, the executive branch of the central government; followed by regional divisions (or states); townships; and then wards or village-tracts. In the economic realm, it proclaimed that all land belonged to the state so that any property could be expropriated if needed. It confirmed also that the state owned the means of production, including natural resources. Nationalization of all industries was consistent with this policy.

The new constitutional order changed little to the military-controlled authoritarian regime. The Revolutionary Council was abolished and replaced with the constitutionally sanctioned Council of State, of which Ne Win became chairman. Almost all of the Council's members were transferred from the Revolutionary Council. Senior military officers dominated all of the state's top positions. The People's Assembly gave an aura of representation but mainly provided a further instrument for the military's dominance.

These changes failed to address or resolve Burma's problems. Insurgency continued unabated, as ethnic minority groups found little comfort in the state's new constitution. The constitution had created seven states and seven divisions to represent ethnic groups, and given them equal status. In reality, however, the state had abandoned federalism and states mainly obtained symbolic recognition rather than any significant powers. As a result, insurgency not only continued but also intensified in 1974 as Karen, Kayah and Shan for the first time united with Burman dissidents against the government.

During 1975 and 1976, a number of riots spread in urban areas. Workers and students protested the deteriorating conditions, high prices and misdistribution leading to shortages of basic foodstuffs. Corruption and mismanagement among government officials and the military made conditions worse. Peasants produced sufficient rice but preferred to sell their produce on the black market rather than through official channels, given the very low prices obtained from the state. Ne Win responded by repressing rioters. Universities were closed down after repeated student demonstrations. The military arrested a large number of protesters, and several were killed. With growing instability, Ne Win changed many administrators at various levels of government but policies remained the same (Silverstein, 1977).

The economy nevertheless improved slightly through a combination of chance and partial acknowledgement of policy failure. The regime maintained state dominance and management of all sectors but Ne Win recognized that some aspects of economic management had failed. Consequently, the World Bank was invited back and bilateral foreign assistance was accepted selectively. Some imports and exports resumed. Growth reached higher levels by the late 1970s but mainly because of the introduction of new, high-yielding rice varieties that had spread across Asia. Oil production also increased as new sources were found (Steinberg, 1999).

Yet it only slowly caught up with pre–Second World War levels as the regime continued to follow rigid policies. Growth reached new bottlenecks in the early 1980s as the state refused foreign involvement in the oil sector and its own technology remained limited. Rice production reached new peaks as the irrigation and appropriate fertilizers remained limited. Teak production had risen under the sponsorship of a World Bank programme but began to peak during this period. Table 2 shows growth rates for Burma, compared to other Southeast Asian countries. While growth rates rose above 5 per cent during the 1970s and early 1980s, the economy contracted in the period 1985–9.

By the late 1980s, a new economic crisis brewed. Imports had risen rapidly to meet the demand for fertilizers and other productive inputs for Burma's agricultural and natural resource sectors. Yet, exports failed to expand sufficiently given production limits reached for several goods. At the same time, debt levels ballooned, particularly as a result of a rapid rise in Japanese foreign assistance that had been allotted mainly in the form of loans. State enterprises drained public funds as they operated at a loss. The economy was strained (Steinberg, 1999).

The 1988 crisis, the rise of opposition and the new SLORC/SPDC regime

Economic and political problems reached a peak in 1988. Opposition to the regime became assertive. Despite the regime's crackdown, it had shown its limits. The military staged a coup and launched a new military-dominated regime, while Ne Win was sidelined. The opposition nevertheless maintained its mobilization as the charismatic figure of Aung San Suu Kyi, the daughter of independence leader Aung San, emerged as a key leader.

The high debt levels and economic problems of the late 1980s forced the regime to adopt policies that made living conditions even worse. The government chose to demonetize, once again, its currency: it replaced existing currency with new paper notes, allegedly to curb the soaring black market. By doing so, prices rose to even higher levels, as people sought to hold commodities rather than cash. In effect, it produced high inflation and even more demand for black market goods (Steinberg, 1999).

This crisis combined with political demonstrations to spark some change. Student protests broke out in the spring of 1988. With growing economic pain, they were joined by many more people. Together demonstrators asked for an end to the regime, and the organization of multi-party elections. It was a mass movement that lasted for several months in spite of some repression. It was the largest set of protests that the regime had faced. In July, Ne Win resigned in the hopes of defusing the crisis, while warning that the armed forces would continue to quell protests.

In September, the military ended the crisis by launching a coup and clamping down forcefully on the widespread protests. Ne Win's resignation had not been sufficient to calm protesters as his replacement, Sein Lwin, was widely hated and definitely not perceived to be a reformer. The new leaders became the targets of demonstrators who continued to demand deeper political change. By September, the armed forces launched a coup, cracked down and killed hundreds of demonstrators while it arrested thousands more. The junta proclaimed the State Law and Order Restoration Council (SLORC) and suspended the BSPP. A group of less well-known, less educated officers under the leadership of General Saw Maung seized the reins of power. At the same time, it was not entirely clear that Ne Win had truly been sidelined. In fact, he remained treated with great respect for the following decade and many observers believed that his influence remained important (Steinberg, 1999).

With the economy in tatters, the regime implemented a few important changes. For the most part, Ne Win and the BSPP had already proposed these measures, given the high levels of debt and severe decline in economic conditions in the preceding years. First, the regime allowed some foreign investment, particularly in the oil and other natural resource sectors. Second, it allowed the establishment of private businesses, although the regime retained high control over most sectors of the economy. It reduced its official commitment to a centrally planned economy and declared itself an open and market economy, although in reality remained far from it. Third, it planned to reform the financial sector to allow a more autonomous banking system. Finally, it regularized the border trade to reap some benefits from the vast black market economy (Steinberg, 2001).

At the same time, the military sought to retain control. It created a number of its own businesses and organizations, such as the Myanmar

Holding Corporation Ltd. It created military procurement factories under its management. Foreign corporations were also required to form joint ventures with military-owned enterprises. The military essentially aimed at reaping vast revenues from the new growth it hoped to create through reform.

As it opened up its borders, foreign assistance declined. In response to the regime's bloody crackdown and assertion of military power, many of the foreign donors who had resumed assistance began instead to impose sanctions. The United States imposed economic sanctions while the Japanese dramatically curtailed their assistance program. Japan and other donors reduced their involvement considerably. In response, China instead expanded its own foreign assistance to Myanmar and became the regime's strongest supporter (Steinberg, 2001).

Although the regime represented mostly continuity, some attempts were made to regain legitimacy by organizing elections. Ne Win had suggested the possibility of moving towards multipartyism when the BSPP was still in place. SLORC decided to move ahead, allowed parties to be formed and scheduled an election for May 1990.

The SLORC's strategy backfired, as it did not anticipate the surge of support for the opposition. Only months before the coup that led to SLORC's creation, Aung San Suu Kyi had returned to Myanmar to care for her ailing mother. As she began to play an active role in demonstrations, her charismatic approach provided a catalyst to unify various opposition forces. She became the general secretary of the National League for Democracy (NLD), which was created soon after. Strong enthusiastic crowds followed Suu Kyi's appearances. Worried about the forthcoming elections in 1990, the regime placed Suu Kyi under house arrest in July 1989. Nevertheless, the NLD won a resounding victory (80.8 per cent) against the military-supported National Unity Party (21.2 per cent). Surprised with this victory, the SLORC refused to recognize the results.

The following two decades remained in a political stalemate as the military increased its power but sought to find new ways of renewing its legitimacy. It argued that a new government could not be formed before a new constitution was adopted. In 1993, it convened a national convention to negotiate the terms of this new constitution. Although the NLD was initially included, negotiations soon stalled as the regime and its opponents held divergent views of Myanmar's future (Thawnghmung, 2003).

Meanwhile, the military tightened its grip over the political and economic system. Expenditure grew considerably in the first part of the 1990s. China provided military aid and training, while businesses owned or controlled by the military funded its increasing ranks and privileges.

Economic conditions improved as the regime continued to move away from its socialist past. Foreign investment increased from $280.57 million in 1990–1 to $1 billion in 1994–5. Thai firms invested heavily in logging and fisheries. Oil sector investments grew considerably. With these new investment sources, joint ventures multiplied. These partnerships often involved military-linked businesses. Farmers continued to benefit from reforms that gave them more production choice and more flexible arrangements for selling their produce to the government (Thawnghmung, 2003).

At the same time, most of the population remained very poor. Figure 2 shows that Myanmar's GDP growth surpassed that of Vietnam, Cambodia and Laos in the late 1990s and 2000s. Nevertheless, it's starting point was so far behind even these relatively poor countries that GDP per capita at $256 remained well below even Laos at $514.

The SLORC also reduced threats from insurgents. It signed cease-fire accords with a number of insurgent groups. Some groups, such as the Shan, Wa, Kachin, Mon, Karen and Pao were given political and economic autonomy in territories they controlled. They were also given the right to bear arms. The regime reaped benefits from their involvement in drug production and trade, particularly of opium. Military officials shared in some of the revenues. At the same time that some groups reached cease-fire agreements with the government, greater military resources and a better ability to target remaining groups gave the regime an edge. In 1995, the military succeeded in overtaking the Karen National Union's (KNU) headquarters in Manerplaw and forced the Karen resistance group to retreat across the border in Thailand. The KNU had been the most significant minority armed group fighting the regime. This victory tilted the balance in favour of the regime.

In the context of this renewed confidence, the regime released in 1995 its most prominent opponent, Daw Aung San Suu Kyi. She had been placed under house arrest prior to the 1990 elections. In 1991, Suu Kyi's struggle against the regime had been rewarded when the Nobel committee awarded her the Nobel Peace Prize. With international recognition and support, an electoral victory that everyone knew the regime had denied, as well as a very strong following, Suu Kyi could not be avoided. The regime sought to contain her influence but could not discard her. As soon as she was released, she resumed her oppositional activities by giving public speeches against the regime's human rights abuses and its disregard for democracy. She also organized NLD meetings, and placed strict conditions on negotiating with the regime. She was placed again under house arrest in 2000.

She was released again in 2002, in a very different context. This time, far from being confident and stronger, the regime appeared much weaker. Years of economic sanctions now took their toll. Foreign investments had all but dried up. The value of the Myanmarese currency had fallen. The economic growth that had begun to appear in the early 1990s soon waned. Inflation reached 60 per cent. External debt ballooned. The state's taxation revenue steadily declined throughout the 1990s, thereby crippling its civil service and increasing its abusive practice of using forced labour for major public works projects. Political pressure also increased as the United Nations spoke of the need for some resolution. It feared that the situation could further deteriorate if the United States decided to impose even stricter sanctions (Englehart, 2005; Steinberg, 2003).

The release coincided with the definitive end of Ne Win and his family's influence. Some of Ne Win's children and grandchildren allegedly conspired to overthrow the regime. More likely, their business interests at times clashed with those of top military officials in the regime. They were detained placed with Ne Win under house arrest. Ne Win died almost unnoticed shortly afterwards. He had been thought to have retained some influence over the regime after 1988 and might well have been an obstacle to releasing Suu Kyi before 2002. Only a year later, she was detained once again and this time remained under house arrest until 2010 (Steinberg, 2003).

It is not entirely clear how or why the regime alternatively arrested and released Suu Kyi. There were several conditions that might have given more confidence or placed greater strain on the regime at particular times. Since the regime's leaders were mindful of their reliance on external assistance and foreign investment, continued economic sanctions and external pressure certainly prevented them from taking harsher measures against Suu Kyi, and might even explain why they wished to be seen, at times, as open to deepening negotiations with the opposition. Periods of more or less stability, agreements with rebel groups, Ne Win's remaining influence, or even subtle shifts in power within the junta might have explained the various patterns of arrests and release from detention.

Beyond Suu Kyi's specific situation, more broadly the regime has been experimenting with various ways of regaining legitimacy. Ever since the coup of 1988, the regime had lost the BSPP's ideological commitment to a Burmese way to socialism to justify its rule. Moreover military dominance after 1988, combined with economic sanctions and a pariah status in the international arena, hampered the regime's ability to seek support for its rule. Shortly after coming to power, the regime announced negotiations for a new constitution. Those negotiations lasted for the following decade but were widely perceived as a ploy to manipulate opposition forces into accepting the regime's own vision for Myanmar.

The NLD pulled out after a few years but then returned informally to negotiation when it appeared that the regime might be willing to compromise. After Suu Kyi's release in 2002, the NLD was less inclined to organize protests and sought instead to reach compromise through dialogue. The regime allowed more freedom of movement to Suu Kyi, who refrained from speaking at large gatherings and confined herself instead to visiting NLD offices and supporters. She continued to emphasize the need to recognize the 1990 elections and supported externally imposed economic sanctions. As a result, few inroads were made through dialogue with the regime. Instead, she was detained placed under house arrest again when a violent clash occurred in Dipaiyin during one of her visits to supporters. NLD leaders were also detained and the regime closed down its offices (Taylor, 2004).

In 2007, the NLD, students groups, human rights activists and others launched protests against the regime. By August, the regime miscalculated. Faced with endemic economic problems and a high budget deficit, it loosened its fuel price subsidy. Within a day, fuel prices doubled and had an immediate impact on food prices as well. In response, protests grew and reached 100,000 demonstrators in mid September, including 10,000 monks. On 26 and 27 September, the regime brutally suppressed the demonstrations and images of military officials arresting and beating up monks spread like wildfire. Despite international pressures, the regime stayed on course and moved its constitutional agenda forward (Thawnghmung & Myoe, 2008).

New constitution, new regime?

From 2008 to 2011, the junta engineered a process of political change whose net outcome remained ambiguous. Were the changes simply window-dressing to secure the lifting of sanctions and give more space to the ruling elite, or were some of the changes genuinely the first steps towards more liberalization and democracy? In May 2008, the regime held a referendum on its newly drafted constitution then proceeded with forming a civilian government in 2011. While new openness to Aung San Suu Kyi and the opposition NLD was widely celebrated, there were still serious doubts about whether changes were genuine as the military remained firmly in power behind the scenes and its privileges were maintained.

The regime announced the resumption of constitutional discussions in 2003. It revived the National Convention that had been suspended in 1996 and announced a new "road map" to democracy. Lieutenant General Thein Sein played a key role in convening it. When the Convention finally met in 2004, the NLD was not included. Its leaders remained mostly imprisoned and its offices still closed. The NLD had also refused to attend as the regime failed to meet its demands, including the release of Aung San Suu Kyi from house arrest. With the opposition weakened, the regime moved ahead with its own constitutional structure. It was ratified by a referendum held in May 2008, only days after Cyclone Nargis struck Myanmar. A total of 92 per cent of voters allegedly supported the new constitution but the NLD and other opposition groups rejected the results and accused the government of holding a rigged plebiscite.

The new constitution essentially preserved military dominance. The military held 25 per cent of seats in parliament. It also assigned military officers to key ministries such as Defence and Home Affairs. Constitutional amendments require more than 75 per cent approval, thereby giving the military de facto veto power. Finally, in a state of emergency, the constitution provides a mechanism for the armed forces to assume control over legislative, executive and judicial authority (Turnell, 2011).

A new civilian government was elected on 7 November, 2010. Reports of fraud, intimidation and irregularities were widespread. In spite of the regime's efforts, the turnout was considered low. The NLD boycotted the election after Aung San Suu Kyi was prevented from running. Although some opposition parties ran, they were not very well known to the broader public. The junta fielded candidates under the banner of the Union Solidarity and Development Party (USDP), and won 76 per cent of the seats while the National Unity Party, also close to the regime, won a significant portion of the rest. The new president, Thein Sein, was the regime's former prime minister. The two vice-presidents were also from the previous government or close to the ruling party. The same group essentially remained in power.

Yet, in 2011, President Thein Sein spearheaded reforms that appeared to signal significant political changes. When several seats were opened for elections, his government allowed not only the NLD to run but Aung San Suu Kyi as well. Restrictions against her were lifted, and she was allowed to campaign and speak freely. On 1 April, the NLD won 43 out of 44 constituencies and around 90 per cent of the votes in these by-elections, marking the first time that Aung San Suu Kyi would enter parliament as an opposition leader.

Against the backdrop of the euphoria surrounding this rapid opening up to the opposition, the United States and European powers began to ease sanctions. They planned to resume aid, while the World Bank and the IMF reopened discussions with the Myanmarese government for the first time in decades. As conditions for new lending were addressed, the regime also began to show a willingness to implement economic reforms. The regime has also made renewed efforts in the last few years to reach ceasefire agreements with various ethnic minority rebels. Most importantly, in January 2012 the government signed an agreement with the Karen, which had been fighting against the regime for 60 years and had refused to sign previously. New ceasefire agreements were signed with other groups as well. On the other hand, the Kachin abandoned their own ceasefire agreement and resumed fighting the year before, as they were frustrated with the lack of progress in implementing promises that were made.

Myanmar's authoritarian regime has remained consolidated partly because of a relatively small middle class and very strong elite unity. The relatively stagnant economy for several decades created low growth. While growth rates have been much higher in the late 1990s and 2000s, they reflected rapidly rising revenues from oil and other resource sectors that the armed forces largely controlled through state-run companies or joint ventures with selective foreign investors. There has been steady growth of an educated middle class that has found some avenues in the small non-governmental sectors but the middle class remained much smaller than in countries such as Thailand or Indonesia. Nevertheless, demonstrations and protests that shook the regime in the late 1980s and, to a lesser extent, in 2007, mobilized the student body, professionals and other groups that were outraged with the government's policies. In the late 1980s, Burma's economy was in such disarray and the economic conditions were so dire that more people were willing to demonstrate out of desperation. Buddhist monks also departed from their usual detachment from politics to express their opposition to the government's policies.

The political elite tied to the regime has remained strong. The military's embeddedness in the regime and the strength of this elite explain in large part the persistent authoritarianism. Englehart argued that part of the military's strength comes from building itself as the only strong institution early on. Civil service was poorly paid, poorly educated in the 1950s, while the military built up its strength in the face of the need to resist intrusion from KMT forces and rising ethnic minority groups. After seizing power, the military maintained a competitive position relative to the civil service, placing military officers in key positions despite their inadequate competence or education. It also built up a parallel administrative structure staffed by military personnel, even during the time that it tried to expand the role of the BSPP. By also failing to adequately pay its civil service, it virtually paralyzed its capacity for service delivery and encouraged, instead, the expansion of patronage networks dependent on close relations with the military (Englehart, 2005).

Unity and cohesiveness within the military has been maintained by two institutional strategies. First, military officers are assigned to particular areas of competence or jurisdiction, and rarely overstep these functions. They are socialized into remaining within their purview so as to not overlap and compete with other officers. There is an internal policing mechanism by which senior military officers intervene swiftly when these unwritten rules are transgressed. Second, the military has taken good care of its officers and soldiers. Incentives include some material benefits for loyal officers and soldiers, as well as relatively clear procedures for promotion. These strategies constitute important means of maintaining the military's unity and coherence (Hlaing, 2009).

Table 12 *Burma/Myanmar*

Population (rank)	Land area (rank)	Main ethnic groups (%)	Main religions (%)	Regime type (transition)	GDP per capita (rank)	GDP growth rate (%) (rank)
54 584 650 (24th) (2012 est.)	653 508 sq km (40th)	Burman 68 Shan 9 Karen 7 Rakhine 4 Chinese 3 Indian 2 Mon 2 Other 5	Buddhist 89 Christian 4 – Baptist 3 – Roman 1 Muslim 4 Animist 1 Other 2	Authoritarian (–1962)[a]	$1 300 (206th) (2011 est.)	5.5 (58th) (2011 est.)

Source: CIA, *The World Factbook*; Polity IV Project, Polity IV Individual Country Regime Trends, 1946–2010.

[a] The year indicates the most recent transition; (+) means a transition towards democracy and (–) denotes a transition towards authoritarianism.

The new constitution, a return to civilian rule and the liberalization after 2011 constitute new departures for Myanmar. The change was highly controlled from the top and the pace of reform came essentially from the regime. While increasing pressure from domestic opposition played a role, other factors were probably more significant. The poor state of the economy, combined with international sanctions, placed important constraints on the regime, which needed to sustain sufficient resources to the armed forces and its supporters. Furthermore, the regime had been searching for new ways of legitimizing its rule ever since the 1988 coup and the 1990 electoral debacle. A return to civilian rule and managed elections allowed the regime to emulate effective formulas used by other authoritarian and semi-authoritarian regimes in the region, while at least temporarily keeping its own pace toward reform.

9 | *Southeast Asia in the twenty-first century*

Southeast Asia in the twenty-first century is a region of contrasts and rapid transformation. Propelled by high growth rates during several decades, many countries of the region have risen from poor to relatively wealthy ones. Singapore, Malaysia, Thailand and Indonesia have modernized rapidly. Their urban areas have expanded and the middle class has grown. Other countries, by contrast, have lagged well behind. The Philippines grew less impressively overall but more steadily in recent years. Wealth inequality remains higher than that of its more prosperous neighbours. Vietnam, Cambodia, Myanmar (Burma) and Laos were left behind. Decades of experimentation with central planning and socialist policies failed to significantly raise living standards. Although the poorest gained minimum safety nets, overall wealth only slowly increased and therefore most of the population remained much poorer than in other parts of the region. The Vietnam War brought further destruction and instability in Vietnam, Laos and Cambodia while civil war in the latter continued to perpetuate destruction and poverty. Vietnam in the 1990s and 2000s began to grow much more rapidly as it implemented market reforms and allowed more critical examination of failed policies of the past. Laos followed suit with its own reforms. Myanmar's radical and ideologically motivated armed forces long prevented its population from prospering. In fact, it was one of the only countries to have several periods of economic setbacks, largely induced by the regime's policies. Recent changes are beginning to produce some results but the country remains far behind others.

Politics in the region have mirrored the divide along these two groups of countries. The poorest were the state-socialist countries. They espoused the socialist experiment, which not only contributed to slowing their economic development but also institutionalized strongly centralized and authoritarian political systems that changed very little once they were established. Southeast Asian communist countries outlived the fall of communist regimes that swept the former Soviet

Union and Eastern Europe. Instead, Vietnam and Laos maintained the supremacy of the communist party and the institutional configurations of communist regimes while slowly introducing more debate, more policy scrutiny and especially economic reforms. Myanmar was already somewhat different, as it adopted its own brand of socialism introduced by a military dominated regime. The military remained dominant although the regime first shed its socialist ideology and experiment with a closed economy, then recently allowed the election of a civilian led government, but still led by former junta leaders. Cambodia also adopted a different path as two competing state-socialist experiments succeeded one another: first the radical Khmer Rouge experimentation with a blend of various socialist projects harshly implemented within a few months with disastrous results; second a more standard communist regime under Vietnamese control. Cambodia was the only country with much political change as the Vietnam-controlled regime failed to garner sufficient power to eliminate its opponents, including royalists and the Khmer Rouge. Civil war ensued, then the United Nations attempted to craft a new democratic regime. Divisive politics contributed to its failure, while Hun Sen, the leader of the former Vietnam-controlled communist regime gained the upper hand over rivals and gradually consolidated his authoritarian rule. Where political change occurred, state-socialism gave way to alternative forms of authoritarian or semi-democratic rule rather than new democracies.

Conversely, the wealthiest countries were non-socialist. Authoritarian regimes were the norm among this group for most of the post-independence period. Indonesia began as a democratic regime in the 1950s but it ended by 1957. Authoritarianism was solidified under the New Order regime of President Suharto after 1965. It lasted until 1998. Singapore and Malaysia stabilized as dominant party regimes. They differed from other authoritarian regimes by the continued supremacy of civilians while armed forces played a prominent role under authoritarian regimes in Indonesia, Thailand and the Philippines. Thailand's security forces long allied with factions in the bureaucracy to control the state. Divisions within the armed forces led to successive coups and counter-coups until the 1980s, when a semi-authoritarian regime under the leadership of a former general gradually loosened its grip and finally allowed a civilian-elected government in 1988. The armed forces have continued however to intervene in politics, most recently in a 2006 coup. Only the Philippines remained mostly democratic although its quality was very low. Wealthy families and political clans have competed for control of various levels of the state, while maintaining their overall dominance over the economy and the political system. The armed forces played a central role mainly during the authoritarian period of President Marcos, which was characterized essentially as a one large political clan seizing the upper hand over the others during a decade or so. Marcos simply went further than others in using the state and the armed forces to advance his friends and family's personal interests.

Democracy has been scarce and of poor quality in the region. Nevertheless, it has begun to take root mainly in wealthier, non-socialist states. To much surprise, given its military-dominated authoritarian past, Indonesia now appears as the bright light in this respect. Since 1998, elections have been held regularly, there has been significant turnover of power between various parties and contenders for the presidency, and civil liberties have been very broad. Thailand has teetered between authoritarian and democratic regimes but since the 1980s has overall been ruled by democratically elected governments, and a significant turnover of power between contenders. The armed forces retreated seemingly from intervening in politics in recent years, most significantly by accepting electoral results in 2010 that returned to power Puea Thai and allowed Yingluck Shinawatra to become prime minister. Thailand resumed a course that was set in the 1990s, when civil liberties were broad, electoral competition lively and democracy seemed to be progressing. The Philippines returned to electoral politics in 1986, when large masses forced Marcos out of power. Mass mobilization blocked other attempts to concentrate power and re-establish authoritarian rule. At the same time, political clans have strongly supported a return of elections and competitive democratic institutions that have served their interests. Their clout remains strong, at the expense of broadening representation and participation of the vast number of poor and marginalized Filipinos. Finally, Malaysia and Singapore, while remaining dominant party systems, have shown signs of pressures to reform and democratize. Certainly Malaysia came close to significant political change with the surprisingly strong showing of Anwar Ibrahim's opposition coalition in the 2008 elections. In Singapore's 2011 elections, the opposition gained six seats and the dominant PAP saw its popular support erode to 60 per cent of votes. While these results did not challenge the PAP's dominance, it shows growing resentment towards the status quo.

This book provides an explanation for this pattern of political change in the region. Broad historical patterns set the stage for the regimes that continue to rule. Yet, some sociological, political and institutional factors also explain patterns of continuity and change.

Ideology and Cold War politics

Ideas and ideological currents informed many of the groups that mobilized and seized power when European colonial rulers left the region. Nationalism strongly influenced groups with existing or growing sense of shared history and identity to seek their own state. Anti-colonial movements rose at a time when nationalism spread throughout Asia. It galvanized groups, some of which had been under colonial rule for several centuries, to identify themselves as modern nations, cobbled together around shared languages, religion or histories. The Indonesian nationalist movement emerged as a prototypical example of how nationalism allowed for disparate groups to imagine themselves as "Indonesian", sharing a regional language of common communication and the experience of Dutch colonial rule. Similar imagination formed the basis of a Filipino nationalist movement that informed the creation and maintenance of an independent Philippines. To different degrees, nationalism also transformed Vietnamese, Khmer, Lao and even Thai identities, as it gave them a new identity as "nations" seeking modern, independent states. After independence, regimes across the spectrum continued to frame these identities in national terms to bolster regime legitimacy and maintain unity. From Indonesia's attempt to articulate a national ideology of Pancasila to the Khmer Rouge or the Burmese armed forces' attempts to articulate their own unique brands of communism, nationalism was used in different shapes and forms to gain popular support, sometimes with positive consequences but other times with more destructive effects.

Communism was another strong ideological current in the first half of the twentieth century. Several movements were formed across the region, often around small groups of intellectuals and students who had travelled to Europe and been inspired by the sweeping promises of communist ideals and the experience of the Russian revolution. While several failed miserably in their initial attempts at societal transformations, others persisted, created external allies and became powerful vehicles for popular mobilization. The Chinese communist movement added further inspiration as it gained ascendency among the peasantry, organized an effective army and finally gained power in 1949. Along similar lines, the Vietnamese communist movement organized an effective army and inspired large numbers of Vietnamese to resist French and later American control. Its influence and organizational skills also spread to the Khmer and Lao communist movements.

Despite its strong appeal, communist ideology alone could not determine where communist movements would succeed in seizing power. Other large movements in Indonesia and the Philippines, for instance, were unable to gain ascendency. The Indonesian communist movement was brutally crushed and eliminated after the Indonesian armed forces seized power in 1965. In the Philippines, President Marcos declared martial law and imposed authoritarian rule partly to counter the rising threat of the New People's Army (NPA), the armed wing of the communist movement. Marcos failed to crush the NPA. Successive governments were also unable to do so, although the NPA never obtained sufficient support to overthrow either Marcos or democratic governments that succeeded him.

The Cold War framed local struggles and had a large impact on where communist movements succeeded. Vietnam became a focal point during the 1960s. With the United States' involvement, Vietnam became a battleground against the spread of communism. Ironically, its involvement contributed to deepening support for the communists, as the Vietnamese population perceived the United States' presence as occupation and suffered dramatically from the war. With support from the Soviet Union and China, the Vietnamese communists won in 1975 and then used their own strategic upper hand to support the Pathet Lao and ensure a communist victory in Laos as well. The Khmer Rouge benefited from the instability and Vietnamese communist victory, as they also seized power that year.

Conversely, the United States strongly supported anti-communist regimes in Indonesia and the Philippines. It disbursed large amounts of aid that contributed to supporting the armed forces and authoritarianism under Suharto's and Marcos' leadership respectively. Anti-communist repression eliminated the communist movement in Indonesia and solidified Suharto's rule. In the Philippines, despite strong backing from the United States, Marcos was unable to defeat the NPA, which continued its activities well beyond the end of the Cold War.

Ideas, ideology and cold war politics therefore set the stage for the division of Southeast Asia into communist and non-communist countries. Poor, peasant-based societies provided fertile ground for communism to spread, with their promise of land reform or more equal distribution of wealth.

Economic development

Economic development has played a strong role in the region's politics but has not quite had expected consequences. Poor and stagnant economies produced very little political change, whereas vast economic transformations over several decades created some pressures for political reform, but not the corresponding democratic politics that one might expect.

With the exception of Singapore, all countries in the region were agrarian economies at the time of independence. Aside from very large majorities of peasants, they had small groups of educated people many of whom had served colonial bureaucracies. Some areas were largely integrated to world markets, especially where colonial rulers had exploited cash crops – oil palm, rubber, coffee, spices – for export to Europe. Some rice basket areas of the region also became important rice exporters. Thailand and Burma, for instance, were top rice producers in the 1940s and 1950s. Significant plantation and cash crop economies developed in parts of Indonesia, the Philippines and Malaysia.

Political scientists and sociologists have long suggested that economic development produces vast transformations that lead to democracy. Countries in the region cast some doubt that this proposition yields strong predictive results. On the contrary, some wealthy countries such as Malaysia and Singapore maintained stable authoritarian regimes despite decades of economic transformation, while some relatively poorer countries such as the Philippines maintained some form of democratic rule. Nevertheless, while other factors might have interfered and prevented democratization in some cases, economic development has produced change in the region and, certainly, the lack of it has been associated with continued authoritarian rule.

The absence of economic development, on the other hand, has been associated with authoritarian rule. State-socialist experiments in the region largely failed to produce economic development. While they managed to raise living standards for some of the poorest peasants, failure to raise agricultural output or to create strong industrial sectors contributed to broad poverty overall. Of course, even within state-socialist economies there were vast differences. The Khmer Rouge destroyed Cambodia's economy with very harsh and radical policies. The Ne Win regime in its early days contributed to impoverishing Burma as it cut off some of its most productive sectors as well as links to markets abroad. In Vietnam, Laos and Cambodia after 1979, communist regimes implemented collectivization and other state-directed socialist practices more cautiously and pragmatically. Nevertheless, they also remained for the most part poorer than other countries in the region. Overall, the poorest countries in the region – Cambodia, Laos, Burma and Vietnam – also remained mostly authoritarian.

Why does economic development produce political change? Over time, when an economy diversifies, it becomes more complex to manage. More importantly, groups with different interests are formed, from various entrepreneurs in a variety of economic sectors, to professionals, students and remaining farmers. Tightly controlled political systems often rule through simplification. They are ill equipped to control and manage increasingly diverse interests. They are more prone to selecting winners, often business groups close to the regime either through patronage or occasionally with the intention of producing economic growth. Strains tend to appear, particularly in regimes where the economy is also tightly controlled.

Business groups and the middle class play an important role in political reform. Unless they are state-run, businesses require stable political environments, predictable rules, protection of their property and expanding markets to thrive. Authoritarian systems can sometimes provide stable environments but can be quite unpredictable. Democracies generally tend to provide better legal protections and more open environments that are favorable to diverse business interests. Business groups that rise outside of authoritarian states' direct protection often participate in reform movements. The middle class, in turn, is more often a driver of political change. Education, comfortable living standards and diverse interests form a preference for more open politics, choice of policies and platforms and more participation in politics. Democracies provide such a political environment.

What has been their role in Southeast Asia? Looking beyond levels of economic development, more directly to the business class and middle class, we can trace why they have sometimes been motors of change but other times not. The case of Thailand in many respects confirms the trend. New business groups, outside of Bangkok, began to enter politics and challenge the narrower grip held by large Bangkok elites and conglomerates. They formed the core of some of the politicians behind parties such as Chart Thai and later Thai Rak Thai. Demonstrations in 1973, 1992 and after 2006 involved a middle class that no longer accepted military-bureaucratic dominance. In Indonesia and the Philippines, the middle class sometimes demonstrated in the streets to trigger political reform. Indonesians demonstrated for days in 1998 and brought down Suharto's regime. The People Power revolution in 1986 ended Marcos' authoritarian rule. The Indonesian middle class had also been working within Golkar and established institutions to gradually pressure for reform. There are signs of similar kinds of middle class pressures in Vietnam since Doi Moi, when the regime introduced economic reforms to economic development. In recent years, it has implemented some gradual political reform allowing more policy scrutiny. In Malaysia, where the United Malays National Organization (UMNO) remains dominant, the Malay middle class has been increasingly divided, thereby feeding the ranks of the rising Pakatan Rakyat (People's Alliance). Although maybe only an initial sign, pressure for change is rising in some authoritarian regimes with a growing middle class.

Nevertheless, the middle class has not always been a driver of change in the region. Scholars of Southeast Asia have pondered over why it seemed unusually quiescent and supportive of authoritarian regimes (Robison & Goodman, 1996; Rodan, 1997). After all, it was growing under Suharto's New Order in Indonesia, and had been large in Malaysia and Singapore, with little corresponding political change. "Performance legitimacy" matters and can sometimes cushion the effects of middle-class preferences for political participation. Sometimes the middle class is willing to forego some political freedoms when authoritarian regimes perform well, and their living standards rise. Singapore and to a lesser extent Malaysia have been the main examples of this trade-off, where the middle class enjoyed rapidly rising wealth and economic opportunities under tightly controlled political regimes. The benefits of comfort outweighed for some time those of freedom to express themselves politically. Furthermore, when the middle class is dependent on the state for its wealth, it is even more likely to accept compromise. Singapore's government consistently provided a host of housing and other social benefits that could be manipulated to foster greater political support. In Malaysia's case, the regime exploited its vast patronage machine through UMNO to nurture Malay support. At the same time, ethnic divisions created a different kind of middle class. For decades, Malaysian Chinese constituted its largest part. They were not likely to demand political change after the 1969 riots. Similarly, much of the middle class during the early days of the Suharto regime was ethnic Chinese, who in Indonesia constituted only a very small percentage of the population. Having been frequently victimized, they also refrained from politics. With the growth of the middle class in both countries, these factors have changed. Indonesia certainly saw a new middle class play a central role in the establishment of a democratic regime after 1998, while Malaysia's has increased pressures for reform.

Furthermore, while the middle class is often at the forefront of political change, others sometimes play an equally important role. The confrontation between red shirts and yellow shirts in Thailand is a good example. Thaksin Shinawatra and the Thai Rak Thai successfully gained support among poor, marginalized Thai from rural areas, particularly from the northeast of Thailand. When the 2006 coup removed Thaksin from power, party supporters were able to mobilize this group. During subsequent years, they maintained a strong presence in the streets of Bangkok. In the Philippines, the urban poor also participated in the People Power movement that first ousted Ferdinand Marcos in 1986, and forced the resignation of President Joseph Estrada in 2001. Although more difficult to organize and mobilize, the working class and rural poor sometimes participate in key demonstrations and movements that contribute to political change.

Overall, economic development has contributed somewhat to democratization in the region. The middle class has been ambiguous in its preference for democracy but, over time, has demanded reform and pushed for political change in several cases in Southeast Asia. Occasionally, it has been joined by business groups that were eager to diversify political representation and gain more power against business rivals tied to authoritarian regimes. Nevertheless, there is no straightforward relationship between economic development and democracy in the region in part because other factors are equally important to explain political change or its absence.

Elites and institutional cohesion

Many regimes have been stable but authoritarian. In many cases, a strongly united elite contributes to their longevity. When ruling elites divide and compete, authoritarian regimes often collapse. While in itself such division does not necessarily lead to democracy, it is often a precondition. Through elections, democracy thereafter provides a framework for elite competition, provided that they are fair and that elites accept the risks of losing power.

Elite unity is often fostered and sustained through various institutional mechanisms, benefits and patronage. Well-structured, tightly controlled and disciplined political parties can streamline benefits, impose sanctions and solidify elite networks that maintain unity. Ideology or strong programmatic visions can help to foster party loyalty. Regimes that have built up strong dominant parties often remain more stable. Armed forces can also produce elite unity when they are centralized and when hierarchical command is routinized and respected. Their dominance and relationship to the broader elite can be key in determining elite unity.

State-socialist regimes in Southeast Asia have shown surprisingly strong elite unity. While in other parts of the world many collapsed with the fall of the Soviet Union in 1989, few changes occurred in Southeast Asia. Communist parties continued to maintain political control in Vietnam and Laos even after both regimes diluted their ideological commitments. They benefited from tightly knit relations between the party and the armed forces, thereby strongly reducing the potential for splits in the ruling elite. Burma showed similar unity mainly because its armed forces were the primary institution ruling its socialist regime. Ideology supported military rule in its early stages but the regime migrated to a more straightforward military regime after the establishment of the SLORC/SPDC regime in 1988. This base provided strong unity within the armed forces, which was maintained through a steady provision of large benefits, patronage and other material benefits for members of the armed forces. Only Cambodia's path produced less elite unity. In this case, Vietnam's external intervention in 1979 prevented a consolidation of the Khmer Rouge regime, which had proceeded to eliminate its opponents and brutally repress any opposition. Their own unity was sustained through ideological commitment, and remained significant once they were removed from power. It prevented the successor state-socialist regime under Vietnam's patronage to gain party dominance and elite unity. Instead, civil war ensued, with a pro-monarchy faction representing yet another oppositional force among the elite. These deep divisions remained after a UN brokered peace agreement established a democratic framework. Instead of stabilizing a new democratic regime, the framework showed greater evidence of deep division and competition within the elite, while Khmer Rouge forces refused to join and chose instead to continue armed struggle. Hun Sen, who became the leader of the Vietnamese supported regime, maintained an advantage with a more institutionalized party and loyalty from military forces. He was able therefore to establish authoritarian rule, while maintaining some token concessions to opponents and an electoral framework to allow some competition.

Other authoritarian regimes benefited from similar mechanisms to maintain elite unity. Singapore's People's Action Party created a system of incentives, rewards and benefits for members and supporters. Its image of a meritocratic, development-oriented party provided a strong programmatic vision that its leader Lee Kuan Yew nurtured for several decades. The PAP maintained this strong base even after leadership succession. In Malaysia, UMNO similarly provided patronage and cohesive networks of benefits to maintain strong elite unity for much of its post-independence period. Even when prominent UMNO politicians split and attempted to form alternative political parties, they were often attracted back. Only in recent years has a more permanent split appeared in the Malay elite, although UMNO's institutional capacities remain strong. Finally in Indonesia, during Suharto's long authoritarian rule, Golkar played a similar role as UMNO. With a strong network of members spread across the archipelago and at all levels of government, it used many of the institutional and organizational mechanisms more often seen in communist parties. This helped maintain some degree of elite unity for three decades. Nevertheless, there was less cohesion between Golkar and the armed forces than in other regimes, and factional splits did occasionally appear with Golkar and the armed forces. Suharto's leadership skills, large amounts of patronage resources, as well shared elite interest in maintaining the regime allowed it to sustain elite unity until the late 1990s.

When and where elite division occurs and leads to political change is not always straightforward. Yet, rarely does political change occur without it. In these Southeast Asian cases, we have seen two trends. In some cases, elite divisions have been endemic, while in others serious divisions occurred prior to political change, confirming O'Donnell and Schmitter's argument that such splits tend to precede the demise of authoritarian regimes (O'Donnell & Schmitter, 1986).

Elites in Cambodia, Thailand and the Philippines have been the most divided. Ever since communists began to challenge the authoritarian rule of King Norodom Sihanouk under the French, Cambodia's elite has been deeply divided. After independence, Sihanouk faced armed resistance from Vietnamese-backed communist groups as well as the embryonic Khmer Rouge. Once victorious in 1975, the latter could not maintain power after Vietnam's intervention. The elite became divided between Vietnamese-backed communists, Khmer Rouge and royalists. Even after a UN peace accord, these divisions remained. In recent years, the Khmer Rouge has finally been defeated, but royalists continue to compete against the greater consolidation of the Cambodian Communist Party's power under Hun Sen. Divisions led to instability and war. They ran too deep to be managed through the fragile democratic framework established under UN auspices.

Thailand's elite also has been divided. Initially different military-bureaucratic cliques competed for power. While change occurred, authoritarianism remained as coups were frequent. As noted above, over time a new business elite and middle class became more active and challenged this military-bureaucratic dominance. New alliances were created as divisions evolved, rather than creating an elite with strong commitments to a democratic political framework. As a result, democratic politics were introduced gradually in the 1980s but were interrupted by mass demonstrations and coups in 1991 and 2006. Overall, the effect has been ambiguous. Elite division created instability but, over time, competing groups appear to accept a democratic framework. Most recently, when monarchists and the Bangkok elite opposed supporters of Thaksin and rural-based business elites, it appeared that elites could become so deeply divided that civil war might erupt. Since 2011, such a scenario appears more remote and even the armed forces appear to have accepted a compromise.

The Philippines is somewhat exceptional given its stable, low-quality democracy. Democratic elections have been common, as well as frequent changes at the executive level. Competition is strong in national, provincial and local elections. The elite is relatively homogenous as dominant families and political clans diversified their economic base but continued to own and control most of the economy. They compete against each other, even sponsoring private militias to protect their interests. Elections have often seen violent attacks. Yet, except for the Marcos era, there was broad agreement on allowing some kind of democratic framework to operate. It has also perpetuated a low-quality democracy, which this elite controls for its private benefit.

Momentary splits in the elite prior to political change have been less frequent but key in some cases. A split in the military and the broader political elite preceded the fall of Suharto's authoritarian regime. Politicians who were once in Golkar, or who supported the regime because of the risks of losing benefits or fears of instability began to more openly demand for reform. Factions became more apparent in the armed forces, where concerns for Suharto's succession grew stronger. When demonstrations broke out in 1998, groups in the military and among the established politicians joined demonstrations and broke ranks with the regime. A similar sequence of events preceded Marcos' downfall in the Philippines. Although frequently attributed to People Power, the regime's breakdown also happened because a key group in the armed forces openly challenged Marcos' rule, and joined forces with other members of the political elite, namely large families that had been sidelined during the Marcos years and even the Catholic church, which broke its conservative support for the state and called for an end to Marcos' rule.

The conditions that sustain elite unity have contributed to authoritarian stability in Southeast Asia. Elite splits that characterized many of the transitions to democracy in Latin America and other regions of the world have been less frequent. Instead, strong, united armed forces, dominant political parties and tight alliances among ruling elites have often been sufficiently strong to outweigh some of the broader pressures for change that economic development might have created.

Nevertheless, there are some signs that democratic politics are becoming more prevalent. Indonesia appears to be the shining light of the region, with regular changeover of governments, broad civil liberties and relatively few pockets of authoritarian resilience. Malaysia and Singapore are both seeing the rise of more challenge and demands for reform than before. Myanmar's new civilian regime is accepting that the opposition participate in politics for the first time since the 1950s. Thailand's armed forces and pro-monarchy elite, after first supporting a coup in 2006 and keeping tight control to avoid pro-Thaksin supporters to regain power, then accepted Yingluck Shinawatra and Puea Thai's election. Even communist Vietnam and Laos continue to implement slow reform towards more accommodation of diverse perspectives and gradually more openness.

Do grass-roots movements create political change?

The mobilization of mass movements often accompanies political change. Images of large-scale demonstrations preceding the downfall of authoritarian regimes have become a familiar scene. Have grass-roots movements been responsible for political change in Southeast Asia? How important have they been?

Scholars of democratization have emphasized the role of mass mobilization in two different ways. First, they recognized a number of cases where mass mobilization played a crucial role in the demise of authoritarian rule. The former Soviet Union and Eastern European communist regimes fell like dominoes when mass movements spread across Europe in 1989. More recently, the Arab Spring saw several cases of mass movements bringing down military-dominated regimes, such as in Tunisia and Egypt. While regimes were toppled and these movements triggered political change, the outcome has not necessarily been a new democracy. Sometimes a new authoritarian regime is established. A second approach to mass mobilization emphasizes its importance but only in conjunction with other, prior triggers of change. O'Donnell and Schmitter, who primarily emphasized the role of elite splits leading to the breakdown of authoritarian regimes in Latin America, also emphasized a crucial role of mass mobilization, and particularly its timing, to explain transition to a new democratic regime. Once an authoritarian regime is weakened by a split in the elite and opens up as a result, the mobilization of civil society can be an important supporting factor in paving the way towards a new democracy. In sum, they still stress an important, but more contingent role for mass mobilization.

Where such mobilization occurred in Southeast Asia, it has more closely resembled the second path rather than the Arab Spring model.

The mass mobilization that accompanied the downfall of Suharto in Indonesia was perhaps the strongest and most sustained. Nevertheless, two factors were prior to mobilization. First, Indonesia was severely hit by the 1997 Asian financial crisis that not only weakened key sectors of the economy and hurt many Indonesians but also limited the regime's resources to sustain its patronage. Second, the ruling elite had already begun to split in anticipation of Suharto's succession and various groups were already jockeying for a strong position before the Asian financial crisis hit. Mass mobilization was therefore a catalyst more than the main cause of the regime's downfall. In the Philippines, "People Power" is often portrayed as bringing down the Marcos regime. While mass mobilization was again crucial, and certainly a tipping point, the ruling elite and even the armed forces had already split. Furthermore, members of this elite skilfully encouraged and manipulated mass mobilization to this effect. Finally, in Thailand, mass mobilization in 1973 certainly contributed to the downfall of the authoritarian regime but against the backdrop of factional divisions within the armed forces.

Mass mobilization on a large scale often failed to bring down regimes but has sometimes placed significant pressure for some reform. In Burma, sustained demonstrations and mass mobilization in 1988 did not end authoritarian rule but contributed to the regime's attempts to legitimize itself through elections in 1990. Ultimately, the regime reconstituted itself under a new name, SLORC, and ignored the election results. Protests in 2007 once again did not break the regime's stronghold but created pressure that contributed to its plans to turn itself into a civilian regime under a new constitution in 2010. In the Philippines, People Power was activated again in 2001 and succeeded in forcing President Estrada's resignation. Mass mobilization, however, was in part the product of elite manipulations to force Estrada out of power. Furthermore, People Power's purported objective of improving democratic practice, making leaders more accountable, and increasing participation was never reached. In Malaysia, the Reformasi movement that paralleled Indonesia's failed to produce any change in the regime. In Southeast Asia, therefore, the outcome of mass mobilization has been mixed.

Although mass mobilization is sometimes associated with a strong and vibrant civil society, it is not always the case. In order to thrive, civil society must be provided with a space where organizations can form and operate independently from the state. Where such a space is constrained and monitored, or when the state intervenes in the functioning of these organizations, it is very difficult to speak of a civil society. When there are large numbers of organizations, they might coalesce and mobilize against the government or its policies. Yet, when mass movements arise, they are not necessarily a product of a dense web of organizations but rather spontaneous and loosely organized.

Most of the mass mobilization that contributed to regime change arose out of very loosely organized networks. Although student organizations were involved in Thailand (1973), Indonesia (1998) or the Philippines (1986), it would be difficult to argue that there was a large number of civil society organizations in any of these cases just prior to this mobilization.

On the other hand, where democracy has flourished, civil society has often grown and become more solidified. The number of organizations grew rapidly in the Philippines, Indonesia and Thailand under democratic regimes. People Power in 2001 was much more linked to a web of organizations in civil society. Demonstrations in Thailand, divided among red shirts and yellow shirts, were also tied to networks of organizations, although these movements were also tied to the ruling elites.

More broadly, civil society organizations have also exerted pressure for more modest reforms. They have become important actors in a variety of issues areas in Indonesia, Thailand and the Philippines. Although space has been restricted in countries such as Malaysia, nevertheless they have been able to lobby favourably for progress on issues such as women's rights, environmental protection or health care. And in even more greatly restricted space, such as Myanmar, there is some evidence that organizations working on development or environmental protection sometimes manage to influence policy as they often provide services that the government is unable or unwilling to offer.

Is Southeast Asia unique?

This book argues that we can explain political change in Southeast Asia by comparing factors across cases. It probed the strength of the proposition that economic development and the growth of the middle class over time leads to democracy. It emphasized how splits in ruling elites often precede political change and how, conversely, where ruling elites are strongly united and consolidated, political change rarely occurs. Furthermore, when ideology or institutions – such as professionalized armed forces or dominant political parties – reinforce this unity, elites tend to remain cohesive and authoritarian regimes solid. This book also made the case that mass mobilization sometimes leads to political change but more often creates pressure for reform or plays a supportive, rather than a determinative, role. These factors explain aspects of political change in many countries. While Southeast Asia's experience differs somewhat from other regions, a focus on comparable factors, rather than unique circumstances, provides much explanatory leverage. The mix of factors, or their character, might best explain regional differences.

While electoral democracies replaced authoritarian regimes in the 1980s and 1990s across Latin America, Africa and former communist states in Eastern Europe, Southeast Asian countries remained mostly authoritarian. Many countries experienced little political change while others changed their authoritarian regimes. Few became democratic. Why have authoritarian regimes been so resilient?

Three main reasons can explain why Southeast Asia differs from other regions. First, the middle class has been more dependent on the state in Southeast Asia than elsewhere. Second, the state has been stronger. Third, economic development has provided "performance legitimacy" to some authoritarian regimes.

In many cases, the middle class has been dependent on the state for progress in their living standards or politically vulnerable. In Singapore, many benefits depended on support for the government. In Malaysia, many members of the middle class are ethnic Chinese, and are unlikely to mobilize against the regime by fear that an alternative government might protect them less. Many Malays, moreover, gained middle-class status by benefiting from the NEP or advancing in state-owned corporations. During the New Order regime of President Suharto, middle-class Chinese-Indonesians were unlikely to mobilize for political change, given their numerically small numbers and their relative protection from the regime. The non-Chinese middle class grew steadily during those years but state corporations employed a good portion of them. The small middle class emerging in Vietnam and other communist states is closely linked to the ruling communist party.

The state in Southeast Asia has been relatively strong. In the case of state-socialist countries, the armed forces and dominant political parties established a solid stronghold on the state in Vietnam and Laos after the war. Burma's armed forces did so as well after they seized power in 1962. Dominant parties in Singapore and Malaysia consolidated and maintained their power. They also developed bureaucracies that were highly functional, particularly in Singapore's case. The Indonesian armed forces were also dominant and strong, and the regime further strengthened its hold over the state by forming Golkar in the image of dominant parties in state-socialist countries. Although weaker than dominant parties in neighbouring countries, Golkar nevertheless helped to strengthen the state along with the armed forces' control. Indonesia's authoritarian rule remained stable as a result for over thirty years.

Economic development has sometimes contributed to the legitimation of authoritarian rule rather than leading to political change. In many respects, steady improvements in living standards, increasing wealth among the business class and stable economies supported authoritarian rule in Singapore, Malaysia and Suharto's Indonesia. Reforms that helped to boost economic growth in Vietnam and Laos also contributed to strengthening the regimes, as more party cadres and business associates reaped the benefits of new sources of development. In combination with other factors, economic development prevented the emergence of crises that sometimes weaken regimes. Nevertheless, economic and financial crises did arise and place a dent in some countries' economic development path and, by extension, regime stability. Most notably, the 1997 Asian financial crisis contributed to the Suharto's downfall and the demise of the New Order regime. It forced a change of government in Thailand, but democracy was already in place and the regime was able to absorb the shock. A particularly severe crisis in Burma momentarily weakened the regime in 1988, and stimulated the mass movements that demanded political change. Nevertheless the regime was able to survive. Subsequent reforms enabled the regime to keep funding the expansion of the armed forces and benefits to its members.

In each case of authoritarian resilience in Southeast Asia, these factors have been important. It is the particular mix, and their character, particularly the factors contributing to elite unity, state strength and the middle class, that explain why political change has been absent in many countries of the region, or has led to a reassertion of authoritarian rule.

Are there factors that are unique to Southeast Asia? Some features, unique historical events or other factors have been important. In some Southeast Asian countries, certain authoritarian forms were almost unique. For instance, Burma's military dominated yet socialist-inspired and autarchic regime had few parallels elsewhere. The Khmer Rouge's radical programme similarly had few useful comparisons. Their character provided some further strength in the Burmese case yet sowed the seeds of its own demise in the latter. Repression, autarchy and radical programmes have rarely been sustainable in any authoritarian context. While Burma's regime remained, it became over time a more typical military-dominated regime.

Significant events can also affect political trajectories. The New Order regime began its rule by sanctioning the elimination of communist supporters. The killing of more than 500,000 people in 1965–6 left deep scars among Indonesians. The regime used the communist threat and exploited the memory of such killings to weaken opposition. In Malaysia, the 1969 riots left lasting worries of potential violence between Malays and Chinese. The regime also used divisions effectively, and frequently reminded Malaysians of the dangers of similar riots. In both cases, the regime used these events strategically to justify their rule and curtail opposition.

Some unique institutions also played a significant role. Most notably, the monarchy in Thailand has been involved in the country's politics. The king intervened directly to end the bloody crackdown in May 1992. Behind the scenes, the monarchy also relied on a network of allies to direct the pace and direction of the country's political change. While less powerful in Cambodia, King Sihanouk managed to rule Cambodia under French colonial rule and for a brief authoritarian interlude during the 1960s. He remained influential, along with Prince Ranariddh, after the Vietnamese removed the Khmer Rouge from power in 1979. He maintained sufficient support to remain a significant player, even if weak, after forming a political party, FUNCINPEC. Without attributing too much explanatory power to the monarchy in both cases, the presence of such an institution has nevertheless been important.

Finally, patrimonialism and bossism have been persistent features of several countries in the region. They helped to sustain authoritarian regimes in Indonesia, the Philippines, Thailand and Burma. In

Malaysia's case, UMNO's sustained dominance persists partly through patrimonial ties. Patrimonialism and bossism have also been chronic features of democracy in the Philippines, Indonesia and Thailand. They are tied to low-quality democracy and certainly played a role under authoritarian rule. Nevertheless, while these features are important and explain some aspects of authoritarian persistence and low-quality democracy, they are not unique to Southeast Asia.

Southeast Asia is a region of vast differences. Strongly divided between communist and non-communist states during the Cold War, the region's countries took very different political paths. The end of the Cold War and changes in the international system framed some of the region's transformation but domestic factors have been more important in explaining political change, or its absence, across various countries. While the region's experience, or that of particular countries, may seem to be unique, we can understand several aspects of political change by focusing on a few, comparable explanatory factors. Unique events and circumstances, as well as particular historical paths are also important. A dialogue between generalizable propositions and detailed political histories yields strong analytical insights to understand the region's vast transformations.

References

Abinales, P. N. (2001) Coalition politics in the Philippines. *Current History*, 100, 154–61.

Adas, M. (1979) *Prophets of Rebellion: Millenarian Protest Movements Against the European Colonial Order*. Chapel Hill: University of North Carolina Press.

Albritton, R. B. (2006) Thailand in 2005: the struggle for democratic consolidation. *Asian survey*, XLVI, 140–7.

Anderson, B. (1988) Cacique democracy and the Philippines: origins and dreams. *New Left Review*, 169, 3–31.

Anderson, B. R. O. G. (1983) *Imagined Communities: Reflections on the Origin and Spread of Nationalism*. London: Verso.

Anderson, B. R. O. G. (1990) *Language and Power: Exploring Political Cultures in Indonesia*. Ithaca, NY: Cornell University Press.

Aspinall, E. (2005) *Opposing Suharto: Compromise, Resistance, and Regime Change in Indonesia*. Stanford, CA: Stanford University Press.

Aspinall, E. (2010) The irony of success. *Journal of Democracy*, 21, 20–34.

Barr, M. (2003) Perpetual revisionism in Singapore: the limits of change. *Pacific Review*, 16, 77–97.

Barr, M. D. (2006) Beyond technocracy: the culture of elite governance in Lee Hsien Loong's Singapore. *Asian Studies Review*, 30, 1–18.

Bedlington, S. S. (1978) *Malaysia and Singapore: The Building of New States*. Ithaca, NY: Cornell University Press.

Beng Huat, C. (2007) Political culturalism, representation and the People's Action Party of Singapore. *Democratization*, 14, 911–27.

Beresford, M. (1993) The political economy of dismantling the "bureaucratic centralism and subsidy system" in Vietnam. In K. Hewison, R. Robison & G. Rodan (Eds.), *Southeast Asia in the 1990s: Authoritarianism, Democracy and Capitalism*. St Leonards, Australia: Allen & Unwin, 213–36.

Beresford, M. (2006) Vietnam: the transition from central planning. In G. Rodan, K. Hewison & R. Robison (Eds.), *The Political Economy of South-East Asia: Markets, Power and Contestation*, 3rd edn. South Melbourne, Australia: Oxford University Press, 197–220.

Beresford, M. (2008) Doi Moi in review: the challenges of building market socialism in Vietnam. *Journal of Contemporary Asia*, 38, 221–43.

Bertrand, J. (2004) *Nationalism and Ethnic Conflict in Indonesia*. Cambridge: Cambridge University Press.

Brownlee, J. (2008) Bound to rule: party institutions and regime trajectories in Malaysia and the Philippines. *Journal of East Asian Studies*, 8, 89–118.

Bunbongkarn, S. (1993) Thailand in 1992: in search of a democratic order. *Asian Survey*, 33, 218–23.

Bunbongkarn, S. (1999) Thailand: democracy under siege. In J. W. Morley (Ed.), *Driven by Growth: Political Change in the Asia-Pacific Region*, rev. ed. Armonk, NY: M.E. Sharpe, 161–75.

Case, W. (2002) *Politics in Southeast Asia: Democracy or Less*. Richmond, UK: Curzon.

Case, W. (2004) New uncertainties for an old pseudo-democracy: the case of Malaysia. *Comparative Politics*, 37, 83–104.

Case, W. (2009a) After the crisis: capital and regime resilience in the ASEAN Three. *Journal of Contemporary Asia*, 39, 649–72.

Case, W. (2009b) Low-quality democracy and varied authoritarianism: elites and regimes in Southeast Asia today. *Pacific Review*, 22, 255–70.

Case, W. F. (2001) Thai democracy, 2001: out of equilibrium. *Asian Survey*, 41, 525–47.

Chandler, D. P. (1991) *The Tragedy of Cambodian History: Politics, War, and Revolution Since 1945*. New Haven, CT: Yale University Press.

Chandler, D. P. (1998) The burden of Cambodia's past. In F. Z. Brown (Ed.), *Cambodia and the International Community: The Quest for Peace, Development, and Democracy*. Singapore: Institute of Southeast Asian Studies, 33–47.

CIA. (n.d.). *The World Factbook*. Available at www.cia.gov/library/publications/the-world-factbook/

Connors, M. K. (1999) Political reform and the state in Thailand. *Journal of Contemporary Asia*, 29, 202–26.

Cribb, R. & Coppel, C. A. (2009) A genocide that never was: explaining the myth of anti-Chinese massacres in Indonesia, 1965. *Journal of Genocide Research*, 11, 447–65.

Crouch, H. A. (1978) *The Army and Politics in Indonesia*. Ithaca, NY: Cornell University Press.

Crouch, H. A. (1996) *Government and Society in Malaysia*. Ithaca, NY: Cornell University Press.

Davidson, J. S. (2009) Dilemmas of democratic consolidation in Indonesia. *Pacific Review*, 22, 293–310.

Dommen, A. J. (1994) Laos in 1993: the revolution on hold. *Asian Survey*, 34, 82–6.

Eaton, K. (2003) Restoration or transformation? "Trapos" versus NGOs in the democratization of the Philippines. *Journal of Asian Studies*, 62, 469–96.

Elson, R. E. (1992) International commerce, the state and society: economic and social change. In N. Tarling (Ed.), *The Cambridge History of Southeast Asia*. Cambridge, UK: Cambridge University Press, 131–95.

Englehart, N. A. (2005) Is regime change enough for Burma? The problem of state capacity. *Asian Survey*, 4, 622–44.

Evans, P. B. (1979) *Dependent Development: The Alliance of Multinational, State, and Local Capital in Brazil*: Princeton, NJ: Princeton University Press.

Feith, H. (1962) *The Decline of Constitutional Democracy in Indonesia*. Published under the auspices of the Modern Indonesia Project, Southeast Asia Program, Cornell University. Ithaca, NY: Cornell University Press.

Fforde, A. (2005) Vietnam in 2004 – popular authority seeking power? *Asian Survey*, 45, 146–52.

Furnivall, J. S. (1948) *Colonial Policy and Practice: A Comparative Study of Burma and Netherlands India*. Cambridge, UK: Cambridge University Press.

Geddes, B. (1999) What do we know about democratization after twenty years? *Annual Review of Political Science*, 2:1, 115–44.

George, C. (2007) Consolidating authoritarian rule: calibrated coercion in Singapore. *Pacific Review*, 20, 127–45.

Gomez, E. T. & Jomo, K. S. (1999) *Malaysia's Political Economy: Politics, Patronage and Profits*. Cambridge, UK: Cambridge University Press.

Goscha, C. E. (1995) *Vietnam or Indochina?: Contesting Concepts of Space in Vietnamese Nationalism, 1887–1954*. Copenhagen, Denmark: NIAS.

Goscha, C. E. (2009) Widening the colonial encounter: Asian connections inside French Indochina during the interwar period. *Modern Asian Studies*, 43, 1189–228.

Gunn, G. C. (2010) Timor-Leste in 2009: cup half full or half empty? *Asian Survey*, 50, 235–40.

Hadiz, V. R. (2010) *Localising Power in Post-Authoritarian Indonesia: A Southeast Asia Perspective*. Stanford, CA: Stanford University Press.

Hedman, E.-L. E. (2006) *In the Name of Civil Society: From Free Election Movements to People Power in the Philippines*. Honolulu: University of Hawai'i Press.

Hlaing, K. Y. (2009) Setting the rules for survival: why the Burmese military regime survives in an age of democratization. *Pacific Review*, 22, 271–91.

Hughes, C. (2009) Cambodia in 2008: consolidation in the midst of crisis. *Asian Survey*, 49, 206–12.

Hutchcroft, P. D. (1998) *Booty Capitalism: The Politics of Banking in the Philippines*. Ithaca, NY: Cornell University Press.

Jackson, K. D. (1978) Bureaucratic polity: a theoretical framework for the analysis of power and communications in Indonesia. In K. D. Jackson & L. W. Pye (Eds.), *Political Power and Communications in Indonesia*. Berkeley: University of California Press, 3–42.

Kerkvliet, B. J. (2005) *The Power of Everyday Politics: How Vietnamese Peasants Transformed National Policy*: Ithaca, NY: Cornell University Press.

Kerkvliet, B. J. T. (2006) Agricultural land in Vietnam: markets tempered by family, community and socialist practices. *Journal of Agrarian Change*, 6, 285–305.

Kiernan, B. (2002) Introduction: conflict in Cambodia, 1945–2002. *Critical Asian Studies*, 34, 483–95.

King, D. & LoGerfo, J. (1997) Thailand: toward democratic stability. *Journal of Democracy*, 7, 102–17.

Landé, C. H. (1965) *Leaders, Factions, and Parties: The Structure of Philippine Politics*. Southeast Asia Studies 6. New Haven, CT: Yale University.

Landé, C. H. (2001) The return of "people power" in the Philippines. *Journal of Democracy*, 12, 88–102.

Leong, H. K. (2000) Citizen participation and policy making in Singapore: conditions and predicaments. *Asian Survey*, 40, 436–55.

Lev, D. S. (1966) *The Transition to Guided Democracy: Indonesian Politics, 1957–1959*. Ithaca, NY: Modern Indonesia Project, Southeast Asia Program, Department of Asian Studies.

Liddle, R. W. (1996) *Leadership and Culture in Indonesian Politics*. Sydney, Australia: Asian Studies Association of Australia in association with Allen & Unwin.

Lieberman, V. B. (2003) *Strange Parallels: Southeast Asia in Global Context, c. 800–1830*. New York: Cambridge University Press.

Lintner, B. (2008) Laos: at the crossroads. *Southeast Asian Affairs*, 2008, 171–83.

Lipset, S. M. (1959) Some social requisites of democracy: economic development and political legitimacy. *American Political Science Review*, 53, 69–105.

Maisrikrod, S. (1994) Thailand 1992: repression and return of democracy. *Southeast Asian Affairs*, 1994, 327–49.

Malesky, E. & Schuler, P. (2009) Paint-by-numbers democracy: the stakes, structure, and results of the 2007 Vietnamese National Assembly election. *Journal of Vietnamese Studies*, 4, 1–48.

Mamdani, M. (1996) *Citizen and Subject: Contemporary Africa and the Legacy of Late Colonialism.* Princeton, NJ: Princeton University Press.

Mauzy, D. K. (1993) Leadership succession in Singapore: the best laid plans. *Asian Survey*, 33, 1163–74.

Mauzy, D. K. & Milne, R. S. (2002) *Singapore Politics Under the People's Action Party.* London: Routledge.

McCargo, D. (2002) Democracy under stress in Thaksin's Thailand. *Journal of Democracy*, 13, 112–26.

McCargo, D. (2005a) Cambodia: getting away with authoritarianism? *Journal of Democracy*, 16, 98–112.

McCargo, D. (2005b) Network monarchy and legitimacy crises in Thailand. *Pacific Review*, 18, 499–519.

McVey, R. T. (1965) *The Rise of Indonesian Communism.* Ithaca, NY: Cornell University Press.

Means, G. P. (1996) Soft authoritarianism in Malaysia and Singapore. *Journal of Democracy*, 7, 103–17.

Mills, C. W. (1956) *The Power Elite.* New York: Oxford University Press.

Moore, B. (1966) *Social Origins of Dictatorship and Democracy: Lord and Peasant in the Making of the Modern World.* Boston, MA: Beacon Press.

Nasution, A. B. (1992) *The Aspiration for Constitutional Government in Indonesia: A Socio-legal Study of the Indonesian Konstituante 1956–1959.* Jakarta, Indonesia: Pustaka Sinar Harapan.

Neher, C. D. (1988) Thailand in 1987: semi-successful semi-democracy. *Asian Survey*, 28, 192–201.

O'Donnell, G. A. (1973) *Modernization and Bureaucratic-Authoritarianism: Studies in South American Politics.* Berkeley, CA: Institute of International Studies.

O'Donnell, G. A. & Schmitter, P. C. (1986) *Transitions from Authoritarian Rule: Tentative Conclusions About Uncertain Democracies*: Baltimore, MD: Johns Hopkins University Press.

Ockey, J. (2002) Civil society and street politics: lessons from the 1950s. In D. McCargo (Ed.), *Reforming Thai Politics.* Copenhagen, Denmark: NIAS, 107–24.

Ockey, J. (2007) Thailand in 2006: retreat to military rule. *Asian Survey*, 1, 133–40.

Pepinsky, T. B. (2007) Malaysia: turnover without change. *Journal of Democracy*, 18, 113–27.

Phongpaichit, P. & Baker, C. (2008) Thaksin's populism [in Thailand]. *Journal of Contemporary Asia*, 38, 62–83.

Polity IV Project. (n.d.). Polity IV Individual Country Regime Trends, 1946–2010, available at www.systemicpeace.org/polity/polity4.htm

Pongsudhirak, T. (2008) Thailand since the coup. *Journal of Democracy*, 19, 140–53.

Porter, G. (1993) *Vietnam: The Politics of Bureaucratic Socialism*, Ithaca, NY: Cornell University Press.

Prasirtsuk, K. (2009) Thailand in 2008: crises continued. *Asian Survey*, 49, 174–84.

Prasirtsuk, K. (2010) Thailand in 2009: colored by turbulence. *Asian Survey*, 50, 203–10.

Putzel, J. (1999) Survival of an imperfect democracy in the Philippines. *Democratization*, 6, 198–223.

Quimpo, N. G. (2009) The Philippines: predatory regime, growing authoritarian features. *Pacific Review*, 22, 335–54.

Reid, A. (1988) *Southeast Asia in the Age of Commerce, 1450–1680*. New Haven, CT: Yale University Press.

Reid, A. (2010) *Imperial Alchemy: Nationalism and Political Identity in Southeast Asia*. New York: Cambridge University Press.

Riggs, F. W. (1966) *Thailand: The Modernization of a Bureaucratic Polity*. Honolulu, HI: East-West Center Press.

Roberts, D. (2007) Democratization, elite transition, and violence in Cambodia, 1991–1999. In B. Kiernan (Ed.), *Conflict and Change in Cambodia*. London: Routledge, pp. 26–44.

Robison, R. (1986) *Indonesia: The Rise of Capital*. Sydney, Australia: Allen & Unwin.

Robison, R. & Goodman, D. S. G. (1996) *The New Rich In Asia: Mobile Phones, Mcdonald's and Middle-class Revolution*: London: Routledge.

Rodan, G. (1997) Civil society and other political possibilities in Southeast Asia. *Journal of Contemporary Asia*, 27, 156–78.

Rodan, G. (2008) Singapore "exceptionalism"? Authoritarian rule and state transformation. In E. Friedman & J. Wong (Eds.), *Political Transitions in Dominant Party Systems: Learning to Lose*. Abingdon, UK: Routledge, 231–51.

Rodan, G. (2009) New modes of political participation and Singapore's nominated members of parliament. *Government and Opposition*, 44, 438–62.

Rueschemeyer, D., Stephens, E. H. & Stephens, J. D. (1992) *Capitalist Development and Democracy*. Chicago, IL: University of Chicago Press.

Samudavanija, C.-A. & Chotiya, P. (1998) Beyond transition in Thailand. In L. J. Diamond & M. F. Plattner (Eds.), *Democracy in East Asia*. Baltimore, MD: Johns Hopkins University Press, 147–70.

Scott, J. C. (1972) Patron-client politics and political change in Southeast Asia. *American Political Science Review*, 66, 91–113.

Scott, J. C. (1976) *The Moral Economy of the Peasant: Rebellion and Subsistence in Southeast Asia*: New Haven, CT: Yale University Press.

Scott, J. C. (1985) *Weapons of the Weak: Everyday Forms of Peasant Resistance*: New Haven, CT: Yale University Press.

Shoesmith, D. (2003) Timor-Leste: divided leadership in a semi-presidential system. *Asian Survey*, 43, 231–52.

Sidel, J. T. (1999) *Capital, Coercion, and Crime: Bossism in the Philippines*: Stanford, CA: Stanford University Press.

Sidel, M. (1995) The emergence of a nonprofit sector and philanthropy in the Socialist Republic of Vietnam. In T. Yamamoto & Nihon Kokusai Koryu Senta (Eds.), *Emerging Civil Society in the Asia Pacific Community: Nongovernmental Underpinnings of the Emerging Asia Pacific Regional Community: A 25th Anniversary Project of JCIE*. Singapore: co-published by the Institute of Southeast Asian Studies (ISEAS) and JCIE in cooperation with the Asia Pacific Philanthropy Consortium (APPC), 293–304.

Silverstein, J. (1977) *Burma: Military Rule and the Politics of Stagnation*. Ithaca, NY: Cornell University Press.

Simonsen, S. G. (2006) The authoritarian temptation in East Timor: nation-building and the need for inclusive governance. *Asian Survey*, 46, 575–96.

Slater, D. (2008) Democracy and dictatorship do not float freely: structural sources of political regimes in Southeast Asia. In E. M. Kuhonta, D. Slater & T. Vu (Eds.), *Southeast Asia in Political Science: Theory, Region, and Qualitative Analysis*. Stanford, CA: Stanford University Press, 55–79.

Steinberg, D. I. (1999) Burma/Myanmar: Under the military. In J. W. Morley (Ed.), *Driven by Growth: Political Change in the Asia-Pacific Region*, rev. ed. Armonk, NY: M.E. Sharpe, 33–58.

Steinberg, D. I. (2001) *Burma, the State of Myanmar*. Washington, DC: Georgetown University Press.

Steinberg, D. I. (2003) Myanmar: reconciliation – progress in the process? *Southeast Asian Affairs*, 2003, 171–88.

Stuart-Fox, M. (1986) *Laos: Politics, Economics, and Society*. London: F. Pinter.

Tarling, N. (1992) *The Cambridge History of Southeast Asia*. Cambridge, UK: Cambridge University Press.

Taylor, R. H. (2004) Myanmar: roadmap to where? *Southeast Asian Affairs*, 2004, 171–84.

Thawnghmung, A. M. (2003) Preconditions and Prospects for democratic transition in Burma/Myanmar. *Asian Survey*, 43, 443–60.

Thawnghmung, A. M. & Myoe, M. A. (2008) Myanmar in 2007: a turning point in the "roadmap"? *Asian Survey*, XLVIII, 13–19.

Thayer, C. A. (2009) Vietnam and the challenge of political civil society. *Contemporary Southeast Asia*, 1, 1–27.

Thompson, M. R. (1995) *The Anti-Marcos Struggle: Personalistic Rule and Democratic Transition in the Philippines*. New Haven, CT: Yale University Press.

Thompson, M. R. (1996) Off the endangered list: Philippine democratization in comparative perspective. *Comparative Politics*, 28, 179–205.

Turnell, S. (2011) Myanmar in 2010. *Asian Survey*, 51, 148–54.

United Nations Main Aggregates Database. (n.d.). Available at http://unstats.un.org/unsd/snaama/selbasicFast.asp

Vasavakul, T. (2003) From fence-breaking to networking: interests, popular organizations and policy influences in post-socialist Vietnam. In B. J. Kerkvliet, R H. K. Heng & D. W. H. Koh (Eds.), *Getting Organized in Vietnam: Moving In and Around the Socialist State*. Singapore: Institute of Southeast Asian Studies, 25–61.

Weiss, M. (2005) Prickly ambivalence: state, society and semidemocracy in Malaysia. *Commonwealth & Comparative Politics*, 43, 61–81.

Weiss, M. L. (2006) *Protest and Possibilities: Civil Society and Coalitions for Political Change in Malaysia*. Stanford, CA: Stanford University Press.

Weiss, M. L. (2008) Civil society and close aproximations thereof. In E. M. Kuhonta, D. Slater & T. Vu (Eds.), *Southeast Asia in Political Science: Theory, Region, and Qualitative Analysis*. Stanford, CA: Stanford University Press, 144–70.

Welsh, B. (2005) Malaysia in 2004: out of Mahathir's shadow? *Asian Survey*, 45 (1), Jan/Feb, 153–60.

World Bank Development Indicators. (n.d.), available at http://data.worldbank.org/data-catalog/world-development-indicators

Wurfel, D. (1988) *Filipino Politics: Development and Decay*: Ithaca, NY: Cornell University Press.

Young, C. (1994) *The African Colonial State in Comparative Perspective*. New Haven, CT: Yale University Press.

Index